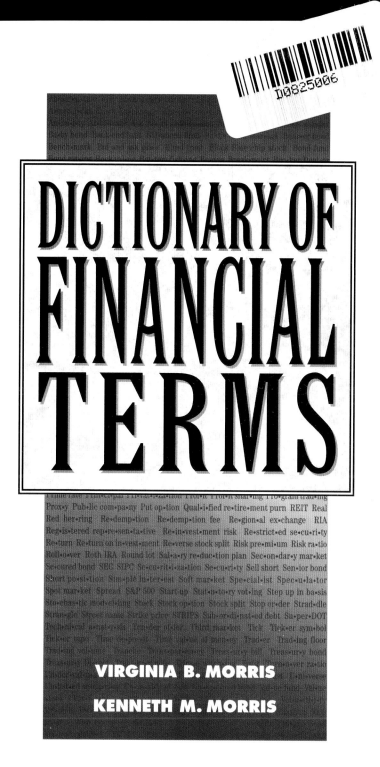

DICTIONARY OF FINANCIAL TERMS

VIRGINIA B. MORRIS

KENNETH M. MORRIS

LIGHTBULB

PRESS

LIGHTBULB PRESS
Corporate Staff

Chief Operating Officer Dean Scharf
Sales and Marketing Carol E. Davis, Germaine Ma, Karen Meldrom

Project Team

Design Director Dave Wilder
Editors Paul Benzon, Sophie Forrester
Copy Editor Sarah Norris
Design Kara W. Hatch
Design Staff Jeff Badger
Production Holly Duthie, Christopher Engel, Edie Evans, Cadence Giersbach, Julie Hair, Mike Mulhern, Thomas F. Trojan, Edie Winograde

SPECIAL THANKS

Tony DeMeo
John E. Herzog, Chairman, Museum of American Financial History
Harvey M. Iwata
Elisa K. Spain, President, EKS Consulting
Morton J. Wagner, Executive Vice President, Salomon Smith Barney (retired)

PICTURE CREDITS

Chicago Board of Trade (page 107); Financial Literacy Center, Inc. (page 146); FPG, New York (page 85); NASDAQ (page 100); Alan Rosenburg, New York (pages 14, 66, 102)

ACKNOWLEDGMENTS

Chicago Board of Trade logo courtesy of The Chicago Board of Trade (page 24); Cirrus logo courtesy of MasterCard International (page 37); The Dow Jones logo courtesy of Dow Jones & Company (page 45); Lipper Index courtesy of Lipper, Inc. (page 87); Moody's logo courtesy of Moody's Investors Service (page 97); Morningstar logo courtesy of Morningstar, Inc. (page 98); NASDAQ logo courtesy of NASDAQ (page 100); NYCE logo courtesy of NYCE Corporation (page 37); NYSE logo courtesy of The New York Stock Exchange (page 104, 145); Standard & Poor's logo courtesy of Standard & Poor's, A Division of The McGraw-Hill Companies (page 134); STAR logo courtesy of STAR Systems (page 37); Value Line logo courtesy of Value Line Publishing, Inc. (page 153)

*I*t's hard to pick up a newspaper or magazine, listen to a news report, or walk by an airport TV monitor without coming across financial terms that sound familiar, but whose precise meanings elude you.

We hear about leading economic indicators, electronic day traders, market caps, bond swaps, upticks and downticks, and a host of other perplexing terms. Knowing what these words mean—for understanding the state of the economy, the intriguing events unfolding on Wall Street, and the investments we've made, or plan to make—has become more a necessity than a vocabulary exercise.

After reviewing dozens of financial dictionaries and online glossaries, we realized that many of the definitions seemed cryptic and legal sounding, and not very practical for everyday use. So we created this easy-to-read financial dictionary, using the techniques that have made our earlier guides so popular— plain, straightforward language, vivid and informative graphics, and most important, explanations that are meaningful to you as an investor.

Since there are many financial terms that can be easily confused (what's the difference between NASD and Nasdaq, or between a market and an exchange, anyway?) we created special pages to help distinguish these similar sounding or frequently confused terms.

To keep the dictionary current, we are also providing updates to existing words, as well as introducing new terms, on our website at *www.lightbulbpress.com*. If you come across financial terms you think others would benefit from knowing about, you can e-mail us at that same website. We'll do our best to include them in future editions.

Virginia B. Morris   Kenneth M. Morris

Acronyms

AAII American Association of Individual Investors

ADR American depositary receipt

AGI Adjusted gross income

AMEX American Stock Exchange

AMT Alternative minimum tax

AON All or none order

APR Annual percentage rate

APY Annual percentage yield

CATS Certificate of accrual on Treasury securities

CBOE Chicago Board Options Exchange

CBOT Chicago Board of Trade

CD Certificate of deposit

CEA Council of Economic Advisors

CFTC Commodity Futures Trading Commission

CMO Collateralized mortgage obligation

COLA Cost-of-living adjustment

CPI Consumer Price Index

CUSIP Committee on Uniform Securities Identifying Procedures

DJIA Dow Jones Industrial Average

DRIP Dividend reinvestment plan

DTCC Depository Trust and Clearing Corporation

ECB European Central Bank

ECN Electronic communications network

ESOP Employee stock ownership plan

FASB Financial Accounting Standards Board

FDIC Federal Deposit Insurance Corporation

FHLMC Federal Home Loan Mortgage Corporation

FICA Federal Insurance Contributions Act

FNMA Federal National Mortgage Association

FOK Fill or kill

FOMC Federal Open Market Committee

FOREX Foreign exchange

GATT General Agreement on Tariffs and Trade

GDP Gross domestic product

GDR Global depositary receipt

GIC Guaranteed investment contract

GNMA Government National Mortgage Association

GTC Good 'til canceled

IMF International Monetary Fund

IPO Initial public offering

IRA Individual retirement account

ISO Incentive stock option

ITS Intermarket Trading System

LEAPS Long-term equity anticipation security

NASD National Association of Securities Dealers

NASDAQ National Association of Securities Dealers Automated Quotation System

NAV Net asset value

NMS National Market System

NYSE New York Stock Exchange

OCC Options Clearing Corporation

OTC Over the counter

P/E Price-to-earnings

P/GF Price-to-growth flow

REIT Real estate investment trust

RIA Registered investment advisor

S&P Standard & Poor's

S&P 500 Standard & Poor's 500-stock Index

SEC Securities and Exchange Commission

SEP Simplified employee pension plan

SIPC Securities Investor Protection Corporation

SLMA Student Loan Marketing Association

SOES Small order execution system

SPDR Standard & Poor's Depositary Receipt

SRO Self-regulatory organization

TIGER Treasury Investor Growth Receipt

UGMA Uniform Gifts to Minors Act

UIT Unit investment trust

UTMA Uniform Transfers to Minors Act

VC Venture capital

YTM Yield to maturity

Special Pages

Acquisition

When one company buys another company outright, or accumulates enough shares to take a controlling interest, the deal is described as an acquisition. The acquiring company's motive may be to expand the scope of its products and services, to make itself a major player in its sector, or to fend off being taken over itself.

To complete the deal, the acquirer may be willing to pay a higher price per share than the price at which the stock has been trading. That means shareholders of the target company may realize a substantial gain—which is one reason that some investors are always on the lookout for companies that seem ripe for acquisition.

Sometimes acquisitions are described, more bluntly, as takeovers and other times, more diplomatically, as mergers. Collectively, these activities are referred to as mergers and acquisitions, or M&A, to those in the business.

Adjusted gross income (AGI)

Your AGI is your gross, or total, income from taxable sources minus certain deductions. Income includes salary and other employment income, interest and dividends, and long- and short-term capital gains and losses. Deductions include unreimbursed business and medical expenses, contributions to a deductible individual retirement account (IRA), and alimony.

You figure your AGI on page one of your federal tax return, and it serves as the basis for figuring the income tax you owe. AGI is also used to establish your eligibility for certain tax or financial benefits, such as deducting your

ADJUSTED GROSS INCOME

Gross income
− Special deductions
ADJUSTED GROSS INCOME

IRA contribution or qualifying for personal tax exemptions.

Advance-decline (A-D) line

The advance-decline line graphs the ratio of stocks that have risen in value—the advancers—to stocks that have fallen in value—the decliners—over a particular trading period. The direction and steepness of the A-D line gives you a general idea of the direction of the market. For example, a noticeable upward trend indicates a growing market and a downward slope indicates a market in retreat. At times, however, there may be no clear trend in either direction.

Advancer

Stocks that have gained, or increased, in value over a particular period are described as advancers. If more stocks advance than decline—or lose value—over the course of a trading day, the financial press reports that advancers led decliners. When that occurs over a period of time, it's considered an indication that the stock market is healthy.

After-hours market

Securities, such as stocks and bonds, that change hands after regular business hours on the organized exchanges are said to trade in the after-hours market. These transactions explain why a security may open for trading at a different price from the one it closed at the day before.

There is a major electronic market in financial futures, where trading in benchmark indexes such as Standard & Poor's 500-stock Index (S&P 500) before the exchanges open for the day is interpreted as an early indicator of stock market activity. As electronic trading systems expand, however, and the trading day is lengthened, the relationship between regular business hours and after-hours seems likely to be redefined.

Agency bond

Some US-sponsored but privately owned corporations, including the Federal National Mortgage Association (FNMA), and certain federal government agencies, including the Government National Mortgage Association (GNMA), raise money by issuing bonds and short-term discount notes for sale to individual and institutional investors.

The money raised by selling these bonds, often referred to as agency securities, is typically used to make reduced-cost loans to specific groups, including students, home buyers, or farmers. Interest you earn on some—but not all—of these securities is exempt from state and local income taxes, but it is always federally taxable.

Bonds issued by the federal agencies are backed by the government's full faith and credit, just as US Treasury securities are, but bonds issued by the sponsored corporations are generally not guaranteed.

MONEY FROM AGENCY BONDS CAN REDUCE THE COST OF:

Education

Home buying

Farming

Agent

A person or institution that handles business and financial transactions between two other people, or between a person and an institution, is described as an agent. The person or institution that authorizes the action is the principal. For example, a brokerage firm employee who acts on your order to buy or sell stock is your agent in that trade, and you are the principal.

Agents, particularly those working for brokerage firms, may also be referred to as financial consultants, account executives, registered representatives, or investment executives.

Aggressive-growth fund

These mutual funds buy stock in companies that show rapid growth potential, including start-up companies and those in hot sectors. While these funds and the companies they invest in can increase significantly in value, they are also among the most volatile. Their values may rise much higher—and fall much lower—than the overall stock market or the mutual funds that invest in the broader market.

All or none order (AON)

When a trading order is marked AON, the broker who is handling the order must either fill the whole order or not fill it at all. However, the order isn't canceled unless it is also marked FOK, or fill or kill.

Alpha

A stock's alpha is an analyst's estimate of the potential price increase in that stock based on the rate at which the company's earnings are growing and other aspects of the company's current performance. For example, if a stock has an alpha of 1.15, that means you would expect a 15% price increase in a year when stock prices in general are flat.

One investment strategy is to look for stocks whose alphas are high, which means the stocks are undervalued and have the potential to provide a strong return. A stock's alpha is different from its beta, which estimates its price volatility in relation to the market as a whole.

Alternative minimum tax (AMT)

This tax law provision was designed to insure that all individuals and companies pay some federal income tax, no matter how many deductions or credits they can claim.

Under the AMT, certain income not usually taxable—income on tax-free bonds, for example—is treated as taxable. People who take major tax deductions, such as interest on a large mortgage, may be surprised to find themselves subject to the AMT.

American Association of Individual Investors (AAII)

The goal of this independent, nonprofit organization is teaching individual investors how to manage their assets effectively. Headquartered in Chicago, the AAII offers publications, seminars, educational programs, software and videos, and other services and products to its members. The AAII website (www.aaii.org) also provides a wide range of information about investing and personal finance.

American depositary receipt (ADR)

Shares of hundreds of major overseas-based companies, including well-known names such as British Petroleum, Gucci Group, Sony, and Toyota, are available on US stock markets as ADRs and trade in US dollars. They are receipts issued by American banks that hold home-country shares of the companies. ADRs let you diversify into international markets without having to purchase shares on overseas exchanges or through mutual funds.

American Stock Exchange (AMEX)

The second-largest floor-based stock exchange in the US after the New York Stock Exchange (NYSE), the AMEX operates a central auction market in stocks (including a large number of overseas stocks) and derivatives, including options on many NYSE-traded and over-the-counter (OTC) stocks.

Although AMEX merged with the electronic Nasdaq Stock Market (Nasdaq) in 1998 to form what's known as the Nasdaq-Amex Market Group, the exchange continues to operate independently.

Amortization

Amortization is the gradual repayment of a debt over a period of time, such as monthly payments on a mortgage or credit card balance. To amortize a loan, your payments must be large enough not only to pay interest that has accrued but also to reduce the principal amount you owe. The word amortize itself tells the story, since it means "to bring to death."

Analyst

A financial analyst tracks the performance of a number of companies or industries, evaluates their potential value as investments, and makes recommendations to buy, sell, or hold specific securities. When the most highly respected analysts express a strong opinion about a stock, there is often an immediate impact on that stock's price as investors rush to follow the advice.

Some analysts work for financial institutions, such as mutual fund companies, brokerage firms, and banks. Others work for analytical services, such as Value Line, Inc., Morningstar, Inc., Standard & Poor's, or Moody's Investors Service, or as independent evaluators. Zacks (www.zacks.com) and First Call (www.firstcall.com) make reports from hundreds of different analysts available on their websites, and analysts' commentaries appear regularly in the financial press, and on radio, television, and the Internet.

Annual percentage rate (APR)

The APR is the annual effective cost of credit on a loan, expressed as a percentage. The APR includes most of a loan's up-front fees as well as the annual interest rate, so it gives a more accurate picture of the cost of borrowing than the interest rate alone. For example, the APR on a car loan or a mortgage, which shows the actual interest you pay, is usually higher than the interest rate you're quoted for the loan.

Annual percentage yield (APY)

Annual percentage yield is the amount you earn on an interest-bearing investment in a year, expressed as a percentage. For example, if in 1999 you earned $60 on a $1,000 certificate of deposit (CD), your APY is 6%.

When the APY is the same as the interest rate that is being paid on an investment, you are earning simple interest. But when the APY is higher than the interest rate, the interest is being compounded, which means you are earning interest on your accumulating interest.

Annual report

By law, each publicly held corporation must provide its shareholders with an annual report showing its income and balance sheet. In most cases, it contains not only financial details but a message from the chairman, a description of the company's operations, and an overview of its achievements.

Most annual reports are glossy affairs that also serve as marketing pieces. Copies are generally available from the company's investor relations office, and annual reports may even appear on the company's website. The company's 10-K report is a more comprehensive look at its finances.

Annuity

Originally, an annuity was simply an annual payment—hence the name. Over time, annuity has come to refer to different kinds of payments, investments, and financial products.

Most commonly, an annuity describes the amount you receive from your pension each year, usually in monthly installments. But, in fact, annuity also refers to the annual income you receive from any source, as well as the source itself. For example, some tax-deferred retirement savings plans are called annuities.

When an annuity is offered as part of a qualified plan, such as a 401(k), a 403(b), or tax-sheltered annuity (TSA), you defer tax on your contribution as well as on any earnings, and you typically begin to receive income from the annuity when you retire.

You can also buy other types of annuities, which provide tax-deferred earnings, a source of regular income, or

both. For example, you can buy a nonqualified deferred annuity while you're working and get income from it when you retire. Or you can buy an immediate annuity when you retire and receive monthly payments as long as you live.

With nonqualified annuities, there are no federal limits on annual contributions and no required withdrawals. You also have a wide choice of products, which can be structured to fit your particular goals and risk tolerance.

Arbitrage

Arbitrage is the technique of simultaneously buying a security at a lower price in one market and selling it at a higher price in another to make a profit on the spread between the prices. Although the price difference may be very small, arbitrageurs, or arbs, trade huge amounts, so they can make sizable profits. But the strategy, which depends on split-second timing, can also backfire if interest rates or prices move in unanticipated ways.

Arithmetic index

An arithmetic index gives equal weight to the percentage price change of each stock that's included in the index. In computing the index, the percentage changes of all the stocks are added, and the total is divided by the number of stocks. The percentage price changes of large companies aren't counted more heavily, as they are in a market-capitalization weighted index. Neither are the percentage price changes of stocks that are selling at higher prices, as they are in a price-weighted index.

While an arithmetic index is a more accurate measure of total stock market performance than an index that stresses relatively few high-priced or large-company stocks, some analysts point out that it may also produce higher total return figures than other indexing methods. The best known arithmetic index in the US is the one computed by Value Line, Inc., which tracks the 1,700 stocks the company analyzes regularly.

Ask

The ask price (a shortening of asked price) is the price at which a market maker or broker offers to sell a security or commodity. The price another market maker or broker is willing to pay for that security is called the bid price, and the difference between the two prices is called the spread.

Bid and ask prices are typically reported to the media for commodities and over-the-counter (OTC) transactions. In contrast, last, or closing, prices are reported for exchange-traded and national market securities. With open-end mutual funds, the ask price is the net asset value (NAV), or the price you get if you sell, plus the sales charge, if one applies.

Asset

Assets are everything you own that has any monetary value, plus any money you are owed. They include money in your checking account, your stocks, bonds, and mutual funds, your equity in real estate, the value of your life insurance policy, and any personal property that people would pay to own. When you figure your net worth, you subtract the amount you owe, or your liabilities, from the value of your assets.

Asset allocation

Asset allocation is a strategy, advocated by modern portfolio theory, for maximizing gains while minimizing risks in your investment portfolio. Specifically, asset allocation means dividing your assets among different broad categories of investments, including stocks, bonds, and cash.

ASSET ALLOCATION

AGGRESSIVE
85% Stocks
10% Bonds
5% Cash

MODERATE
65% Stocks
25% Bonds
10% Cash

CONSERVATIVE
40% Stocks
40% Bonds
20% Cash

Choosing an asset allocation model, or what percentage of your portfolio to allocate to each investment category, depends on many factors, such as how much time you have to invest, your tolerance for risk, the direction of interest rates, and the market outlook. Many experts advise you to adjust or rebalance your portfolio at least once a year to bring it in line with your model as well as to realign your model as your financial goals change. Brokerage firms regularly revise the allocations they are recommending to take changing economic conditions and their sense of future developments into account.

Asset-backed bond

These bonds, also known as asset-backed securities, are backed by loans or by money owed to a company for merchandise or services purchased on credit. For example, an asset-backed bond is created when a securities firm bundles some type of debt, such as mortgages or car loans, and sells investors the right to receive the payments that consumers make on those loans.

Asset class

Different categories of investments, such as stocks, bonds, and cash or cash equivalents, are sometimes described as asset classes. When you allocate the assets in your investment portfolio, you decide what proportion of the total value will be invested in different asset classes. Investments such as real estate, collectibles, and precious metals are also generally considered asset classes. So are futures contracts, options, and mutual funds that follow certain alternative investment strategies more typically associated with hedge funds.

Asset management account

These all-in-one investment accounts, also known as central asset accounts, provide the financial advantages of an investment account combined with the convenience of a checking account. Offered by many brokerage firms and mutual fund companies, asset management accounts generally offer check-writing and ATM privileges, credit cards, direct deposit, and automatic transfer from one account to another as well as access to reduced-rate loans and other perks.

There are usually annual fees and minimum account requirements. Cash is invested or swept into a money market fund that earns more than low- or no-interest checking or savings accounts. You'll find that individual companies use different proprietary names for their accounts, but all of the accounts tend to share similar characteristics.

At the money

At the money is another way of saying at the current price. Options whose exercise price is the same or almost the same as the current market price of the underlying stock or futures contract are considered at the money.

Auction market

Auction market trading, also known as open outcry, is the way the major stock and commodity exchanges, such as the New York Stock Exchange (NYSE) and the Chicago Board of Trade (CBOT), have

traditionally handled buying and selling. Buyers compete against buyers, and sellers against sellers, to get the best price.

In contrast, the Nasdaq Stock Market (Nasdaq) is described as a negotiated market because the differences between what buyers are offering and sellers are asking are recorded electronically, and the final price is determined by the market maker.

Audit

An audit is a professional, independent examination of a company's financial statements and

accounting documents according to generally accepted accounting principles. An IRS audit, in contrast, is an examination of a taxpayer's return, usually to question the accuracy or acceptability of the information the return reports.

Average

A stock market average is a mathematical way of showing the price changes in representative stocks. It is designed to reflect the general movement of the broad market or a certain segment of the market. A true average adds the prices of the stocks it covers and divides that amount by the number of stocks.

However, many averages are weighted, which means they count stocks with the highest prices or largest market capitalizations more heavily than they do others. That's to account for differences in their impact on the markets and on the economy in general. The most widely followed average is the price-weighted Dow Jones Industrial Average (DJIA), which measures the performance of 30 industrial stocks.

Average annual yield

This figure, expressed as a percentage, is your average yearly income on an investment. You can calculate the average annual yield by adding all the income you received on an investment and dividing that amount by the number of years the money was invested. So if you receive $60 interest on a $1,000 bond each year, the average annual yield is 6% ($60 ÷ $1,000 = 0.06, or 6%).

Baby bond

Bonds whose par values are less than $1,000 are often described as baby bonds, or, in the case of municipal bonds, as mini-munis. Small companies that may not be able to attract institutional investors, such as banks and mutual fund companies, may offer smaller-denomination bonds to raise cash from individual investors. Some municipalities also use baby bonds

to foster involvement in government activities by making it possible for more people to invest.

Baccalaureate bond

These zero-coupon bonds are designed to help families meet college tuition costs. They are usually sold in small denominations, so that buyers can buy several, and have staggered maturity dates to fit a tuition payment schedule. In some states, baccalaureate bond hold-ers receive a bonus if they use the bonds

to pay tuition at an in-state school.

Back-end load

Some mutual funds impose a load, or sales charge, when you sell shares in the fund. That's called a back-end load, or a contingent deferred sales load. Typically, the charge, which is a percentage of the value of the assets you have in the fund, applies only during the first few years you own your shares. In most cases, too, the percentage you pay declines each year during that period and then is dropped.

Shares in back-end load funds are sometimes described as Class B shares to distinguish them from front-end load funds, which are known as Class A shares, and level-load funds, called Class C shares.

Balance of trade

The difference between the value of a country's imports and exports during a specific period of time is called the balance of trade. If a country exports more than it imports, it has a surplus, or favorable balance of trade. A trade deficit, or unfavorable balance, occurs when a country imports more than it exports.

Balanced fund

Balanced funds are mutual funds that invest in a combination of common stock, preferred stock, and bonds to meet their dual investment goal of seeking a strong return while minimizing risk.

In a surging stock market, a balanced fund is unlikely to perform as well as a fund invested solely in stocks. But in a downturn, it is likely to produce a stronger return, since losses in its equity investments are offset by fixed-income investments. Balanced funds also generally produce more income than straight stock funds.

Bankruptcy

When you file a petition of bankruptcy, you acknowledge that you are insolvent, or unable to pay your debts. If you file for Chapter 7, or liquidation bankruptcy, most of your assets are sold to repay the debts. A court-appointed trustee oversees settling creditor claims, which are usually not repaid in full. However,

some debts are not reduced by a declaration of bankruptcy, including past due federal income taxes, alimony, and higher-education loans.

With Chapter 11 bankruptcy, also called reorganization bankruptcy, you work with the court and your creditors to set up a plan to pay off some or all of the debt over a specific period of time, such as three to five years.

While bankruptcy damages your credit rating and exposes your finances to public scrutiny, it can be a way to get out from under the burden of debt and make a new financial start. It may also be a way to hold on to your home, even in a Chapter 7 bankruptcy, since you are not required to liquidate it or a car you need to get to work. Similarly, when you hear that a company is reorganizing or is "in Chapter 11," it means it has filed for bankruptcy.

Chapter 11

Basis

The basis is the total cost of buying an investment or other asset, including the price plus commissions and other charges. If you sell, you subtract the basis from the selling price to determine your capital gain or capital loss. If you give the asset away and the recipient sells it, the basis is the same amount you would have used. But if you leave the asset in your will, the person who receives it gets a step up in basis, which means the basis of the asset is reset to its market value as of the time of your death. When your investment is in real estate, basis is generally described as cost basis.

Basis point

Yields on bonds, notes, and other fixed-income investments fluctuate regularly, typically changing only within hundredths of a percentage point. These small variations are measured in basis points, or gradations of 0.01%, or one-hundredth of a percent, with 100 basis points equaling 1%. For example, when the yield on a bond changes from 12.72% to 12.65%, it has dropped seven basis points.

The term is also used to describe small changes in the interest rates charged for mortgages or other loans, and to indicate your percentage of ownership in certain kinds of investments, where each basis point equals 0.01% of the whole investment.

Bear market

A bear market indicates a prolonged downturn in the financial markets, when prices fall by 15% or more (though some experts think a 10% drop indicates a bear market, and others talk in terms of a 20% drop).

A bear market in stocks occurs when investors sell off shares because they anticipate worsening economic conditions and falling profits. The longest bear market of the 20th century ran from April 1939 to April 1942, and the one that registered the greatest loss—86%—began in April 1930, after the crash of 1929, and lasted until August 1932. A bear market in bonds is usually brought on by rising interest rates.

Bearer bond

Unlike most bonds issued in the US since 1983, which are registered electronically, a bearer bond is a certificate that states the security's par value and the rate at which its interest will be paid. It comes with detachable coupons that must be presented to the issuer to receive the interest payments, which explains why a bond's interest rate is often referred to as its coupon rate.

A bearer bond isn't registered, and there's no record of ownership, which means it can be sold or redeemed by the person or organization that holds it. Similarly, whoever presents a coupon is entitled to an interest payment.

Benchmark

Originally a benchmark was a surveyor's mark indicating a specific height above sea level. But it has come to have a much broader meaning in the world of investing.

A stock market benchmark, for example, is an index or average whose movement is considered a general indicator of the direction of the overall market, against which investors and financial professionals often gauge their market expectations and judge the performance of individual stocks or market sectors. For example, the Standard & Poor's 500-stock Index (S&P 500) and the Dow Jones Industrial Average (DJIA) are the most widely followed benchmarks, or indicators, of the US market. There are also benchmarks for international markets, and for other types of investments such as bonds, mutual funds, and commodities.

In a somewhat different way, the changing yield on the 30-year US Treasury bond is also considered a benchmark of investor attitudes. For example, a lower yield is an indication that investors are putting money into bonds, driving up the price, possibly because they expect stock prices to drop.

Beneficiary

A beneficiary is a person or organization that receives income or inheritance from a will, life insurance policy, retirement plan, trust, or other financial arrangement.

Beta

Beta is a measure of an investment's relative volatility. The higher the beta, the more sharply the value of the investment can be expected to fluctuate in relation to a market index. For example, Standard & Poor's 500-stock Index (S&P 500) has a beta coefficient (or base) of 1. That means if the S&P 500 moves 2% in either direction, a stock with a beta of 1 would also move 2%. Under the same market conditions, however, a stock with a beta of 1.5 would move 3% (2% increase x 1.5 beta = 0.03, or 3%). But a stock with a beta lower than 1 would be expected to be more stable in price and move less.

Betas as low as 0.5 and as high as 4 are fairly common, depending on the sector and size of the company. However, in recent years, a number of experts have disputed the validity of assigning and using a beta value as an accurate predictor of stock performance.

Bid

The bid is the price a market maker or broker is willing to pay for a security, such as a stock or bond, at a particular time. The bid and ask price together constitute a stock quotation.

Bid and ask price

Better known as a quotation or quote, the bid is the price a market maker or broker offers to pay for a security, and the ask price is the price at which a market maker or dealer offers to sell. The difference between the two prices is called the spread.

Big Board

The Big Board is the nickname of the New York Stock Exchange (NYSE), the oldest and largest stock exchange in the nation and the largest in the world. Common and preferred stock, bonds, warrants, and rights are all traded on the Big Board, which dates back to 1792.

Blind trust

When a third party, such as an investment advisor or other trustee, has complete control of the assets held in a trust, it is called a blind trust. Elected officials often set up blind trusts to reassure the public that political decisions are not being made for personal financial benefit, since the officials have given up control over how their investments are being managed, or even what those investments are.

Block trade

When at least 10,000 shares of stock or bonds valued at $200,000 or more are bought or sold in a single transaction, it is called a block trade. Institutional investors, including mutual funds and pension funds, typically trade in this volume, and most individual investors do not.

Blue chip stock

Blue chip stocks are the common stock of large, nationally recognized

companies. Blue chip companies have a reputation for quality products and services and a long-established record of earning profits and paying dividends to investors, regardless of the economic climate. In the UK, this caliber of stock is known as alpha stock. Mutual funds that invest in this type of stock are known as blue chip funds.

Bond

Bonds are debt securities issued by corporations and governments. Bonds are, in fact, loans that you and other investors make to the issuers in return for the promise of being paid interest, usually but not always at a fixed rate. The issuer also promises to repay the debt on time and in full. Because bonds pay interest on a regular basis, they are also described as fixed-income investments.

Bond fund

These mutual funds invest in bonds to produce income. Unlike individual bonds, bond funds have no fixed maturity date and no guaranteed interest rate. Nor do they promise to return your principal. Their appeal is that you can usually invest a much smaller amount of money than you would need to buy a bond on your own, making it easier to diversify your portfolio.

There is a great variety of bond funds, each with a specific investment strategy. For example, some funds invest in long-term, and others in short-term, bonds. Some buy government bonds, while others buy corporate bonds or municipal bonds. Finally, some buy investment-grade bonds, while others focus on high-yield bonds. In other words, you could buy a long-term, investment-grade municipal bond fund, a short-term, high-yield corporate bond fund—or almost any other combination.

HOW A BOND WORKS

When you invest in a bond, you loan money, which you expect to be repaid with interest.

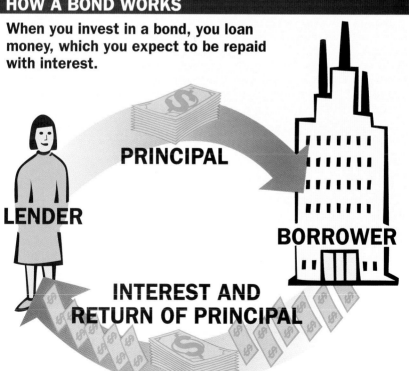

PRINCIPAL

LENDER

BORROWER

INTEREST AND RETURN OF PRINCIPAL

RATING A BOND: A KEY TO THE CODE

Moody's	S&P's	Meaning
Aaa	AAA	Best quality
Aa	AA	High quality
A	A	High-to-medium quality
Baa	BBB	Medium quality
Ba	BB	Some speculative element
B	B	At risk of default
Caa	CCC	Poor quality
Ca	CC	Highly speculative quality
C	C	Lowest-rated
•	D	In default

Bond rating

Independent agencies, such as Standard & Poor's (S&P) and Moody's Investors Service, assess the likelihood that bond issuers—whether corporations or governments—are likely to default on their loans or interest payments. Ratings systems differ from one agency to another but usually have at least 10 categories, ranging from a high of AAA (or Aaa) to a low of D. Bonds ranked BBB (or Baa) or higher are considered investment-grade bonds.

Bond swap

In a bond swap, you buy one bond and sell another at the same time. You might do a swap for several reasons, such as selling one bond at a loss at year's end to get a tax write-off while buying another to keep the same portion of your portfolio allocated to bonds. You might also sell a bond with a lower rating to buy one with a higher rating, or you might sell a bond that's close to its maturity date so you can put the money into a bond that won't mature for several years.

Book-entry security

These securities are electronic versions of stock and bond certificates. Instead of printing a certificate and mailing it to you, the issuing company records the details of your purchase in its computer files. When you sell the security, the records are updated, deleting you as an owner and adding the purchaser. That means you don't have to keep track of paper documents, and they can't be lost or stolen. The Depository Trust Company (DTC) acts as a clearinghouse for book-entry securities.

Book value

Book value is the net asset value (NAV) of a company's stocks and bonds. Finding the NAV involves subtracting the company's short- and long-term liabilities from its assets to find net assets, and then dividing by the number of shares of common stock, preferred stock, or bonds to get the NAV per share or per bond.

Book value is sometimes cited as a way of determining whether a company's assets cover its outstanding obligations and equity issues. Further, some investors and analysts look at the price of a stock in relation to its book value, which is provided in the company's annual report, to help identify undervalued stocks. Other investors discount the relevance of this information.

Bottom fishing

Investors using a bottom-fishing strategy look for stocks that they consider undervalued because the prices are low. The logic of bottom fishing is that stock prices sometimes fall further than a company's actual financial situation warrants, especially in the aftermath of bad news, and can rebound dramatically, providing a healthy profit.

Bottom-up investing

When you use a bottom-up investing strategy, you focus on the potential of individual stocks, bonds, and other investments. Using this approach, for example, means you pay less attention to the economy as a whole, or to the prospects of the industry a company is in, than you do to the company itself.

In making decisions based on bottom-up investing, you read research reports, examine the company's financial stability, and evaluate what you know about its products and services in great detail.

Bourse

Bourse is the French term for a stock exchange, meaning, literally, purse. The national stock market of France, a totally electronic market, is known as the Paris Bourse. The term is used throughout Europe and worldwide as a synonym for stock exchange, though it generally isn't used in the US.

Brady bond

These bonds of Latin American countries, named for former US Secretary of the Treasury Nicholas Brady, are issued in US dollars and backed by US Treasury zero-coupon bonds. The bonds were originally issued in exchange for commercial bank loans that were in default, and their changing prices in the secondary market reflect the level of confidence investors have in the economies of the issuing nations.

Breakpoint

Mutual funds that charge a percentage of the amount you invest as a front-end load, or sales charge, when you buy shares may reduce that percentage if you make a large investment. The dollar amount at which the reduction applies is known as a breakpoint.

In most cases, the first breakpoint is $25,000, with further reductions for each additional $25,000 or $50,000 purchase. For example, if the standard load were 5.5%, it might drop to 5.25% at $25,000, to 5% at $50,000, and perhaps to as low as 2.5% with an investment of $250,000.

In calculating breakpoints, some fund companies will combine the value of all of your investments in the mutual funds they offer. So, for example, if you had $45,000 invested in various funds and added $5,000 to one of them, you might qualify for the reduced sales charge because the total value of your investment reached the breakpoint of $50,000.

Broker

A broker works for a brokerage firm, handling client orders to buy or sell stocks, bonds, commodities, and options in return for a commission. Brokers are licensed in the state where they work and become registered representatives by passing a uniform examination administered by the National Association of Securities Dealers (NASD). Many brokers provide a range of investor services, including financial planning and advice on specific buy and sell decisions.

Broker/Dealer

Broker/dealers have a dual financial role. As brokers, they act on buy and sell orders from their clients. As dealers, they buy and sell securities for their brokerage firm's account. The securities a firm owns may be sold to the firm's clients, sometimes at a more favorable price than if those securities had to be purchased in the open market. They may also be sold to other firms wanting to fulfill a client's buy order. Or the securities a dealer buys may become part of the firm's own investment portfolio.

Brokerage account

To buy and sell securities through a broker/dealer or other financial services firm, you establish an account, generally known as a brokerage account, with that firm.

Investment Rating Systems

How can one analyst's winner be another analyst's also-ran?

With the recent explosion of investment information, there's a virtually infinite supply of resources—both in print and online—that rate, rank and analyze securities. But what do you do when one analyst's strong buy is another's sell, or when one rating system puts an investment at the front of the pack and another relegates it to the middle of the field?

Knowing the Score

Investment rating services extensively research the mutual funds they evaluate and provide in-depth analyses of their findings.

Lipper, Inc. uses letters of the alphabet, with A as the highest score and E as the lowest. Value Line, Inc. uses a five-point scale, with one at the top and five at the bottom. Morningstar, Inc. uses stars, assigning five stars to the highest-ranked funds and one star to the lowest-ranked. The rating criteria vary from company to company, though, so a five-star fund doesn't always get an A.

These scores can usually give you a good preliminary reading of a fund's past performance over several different time periods. Some rankings are provided in relation to a broad category, such as domestic funds, and others, like Lipper's, in relation to a more specific peer group, such as small-cap value funds or large-cap growth funds.

Deeper Analysis

When they assign their mutual fund rankings, Lipper, Morningstar, and Value Line consider the level of risk the fund takes in producing its return.

For example, Lipper uses a classification structure that categorizes equity funds using five possible levels of market capitalization and five possible levels of risk, or aggressiveness. Then it evaluates funds against others that fit into the same category. The top 20% get an A.

Morningstar provides an integrated ranking. To determine the number of stars a mutual fund merits, the company calculates a separate risk score and return score for each fund in each of the time periods it is evaluating and subtracts the risk score from the return score. Using those results, Morningstar assigns five stars to funds that end up in the top 10% of the category to which they are assigned.

Value Line provides two rankings for each fund it follows. They may be the same—both twos, for example—but it's likely that they will be different. The performance ranking evaluates the consistency of a fund's risk-adjusted performance against other funds in the same category, assigning a one to the top 10% of funds in each category. The risk ranking, on the other hand, is based on volatility, and is figured using standard deviation. The 10% of funds with the greatest volatility are given a five, and the 10% with the lowest are given a one.

The ABCs of Bond Ratings

Bond ratings tell a slightly different story. When you buy a bond, you're making a loan to the bond issuer, and what you want to know is whether the interest will be paid on time and whether you'll get your investment principal back at maturity. So a bond rating is in effect a credit rating, or an assessment of how likely the issuer is to be able to pay.

The best-known bond rating services are Standard & Poor's, Moody's Investors Service and A.M. Best & Company. Each rates bonds from A to C, with AAA (or Aaa) indicating the best quality and least risk and C indicating poor quality with high risk. Each service uses a slightly different lettering scale, and their conclusions may vary a grade or two because each emphasizes slightly different factors. But interpreting what they're telling you isn't hard or confusing.

Keep in mind, though, that these are ratings—they aren't recommendations for or against buying a bond. And they aren't directed toward any particular type of investor. Finding the bonds that are right for you depends on knowing what your investment goals are and how much risk you are willing to take.

Stock Answers

If you're investigating stocks you'll discover the nifty 50 (the stocks institutional investors choose), the magic 25 (*Individual Investor* magazine's favorites), and the Dogs of the Dow

(the 10 highest-yielding stocks in the Dow Jones Industrial Average). If you visit financial websites, you'll come across Stocks of the Day, Hot Picks, or maybe even Fanny's Favorites.

But the information that seems the easiest—analysts' recommendations to buy, hold or sell—can be the most perplexing because it's hard to know how they come to their conclusions. More confusing, one analyst's buy can be another's sell.

The solution many experts suggest, if you're seriously looking for advice, is to look for one or more analysts or analytical systems with good track records who follow stocks you're interested in. You may want to give some weight to what they say.

Rating or Ranking?

Although the terms rating and ranking are often used interchangeably, they mean different things. A rating is based on how well an investment, such as a bond, meets a certain standard or set of criteria. A ranking states the relative standing of two or more similar investments, suggesting that one is stronger, or riskier, or higher in whatever is being measured, than the other.

In a traditional full-service broker-age firm, a registered representative or account executive who works for the firm handles your buy and sell instructions and often provides investment advice. If your account is with a discount firm, you are more likely to give your orders to whomever answers the telephone when you call. And if your account is with a brokerage firm that is online, you give orders and get confirmations electronically.

In all three cases, the firm provides updated information on your investment activity and portfolio value, and handles the required paperwork. And in some cases, your brokerage account may be part of a larger package of financial services known as an asset management account.

Brokerage firm

Brokerage firms are licensed by the Securities and Exchange Commission (SEC) to buy and sell securities for clients and for their own accounts. When a brokerage firm sells securities it owns, it is said to be acting as a principal in that transaction.

Firms frequently maintain research departments for their own and their clients' benefit, and increasingly they provide a range of financial products and services, including financial planning, asset management, and educational programs. Online brokerages, discount brokerages, and even some traditional full-service brokerage firms allow customers to trade over the Internet and provide a wealth of investment information on their websites.

Bull market

A prolonged period when stock prices as a whole are moving upward is called a bull market, although the rate at which those increases occur can vary widely both from bull market to bull market and during the period a bull market lasts. Well-known bull markets began in 1923 and 1964, and the most recent prolonged bull market started in 1990 (or, by some reckonings, in 1982).

Buy and hold

Buy-and-hold investors take a long-term view of their investments, usually keeping a bond from date of issue to date of maturity and holding onto shares of a stock through bull and bear markets. Over time, they expect the stock's value to increase substantially. Buy and hold is one of two basic investing styles, and is the opposite of market timing.

Buyback

When a company purchases shares of its own publicly traded stock or its own bonds in the open market, it's called a buyback. The most common reason a company buys back its stock is to make the stock more attractive to investors by increasing its earnings per share. While the earnings stay the same, the earnings per share increase because the number of shares has been reduced.

Companies may also buy back shares to pay for acquisitions that are financed with stock swaps, to make stocks available for employee stock option plans, to decrease the risk of a hostile takeover by reducing the number of shares available for sale, or to discourage short-term trading in its stock by driving the price of the outstanding shares upward.

Companies may buy back bonds when they are selling at discount, which is typically the result of rising interest rates. By paying less than par in the open market, the company is able to reduce the cost of redeeming the bonds when they come due.

Cafeteria plan

Some employers offer cafeteria plans, more formally known as flexible spending plans, which give you the option of participating in a range of tax-saving benefit programs. If you enroll in the plan, a percentage of your pretax income is withheld from your paycheck, up to the limit the plan allows, and is then allocated to the parts of the plan you want to participate in.

For example, you can set aside money to pay for medical expenses that aren't covered by insurance, for child care, or for additional life insurance coverage. As you incur these kinds of expenses, you are reimbursed from the amount you have put into the plan.

Since you owe no income tax on the money you contribute, you actually have more cash available for these expenses than if you were spending after-tax dollars. However, you must estimate the amount you're going to contribute before the tax year begins, and you forfeit any money you've set aside but don't spend. For example, if you've set aside $1,500 for medical expenses but spend only $1,400, you lose the $100.

Call

In the securities market, a call is an issuer's right to redeem bonds it has sold before the date they mature. In a related use of the term, when a bank makes a secured loan, it reserves the right to demand full repayment of the loan—referred to as calling the loan—should the borrower default on interest payments.

Call option

Buying a call option gives you the right to buy a fixed quantity of an underlying investment at a specified price—called the strike price—within a specified time period. For example, you might buy a call option on 100 shares of a stock or on a stock index if you expected the price to increase substantially but preferred not to tie up your money by making the actual purchase. If the price of the stock or index went up, you could exercise the option and buy at less than the market price. But if the price didn't change or it dropped, you could simply let the option expire.

In contrast, you can sell a call option—known as writing a call. That gives the buyer the right to buy the underlying investment from you at the strike price. If you write a call, you are obliged to sell if the option is exercised.

Callable bond

A callable bond can be redeemed by the issuer before it matures, under the terms of the bond agreement, or deed of trust. Usually the issuer pays the bondholder a premium, or an amount above the par value of the bond, when it is called.

Bonds are typically called when interest rates fall sharply, and issuers can save money by paying off existing debt and offering new bonds at lower rates. Before you purchase a bond, you can check with your broker to see if it's callable. Or, if the bond is listed in the bond tables provided in the financial press, you can check there.

Cap

A cap is a ceiling, or the highest level to which an interest rate can rise over a specified period of time. Caps are often applied to variable- or floating-rate bonds or to adjustable-rate mortgages (ARMs). For example, your ARM contract may specify a 2% annual cap and a 6% lifetime cap on interest rates. That means that the interest rate cannot go up more than 2% each year or more than 6% over the entire life of the mortgage.

Capital

Capital is any asset that is used to generate income or make a long-term investment. For example, the money you use to buy shares in a mutual fund is considered capital. So is the money you use to make a down payment on a house. Businesses use capital, which is often money from loans or earnings, for reinvestment, expansion, and acquisitions.

Capital appreciation

Any increase in an asset's fair market value is called capital appreciation. For example, if a stock increases in value from $30 a share to $60 a share, it shows capital appreciation. Some stock mutual funds that invest for aggressive growth are called capital appreciation funds.

Capital gain

When you sell an asset at a higher price than you paid for it, the difference is your capital gain. For example, if you buy 100 shares of stock for $20 a share and sell them for $30 a share, you realize a capital gain of $10 a share, or $1,000 in total. If you had owned the stock for at least a year before selling it, you would have a long-term capital gain. In contrast, if you had held the stock for less than a year, you would have a short-term capital gain.

Long-term capital gains are taxed at a lower rate than your other income. Currently, long-term capital tax rates are 20% for anyone whose marginal federal tax rate is 28% or higher, and 10% for anyone whose marginal rate is 15%. Even lower rates are scheduled to take effect for assets purchased in 2000 or later and held at least five years. The idea behind lower capital gains tax rates is to stimulate investments in business.

CAPITAL GAIN	
What you sold for	$3,000
− What you paid	− $2,000
CAPITAL GAIN	$1,000

Capital gains distribution

When mutual fund companies sell investments that have increased in value, the profits, or capital gains, are passed on to their shareholders as capital gains distributions. These distributions are made on a regular schedule, generally at the end of the year. Most funds offer the option of automatically reinvesting all or part of your capital gains distributions to buy more shares.

Capital loss

When you sell an asset for less than you paid for it, the difference is your capital loss. For example, if you buy 100 shares of stock at $30 a share and sell when the price has dropped to $20 a share, you will realize a capital loss of $10 a share, or $1,000.

Although nobody wants to lose money on an investment, there is a silver lining: You can offset capital losses against capital gains in computing your income tax. And if you have a net capital loss in any year—that is, your losses are greater than your gains—you can usually deduct up to $3,000 of this amount from regular income on your tax return. You may also be able to deduct net capital losses above $3,000 on future tax returns.

CAPITAL LOSS	
What you paid	$3,000
− What you sold for	− $2,000
CAPITAL LOSS	$1,000

Capital market

The physical and electronic markets where equity and debt securities are traded, as well as the commodities exchanges and the over-the-counter (OTC) markets, are called capital markets. When you place an order through a brokerage firm, trade online, or use a dividend reinvestment plan (DRIP), you're participating in a capital market. The term is also used to describe the direct sale of stocks and bonds by an issuer to an institutional investor, such as a mutual fund company.

Cash balance pension

A cash balance pension is an employer-sponsored retirement plan that resembles defined benefit plans in some ways and defined contribution plans, such as 401(k)s, in others. As with defined benefit plans, the employer makes a contribution in each employee's name and guarantees a return, typically promising to pay interest at a rate linked to the rate being paid on US Treasury bonds.

Like 401(k)s, the plan is portable, which means any employee who leaves the company can move the assets that have accumulated in his or her name into a new employer's plan, or into a rollover IRA. The employee also has the option of leaving the assets in the plan, where they will continue to earn interest.

Cash balance plans have advantages for younger employees since a percentage of their earnings is added to the plan each year and can compound over time. The plans also benefit employees who change jobs during their careers.

On the other hand, employees who have stayed at the same job for many years and whose employer switches from a traditional defined benefit plan to a cash balance plan are likely to receive substantially less pension income from a cash balance plan than from a traditional plan. That's because traditional plans typically figure pension income based on the worker's salary in the final three to five years before retirement, when salaries tend to be highest.

Cash equivalent
Low-risk investments, such as money market funds or short-term certificates of deposit (CDs), are considered cash equivalents. The Financial Accounting Standards Board (FASB), which is responsible for establishing national accounting standards, defines cash equivalents as highly liquid securities with maturities of less than three months. Liquid securities typically are those that can be sold easily with little or no loss of value.

Cash market
In a cash market, also known as a spot market, buyers pay the current market price for securities, currency, or commodities "on the spot," just as you would pay cash for groceries or other consumer products. Ownership is transferred promptly, and payment is made upon delivery. A cash market is the opposite of a futures market, where commodities or financial products are scheduled for delivery and payment at a set price at a specified time in the future.

Ceiling
If there is an upper limit, or cap, on the interest rate you can be charged on an adjustable-rate loan, it's known as a ceiling. Even if interest rates in general rise higher than the interest-rate ceiling on your loan, the rate you're paying can't be increased above the ceiling.

However, according to the terms of some loans, lenders can add interest comparable to what a jump in rates would add to your loan repayment, a situation known as negative amortization. That means, despite a ceiling, you don't escape the consequences of rising rates, though repayment is postponed, often until the end of the loan's original term.

Ceiling can also refer to a cap on the amount of interest a bond issuer is willing to pay to float a bond, and to the highest price a futures contract can reach on any single trading day before the market locks up, or stops trading, that contract.

Central bank
Most countries have a central bank, which issues the country's currency, holds the reserve deposits of other banks in that country, and either initiates or carries out the country's monetary policy, including keeping tabs on the money supply. In the US, the 12 regional banks that make up the Federal Reserve System act as the central bank. This structure was deliberately developed to ensure that no single region of the country could control economic decision making.

Certificate of accrual on Treasury securities (CATS)
CATS are US Treasury zero-coupon bonds that are sold at deep discount to par, or their face value. Like other zeros, the interest isn't actually paid during the bond's term but accumulates so that you receive face value at maturity. You can use CATS in your long-term portfolio to provide money for college tuition or retirement, for example.

As with other zeros, CATS prices can be volatile, so you run the risk of losing some of your principal if you have to sell before maturity. And like other federal government issues, the interest is free of state and local income tax but subject to federal income tax.

Certificate of deposit (CD)

CDs are time deposits offered by banks and guaranteed by the Federal Deposit Insurance Corporation (FDIC) up to $100,000 for each depositor. You generally earn compound interest at a fixed rate, which is determined by the current interest rate and the CD's term, which can range from a week to several years.

However, rates can vary significantly from bank to bank, and some banks also offer hybrid CDs whose earnings are tied to a stock index like Standard & Poor's 500-stock Index (S&P 500), or offer an adjustable rate. You usually have to pay a penalty if you withdraw funds before your CD matures—often equal to the interest that has accrued up to the time you make the withdrawal.

Chicago Board of Trade (CBOT)

Established in 1848 to stabilize and organize the midwestern grain trade, the CBOT is the world's oldest and largest futures exchange.

Chicago Board Options Exchange (CBOE)

Founded in 1973, the CBOE is the world's second-largest securities exchange and the largest options exchange. More than 91% of all index options traded in the US are traded on the CBOE.

Churning

If a broker does excessive buying and selling within your investment account, it's known as churning. One indication that your account is being churned is that you end up paying more in commissions than you earn on your investments. Churning is illegal but is often hard to prove.

Circuit breaker

After the stock market crash of 1987, stock and commodities exchanges established a system of trigger-point rules, known as circuit breakers, to temporarily restrict trading in stocks, stock options, and stock index futures when prices fall too far, too fast.

Currently, trading is halted when the market, measured by the Dow Jones Industrial Average (DJIA), drops 10%. But trading could resume, depending on the time of day the drop occurs. If the Dow drops 20%, trading ends for the day. The actual number of points the Dow would need to drop is set twice a year (in January and June) based on the average value of the Dow in the previous month.

The circuit breakers have been triggered only once—on October 27, 1997, when the Dow fell 554 points, or 7.2%, and the trigger levels were lower. In fact, the market has dropped as much as 10% only three times since 1915.

Clearinghouse

Clearing corporations, or clearinghouses, provide operational support for brokerage firms and exchanges, and help ensure the integrity of securities trading in the US and other open markets. For example, when an order to buy or sell securities, futures, or options has been filled, the clearinghouse compares the details of the trade, delivers the product, and ensures that payment is made to settle the transaction.

Closed-end fund

Closed-end mutual funds raise capital only once, by issuing a fixed number of shares. They are traded on an exchange, as stocks are, and their prices fluctuate, based on supply and demand as well as on changes in the value of their underlying holdings. Closed-end funds are also known as exchange-traded funds.

Closely held

A closely held corporation is one in which a handful of investors, often the people who founded the company, own a majority of the outstanding stock.

Closing price

The closing price of a stock, bond, option, or futures contract is the last trading price before the exchange or market on which it is traded closes for the day. With after-hours trading, however, the opening price at the start of the next trading day may be different from the closing price the day before. When a security is valued as part of an estate or charitable gift, its value is set at the closing price on the day of the valuation of the estate.

Collateral

Assets with monetary value, such as stocks, bonds, or real estate, that are used to guarantee a loan are considered collateral. If the borrower defaults and fails to fulfill the terms of the loan agreement, the collateral, or some portion of it, becomes the property of the lender.

For example, if you borrow money to buy a car, the car is the collateral. If you default, the lender can repossess the car and sell it to recover the amount you borrowed. Loans guaranteed by collateral are also known as secured loans.

Collateralized mortgage obligation (CMO)

CMOs are bonds backed by mortgages. Issuers of CMOs subdivide  pools of mortgages into investments called tranches, which are then packaged and sold with different interest rates and maturity dates. CMOs usually involve high-quality mortgages, or those guaranteed by the government.

While their yield may be lower than those of other mortgage-backed investments, one attractive feature of CMOs is that they are not usually redeemed, or called, before maturity. But if interest rates drop sharply, repayment can be sped up.

Collectible

When you invest in objects rather than in assets such as stocks or bonds, you are putting your money into collectibles. Collectibles can run the gamut from fine art, antique furniture, stamps, and coins to baseball cards and Barbie dolls.

Their common drawback, as an investment, is their lack of liquidity. If you need to sell your collectibles, you may not be able to find a buyer who is willing to pay what you believe your investment is worth. In fact, you may not be able to find a buyer at all. On the other hand, collectibles can provide a sizable return on your investment if you have the right thing for sale at the right time.

Commercial bank

Commercial banks offer a full range of retail banking products and services, such as checking and savings accounts, loans, and certain investments to individuals and businesses. Between 1933 and 1999, commercial banks could not underwrite securities.

However, with the repeal of parts of the Glass-Steagall Act, many commercial banks can act as broker/dealers, which means they can sell securities, mutual funds, and variable annuities, and provide other investment services.

Commercial paper

To help meet their immediate needs for cash, banks and corporations sometimes issue unsecured, short-term debt instruments known as commercial paper. Commercial paper can be a good place for investors—institutional investors in particular—to park cash temporarily. That's because commercial paper is liquid and essentially risk-free, since it is typically issued by profitable, long-established organizations.

Commission

Securities brokers and other sales agents charge a commission for their services, which is a sales charge on each transaction. With traditional, full-service brokers, the charge is usually a percentage of the total cost of the trade, though some brokers may offer favorable rates to heavy traders.

Online brokerages, on the other hand, usually charge a flat fee for each transaction, regardless of the value of the trade. The flat fee may have certain limits, however, such as the number of shares being traded at one time. Except for mutual funds, new issues, and thinly traded securities, the maximum commission a broker can charge is 5%.

Committee on Uniform Securities Identifying Procedures (CUSIP)

CUSIP assigns codes and numbers to all US exchange-traded securities. The

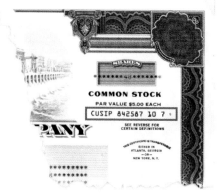

CUSIP identification number is used to track the securities when they are bought and sold. You'll find the CUSIP number on a confirmation statement from your broker, for example, and on the face of a stock certificate.

Commodity

Commodities are bulk goods and raw materials, such as grains, metals, livestock, oil, cotton, coffee, sugar, and cocoa, that are used to produce consumer products. The term also describes financial products, such as currency or stock and bond indexes, that are the raw materials of trade.

Commodities are bought and sold on the cash market, and they are traded on the futures exchanges in the form of futures contracts. Commodity prices are driven by supply and demand: When a commodity is plentiful—tomatoes in August, for example—prices are comparatively low. When a commodity is scarce because of a bad crop or because it is out of season, the price will generally be higher.

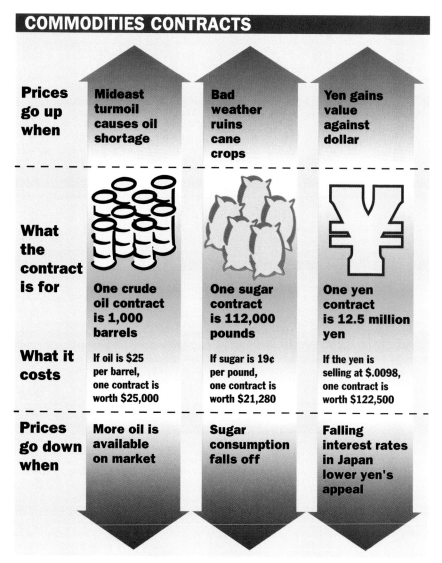

COMMODITIES CONTRACTS

Prices go up when	Mideast turmoil causes oil shortage	Bad weather ruins cane crops	Yen gains value against dollar
What the contract is for	One crude oil contract is 1,000 barrels	One sugar contract is 112,000 pounds	One yen contract is 12.5 million yen
What it costs	If oil is $25 per barrel, one contract is worth $25,000	If sugar is 19¢ per pound, one contract is worth $21,280	If the yen is selling at $.0098, one contract is worth $122,500
Prices go down when	More oil is available on market	Sugar consumption falls off	Falling interest rates in Japan lower yen's appeal

Commodity Futures Trading Commission (CFTC)

The CFTC is an independent agency that regulates the US commodity futures and options markets. The agency's

five commissioners, who are appointed by the president for staggered five-year terms, are responsible for maintaining fair and orderly markets, enforcing market regulations, and protecting customers from fraudulent or abusive trading practices.

Commodity exchanges also regulate themselves, but any new rules they want to introduce, or any changes they want to make to existing rules, must be approved by the CFTC before they go into effect.

Common stock

When you own common stock, you own shares in a corporation. Your shares give you voting rights to elect a company's board of directors, but unlike holders of preferred stock, you are not guaranteed dividend payments. However, common stock has historically

produced a stronger long-term total return than any other investment category through a combination of dividend payments and increases in value (known as capital appreciation).

Community property

In nine US states any assets, investments, and income that are acquired during a marriage are considered community property, or owned jointly by the married couple. For example, if you're married, live in one of these states, and buy stock, half the value of that stock belongs to your spouse even if you paid the entire cost of buying it.

In a divorce, the value of the community property is divided equally. However, property you owned before you got married or that you received as a gift is generally not considered community property. (The community property states are Arizona, California, Idaho, Louisiana, Nevada, New Mexico, Texas, Washington, and Wisconsin.)

Competitive trader

A competitive trader, also known as a registered competitive trader or a floor trader, buys and sells stocks for his or her own account on the floor of the New York Stock Exchange (NYSE). Traders must follow very specific rules governing when they can buy and sell. But since they trade in large volumes and do not pay commissions on their transactions, they are able to profit from even small differences in the price they pay and the price they get when they sell.

Composite trading

Composite trading figures report the price changes, closing prices, and the total daily trading volume for stocks, warrants, and options listed on the New York Stock Exchange (NYSE) or the American Stock Exchange (AMEX).

In addition, the NYSE total also includes transactions on exchanges in Boston, Chicago, Cincinnati, and Philadelphia, and on the Pacific Exchange in California. Since trading continues on some of those exchanges after the close of business in New York, the composite figures give a comprehensive picture of the day's activities.

COMPOUND INTEREST VERSUS SIMPLE INTEREST

$100 invested at 10% interest	▶ Compound	▶ Simple
Start	▶ $100.00	▶ $100.00
After 1 Year	▶ $110.00	▶ $110.00
After 2 Years	▶ $121.00	▶ $120.00
After 3 Years	▶ $133.10	▶ $130.00
After 4 Years	▶ $146.41	▶ $140.00
After 5 Years	▶ $161.05	▶ $150.00
GROWTH RATE	▶61.1%	▶50%

Compound interest

When the interest you earn on an investment also earns interest, it is said to be compound interest. Without compounding, you earn simple interest, and your investment doesn't grow as quickly.

For example, if you earn 10% interest on $100 every year for five years, you'll have $110 after one year, $121 after two years, $133.10 after three years, and $161.05 after five years—for total growth of 61.1% on your investment. With simple interest, you would have earned $150 after five years, for 50% growth. The $11.05 difference is the effect of compounding. Compound interest earnings are reported as annual percentage yield (APY), though the compounding can be figured annually, monthly, or daily.

Comptroller of the Currency

The Office of the Comptroller of the Currency, housed in the US Department of the Treasury, charters, regulates, and oversees national banks. The comptroller ensures bank integrity, fosters economic growth, promotes competition among banks, and guarantees that all Americans have access to adequate financial services by enforcing the Community Reinvestment Act and federal fair lending laws, which mandate that access. The comptroller is appointed by the president of the United States and confirmed by the Senate.

Confirmation

When you buy or sell a stock, your brokerage firm will send you a document showing what you bought or sold, the price, the trade and settlement date, and the commission. You'll also receive confirms when you buy or sell a bond, and to reaffirm orders you place, such as a good 'til canceled order to buy or sell a certain stock. In addition activity in your trading account, such as stock splits, spinoffs, or mergers will trigger a confirmation notice.

Conscience fund

If you prefer to invest in companies whose business practices are in keeping with your social, political, or environmental values, you can buy mutual funds described as green, socially responsible, or conscience funds. For example, you can choose funds that put money into companies that have exceptional environmental or social records, or those that refuse to invest in the tobacco or weapons industries.

In late 1999, there were more than 60 funds in this rather loosely defined category, up from 12 in 1990. While some fund companies offer conscience funds exclusively, others offer them as part of a broader fund mix.

Consumer Confidence Index

Released each month by The Conference Board, an independent, not-for-profit business research organization, the Consumer Confidence Index measures how a representative sample of 5,000 US households feel about the current state of the economy, and what they anticipate the future will bring.

The survey focuses specifically on the participants' impressions of business conditions and the job market. When consumer attitudes are positive because they think the economy is growing and they have a sense of job security, they are more likely to spend money, which contributes to the very economic growth they anticipate. But if consumers are worried about their jobs, they may spend less, contributing to an economic slowdown.

Consumer Confidence Index

Consumer Price Index (CPI)

The consumer price index is a monthly gauge of inflation that measures changes in the prices of basic goods and services, such as housing, food, clothing, transportation, medical care, and education.

Compiled monthly by the US Bureau of Labor Statistics, the CPI—often incorrectly referred to as the cost-of-living index—is used as a benchmark for making adjustments in Social Security payments, wages, pensions, and tax brackets to keep them in tune with the buying power of the dollar.

Contango

The price of a futures contract tends to reflect the cost of storage, insurance, financing, and other expenses incurred by the producer as the commodity awaits delivery. So typically, the further in the future the maturity date, the higher the price of the contract. That relationship is described as contango.

If the opposite is true, and the price of a longer-term contract is lower than the price of one with a closer expiration date, the relationship is described as backwardation.

Contingent deferred sales load

Some mutual funds impose a sales charge, called a back-end load or contingent deferred sales load, when you sell shares in the fund within a certain period of time after you buy them. That period, which might be as short as a few months or as long as several years, is determined by the fund.

The charge is a percentage of your investment amount and may be the same—say 1%—during the entire period it applies, or it might begin at a higher percentage and decline each year until it disappears entirely, typically over five to seven years. Information about the charge and how long it's levied is provided in the fund's prospectus.

Contrarian

An investor who marches to a different drummer is sometimes described as a contrarian. In other words, if most in-

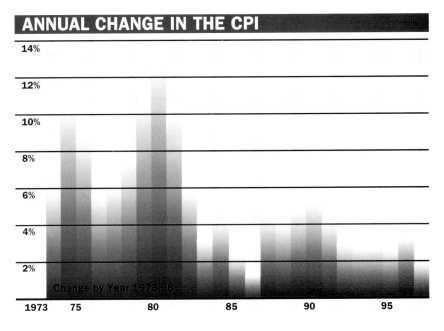

ANNUAL CHANGE IN THE CPI

Change by Year 1973-98

Measuring the Economy

The economy is always being weighed and measured to see if it's healthy.

The health of the economy is affected by so many factors, and its performance is measured in so many ways, that it can be hard to sort out what all the information tells—or doesn't tell—you.

Gross Domestic Product

The Gross Domestic Product, or GDP, measures a country's economic well-being in terms of the dollar value of the goods and services that are produced over a given period of time, usually a year. In the US, the Department of Commerce calculates GDP by subtracting the cost of raw materials from the selling prices of new goods and services. That amount is what's being pumped back into the economy as income to the producers.

Nominal and Real

Changes in the GDP are calculated two different ways to account for the effect of inflation on the value of the dollar. The first calculation is in current dollars and produces what is called the nominal GDP. Current-dollar or nominal GDP measures the value of production in sale prices at the time of production, which are typically higher than they were in previous years. That makes it difficult to determine to what extent increases in production, as opposed to higher prices, contribute to any increase in the GDP.

The second method uses a fixed value for the dollar, or what it was worth in the arbitrarily chosen baseline year of 1987, and produces what is known as the constant-dollar or real GDP. Real GDP is a more accurate measure of growth because one of the variables—the value of the dollar—is kept constant from year to year.

Whatever Happened to GNP?

Before 1991, US experts used the Gross National Product (GNP) as the primary economic yardstick. But to be consistent with the United Nations System of National Accounts, they switched to the GDP. The basic difference is that GDP measures earnings within the country where they're created, whether by domestic or overseas companies. The GNP measures earnings produced both at home and abroad by US citizens and corporations, but not earnings produced in the US by overseas companies.

Limitations of the GDP

While many experts consider the GDP the most comprehensive measure of economic growth, critics say it has some limitations. For example, it doesn't account for goods and services created outside of organized markets. All sorts of transactions, from a waiter's unreported tips to a small farmer's self-sufficiency, go unnoticed. Further, it doesn't include purchases of goods produced in the past, or purchases of stocks and bonds. There's no way to tell how much activity falls into these categories, and thus no way to know how accurate (or inaccurate) a measure of the total economy the GDP is.

Consumer Price Index

The Consumer Price Index, or CPI, measures the monthly change in the prices of 80,000 goods and services that reflect the spending habits of the average urban American consumer. Changes are measured against the cost of the same or comparable goods and services in 1982. The CPI is the the most widely used measure of inflation: Among other things, it's used as a benchmark for a variety of economic decisions, such as negotiating new labor contracts and calculating increases in Social Security benefits.

The Index of Leading Economic Indicators

The Index of Leading Economic Indicators is released every month by The Conference Board, a business research group. The Index is designed to predict short-term changes in the economy by computing a weighted average of ten economic indicators, including the average number of hours worked in the manufacturing sector of the economy, the weekly claims for unemployment, new orders for consumer goods, and the number of building permits issued for private homes as well as information on interest rates, stock prices and the money supply.

Experts generally consider three consecutive increases in the Index a sign of growth, and three consecutive drops a sign of decline and potential recession.

The Index has a mixed record. On the one hand, it has rarely failed to predict peaks in economic growth, and it has correctly forecast all eight recessions since 1950. But it has also signaled a number of recessions that never materialized, including one every year from 1992 through 1995, a time span that saw the economy surge.

Consumer Confidence Index

The Conference Board also releases the Consumer Confidence Index every month. This index measures how 5,000 US households feel about the current state of the economy as well as what the future might bring. It focuses mainly on their sense of job security and their willingness to spend money.

The Consumer Confidence Index doesn't just predict the country's financial well-being—it affects it as well. When people see that consumer confidence is high, they're often more likely to spend money, which creates the very economic growth that high confidence anticipates. However, the reverse is also true: Slipping confidence can perpetuate economic sluggishness.

(Not) The Cost of Living

Although the CPI is frequently referred to as a cost-of-living index, it isn't. It measures only changes in price, not the changes in buying patterns and lifestyle that people often make in response to price shifts. It also can't evaluate the changing quality or supply of the things you buy—which also affects their price.

Some experts also question the accuracy and effectiveness of the way the CPI is currently calculated. Many experts feel that it overstates inflation, causing increased Social Security payments and cost-of-living raises, and thus actually adds to inflation.

vestors are buying stocks, a contrarian is concentrating on building a bond portfolio or putting more money into cash investments. This approach is based on the idea that if everybody expects something to happen, it probably won't.

In addition, the contrarian believes that if other investors are fully committed to a certain type of investment, they're not likely to have cash available if a better one comes along. But the contrarian would. Contrarian mutual funds use this approach as their investment strategy, concentrating on building a portfolio of out-of-favor (and therefore often undervalued) investments.

Convertible bond

Convertible bonds are corporate bonds that you can convert into common stock of the company that issues them rather than redeeming them for cash when they mature.

These bonds have a double appeal for investors concerned about volatility and high stock prices: Their prices go up if stock prices go up but usually drop less than the underlying stock price if that price should fall. And while convertible bonds typically provide lower yields than regular bonds, they provide higher yields than the underlying stock. You can buy convertibles through a broker or choose a mutual fund that invests in them.

Cornering the market

If someone tries to buy up as much of a particular investment as possible in order to control its price, that investor is trying to corner the market. Not only is it difficult to make this strategy work, but the practice is illegal in US markets.

Corporate bond

The debt securities issued by publicly held corporations to raise money for expansion or other business needs are known as corporate bonds. Corporate bonds typically pay a higher rate of

interest than government bonds but the interest is generally taxable.

You can buy these bonds directly through brokers, usually at a par value of $1,000, or by investing in a mutual fund that specializes in corporate bonds.

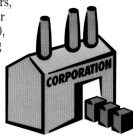

Correction

A correction is a drop—usually a sudden and substantial one—in the price of an individual stock, bond, commodity, index, or the market as a whole. Market analysts anticipate market corrections when security prices are high in relation to company earnings, but they can't predict the drops accurately.

There were major market corrections in October 1987 and March 1994, but in those cases, the market rebounded within a relatively short period of time. When a market correction is greater than 10% to 15%, some analysts consider the correction the beginning of a bear market.

Cost basis

The cost basis is the original price of an asset—usually the purchase price plus commissions—which you use to calculate capital gains and capital losses, depreciation, and return on investment. If you inherit assets, however, such as stocks or real estate, your cost basis is the asset's value upon the date of death of the person who left it to you (or the date on which the estate is valued). This valuation is known as a step up in basis.

COST BASIS	
Original purchase price	$2,000
+ Commission	+ $60
COST BASIS	$2,060

For example, if you buy a stock at $20 a share and sell it for $50 a share, your cost basis is $20. If you sell, you owe capital gains tax on the $30-a-share profit. However, if someone left you stock that was bought at $20 a share but was valued at $50 a share when that person died, your cost basis would be $50 a share, and you would owe no tax if you sold it at that price.

Cost-of-living adjustment (COLA)
COLAs are increases in wages, Social Security, and some pension benefits designed to offset the impact of inflation. They are usually pegged to increases in the consumer price index (CPI). Only a few private pensions provide COLAs, but  federal government pensions and Social Security are usually adjusted annually to keep pace with increased living costs.

Council of Economic Advisors (CEA)
The Council of Economic Advisors' job is to assist and advise the president of the United States on economic policy. The CEA differs from other government agencies in its academic orientation and emphasis on contemporary developments in economic thought.

The Council consists of a chairman and two staff members, appointed by the president and confirmed by the Senate, plus a staff of about 10 economists and 10 younger scholars. The Council's chairman frequently speaks on behalf of the administration on its economic issues and policies.

Countercyclical stock
Stocks described as countercyclical tend to provide stronger returns when the economy is slowing down or staying flat. Companies whose stocks fall into this category are those whose products are always in demand—such as food or utilities—or whose services reduce the expenses of other companies, such as temporary office help, or financial services companies that offer money market mutual funds and other cash-equivalent investments.

Experts suggest including some countercyclical stocks in your equity portfolio to balance the potential volatility of cyclical investments—

which tend to gain value as the economy expands—and to provide regular income, if not growth potential, in economic downturns.

Coupon
Originally, bonds were issued with detachable coupons, which you clipped and presented to the issuer or the issuer's agent—typically a bank or brokerage firm—to collect your interest payment. They're also known as bearer bonds because the bearer of the coupon is entitled to the interest.

Although most new bonds are registered, the term coupon has stuck as a synonym for interest in phrases like the coupon rate. When interest accumulates rather than being paid during the bond's term, the bond is known as a zero-coupon.

Coupon rate
The coupon rate is the interest rate that the issuer of a bond or other debt security promises to pay during the term of a loan. For example, a bond that is paying 6% annual interest has a coupon rate of 6%.

The term is derived from the practice, now discontinued, of issuing bonds with detachable coupons. To collect a scheduled interest payment, you presented a coupon to the issuer or the issuer's agent. Today, coupon bonds are no longer issued. Most bonds are registered, and interest is paid by check or, increasingly, by electronic transfer.

Covered option
When you sell options on stocks that you own, they're known as covered options. That means, at the very worst, if someone exercises the option, you can turn over the stocks you own to meet your obligation to sell. Covered options are the opposite of naked options, where you don't own the underlying stock.

One appeal of selling a covered option is that you collect the premium and don't risk unexpected losses caused by having to buy the stock at market price in order to meet your obligation to sell. It can also be a good technique for receiving income from stocks that pay few or no dividends.

Crash

A crash is a sudden, steep drop in stock prices. The downward spiral is intensified as more and more investors, seeing the bottom falling out of the market, try to sell their holdings before these investments lose all their value.

The two great US crashes of the 20th century, in 1929 and 1987, had very different conse-quences. The first was followed by a period of economic stagnation and severe depression. The second had a much briefer impact. While some investors suffered huge losses, recovery was well underway within three months.

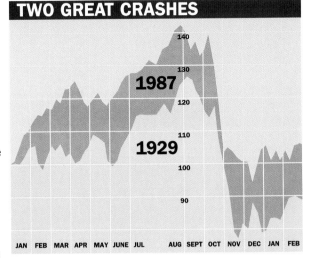

TWO GREAT CRASHES

1987

1929

140 130 120 110 100 90

JAN FEB MAR APR MAY JUNE JUL AUG SEPT OCT NOV DEC JAN FEB

Credit

Credit generally refers to the qualifica-tions of a person or organization to borrow money, as well as the arrange-ment that's made for repaying the loan and the terms of the repayment sched-ule. If you are well qualified to obtain a loan, you are said to be "credit-worthy."

Credit is also used to mean positive cash entries in an account. For exam-ple, your bank account may be credited with interest. In this sense, credit is the opposite of debit, which means money is taken from your account.

Credit rating

Your credit rating is an independent statistical evaluation of your ability to repay debt based on your borrowing and repayment history. Credit grantors use a point system to evaluate your credit history, often on a scale of 0 to 9, or 9 to 0.

If you always pay your bills on time, you are likely to have good credit and therefore may receive favorable terms on a loan or credit card, such as rela-tively low interest rates. If your credit rating is poor because you have paid bills late or have defaulted on a loan, you are likely to get less favorable terms or may be denied credit altogether.

A corporation's credit rating is an assessment of whether it will be able to meet its obligations to bond holders and other investors. Credit rating sys-tems for corporations generally range from AAA or Aaa at the high end to D (for default) at the low end.

Credit report

Credit reporting agencies provide potential lenders with your financial history to help them evaluate whether you are a good credit risk and the likeli-hood that you will default on a loan. The three major agencies—Experion, Equifax, and Transunion—don't evalu-ate the information, and the lenders set their own criteria for making loans. But certain types of information, such as late payments, are generally seen as an indication of potential risk.

You have a right to see your credit history if you have been turned down for a loan. You may also question any information the credit reporting agency has about you and ask that errors be corrected. If the information isn't changed when you request it, you have the right to attach a comment or expla-nation, which must be sent out with future reports.

Credit union

Credit unions are financial cooperatives set up by employee and community associations, labor unions, church groups, and other organizations. They are created to provide affordable finan-cial and lending services to members of the sponsoring organization, or, in some cases, to rural or economically disadvantaged areas, where commercial banks may be scarce or prohibitively expensive.

Because they are not-for-profit, credit unions tend to charge lower fees and lower interest rates on loans than commercial banks while paying higher interest rates on savings and investment accounts. The services offered at large credit unions can be as comprehensive as those at large banks. At smaller credit unions, however, services and hours may be more limited, and deposits may not be insured. Credit unions enjoy a reputation for superior customer service, which may be part of the reason why more than 76,000,000 people across the nation are members.

Crossed market

A market in a particular stock or option is described as crossed when a bid to buy that stock or option is higher than the offer to sell it, or when an offer to sell is lower than a corresponding bid to buy. A crossed market reverses the normal relationship of a stock quotation in which the bid price is always lower than the ask price.

Although it is illegal for market makers to cross a market deliberately, the situation may occur when individual investors place after-hours market orders over the Internet for execution at opening, or when investors participate directly in the market through an electronic communications network

(ECN). The National Association of Securities Dealers (NASD) has introduced a set of pre-opening procedures for market makers on the Nasdaq Stock Market to help prevent the confusion, and potential inequalities in pricing, that a crossed market can produce.

Cumulative voting

With this method of voting for a corporation's board of directors, you may cast the votes you're entitled to (generally one for each share of company stock you own times the number of directors to be elected) any way you choose. For example, you can either split your votes equally among the nominees, or you can cast all of them for a single candidate.

Cumulative voting is designed to give individual stockholders greater influence in shaping the board than they would ordinarily have if their votes had to be spread among all the candidates, as is the case with statutory voting.

Currency fluctuation

A currency has value, or worth, in relation to other currencies. For example, if demand for a particular currency is high because investors want to put money into that country's stock market or want to buy that country's exports, the price of its currency will increase. Just the opposite will happen if that country suffers an economic slowdown, or investors lose confidence in its markets.

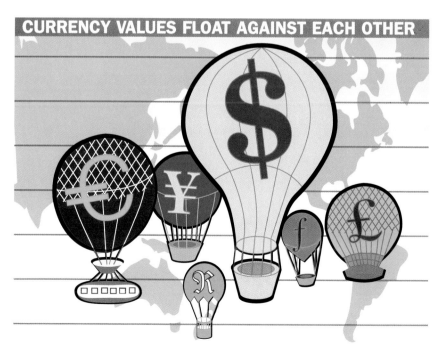

CURRENCY VALUES FLOAT AGAINST EACH OTHER

While some currencies fluctuate freely against each other, such as the Japanese yen and the US dollar, others are pegged, or linked, to the value of another currency, such as the US dollar or the euro, or to a basket, or weighted average of currencies.

Currency trading

The global currency market—in which roughly $1.5 trillion a day changes hands—is by far the largest financial market in the world. Banks, other financial institutions, and multinational corporations buy and sell currencies in enormous quantities to handle the demands of international trade. In some cases, traders seek profits from minor fluctuations in exchange rates or speculate on currency fluctuations.

Current yield

Expressed as a percentage, current yield is a measure of your actual rate of return on an investment. If you own a bond, current yield is calculated by dividing the coupon rate by the purchase price and multiplying by 1,000.

For example, if you paid $800 for a bond with a coupon rate of 10%, the current yield is 12.5%. If you paid $1,200, the current yield would be 8.33%. And if you paid par, or $1,000, the current yield would be 10%, the same as the coupon rate. If you own a stock, the current yield is the annual dividend divided by its market price.

CURRENT YIELD: BONDS

$$\frac{\text{Coupon rate}}{\text{Purchase price}} \times 1{,}000 = \text{BOND CURRENT YIELD}$$

for example

$$\frac{.10}{800} \times 1{,}000 = .125 = 12.5\%$$

CURRENT YIELD: STOCKS

$$\frac{\text{Annual dividend}}{\text{Market price}} = \text{STOCK CURRENT YIELD}$$

for example

$$\frac{\$2.28}{\$27.50} = .0829 = 8.29\%$$

Custodial account

If you want to make investments for a minor, or transfer property you already own to that person, you can open a custodial account with a bank, brokerage firm, or mutual fund company. You name an adult custodian for the account—either yourself or someone else—who is responsible for managing the account until the child reaches the age of majority (18 or 21, depending on the state and the type of account you choose). At that point, the child has the legal right to control the account and use the assets as he or she chooses.

There may be some tax advantages in transferring assets to a minor. If the child is under 14, up to $650 in earnings in the account are free of federal income tax, and earnings between $650 and $1,300 are taxed at the child's income tax rate (typically the lowest rate). Any earnings above $1,300 are taxed at the parents' top marginal tax rate. But if the child is 14 or older, earnings are taxed at the child's rate—again, typically the lowest rate.

Cyclical stock

Cyclical stocks tend to rise in value during an upturn in the economy and fall during a downturn. They usually include stocks in industries that flourish in good times, including airlines, automobiles, and travel and leisure.

In contrast, stocks in industries that provide necessities such as food, electricity, gas, and health care products, or those that provide services that reduce the expenses of other companies, tend to be more price-stable. Those stocks are sometimes called countercyclicals.

Daily trading limit

The daily trading limit is the most that the price of a futures or options contract can rise or fall in a single session before trading in that contract is stopped for the day.

Trading limits are designed to protect investors from wild fluctuations and the potential for major losses. They're comparable to the circuit breakers established by stock exchanges to suspend trading when prices fall by a specific percentage.

Date of maturity

The date of maturity, or maturity date, is the day on which the term of a bond or other debt ends, and the principal and final interest payment are payable, or due. If you're the borrower rather than the lender, as you would be if you had a car or education loan, the date of maturity is the day your final payment is due.

Day order

A day order is an instruction you give to your broker to buy or sell a security at a particular price before the end of the trading day. The order expires if it isn't filled. The opposite is a good 'til canceled (GTC) order.

Day trader

When you buy and sell an investment within a very short time, frequently as short as a few hours, you're considered a day trader. The strategy is to take advantage of rapid price changes to make money quickly. In the past, professional investors did most of the day trading, but as online trading has gained popularity, many more individuals, usually

referred to as electronic day traders, are trying it as well.

The risk is that you can lose money as well as make it, since no one can predict how prices will change. That risk is compounded by the fact that the technology does not always keep pace with investors' orders, so you might authorize a sell at one price and then have to wait while the price drops much further before your order is executed.

Dealer

Dealers—also known as principals—trade securities for their own investment accounts or for the account of the brokerage firms where they work. Securities purchased for a particular firm's account may, in turn, be sold by the firm's brokers to investors who are clients of the firm. As a result, the term broker/dealer is frequently used to describe people or firms that handle both types of transactions.

Debenture

A debenture is an unsecured bond. Most bonds issued by large corporations are, in fact, debentures, which are backed by the corporation's reputation rather than secured by any collateral, such as the company's buildings or its inventory. Although debentures sound riskier than secured bonds, they generally aren't, since they are usually issued by well-established companies with good credit ratings.

Debit

A debit is the opposite of a credit. For example, it can be an account balance representing money you owe a lender, or it can be the amount you owe your broker for securities you have bought on margin.

A debit card differs from a credit card, since it allows you to take money out of your bank account electronically, either as cash or as an on-the-spot payment to a merchant, rather than borrowing the money from the card issuer.

Debt

A debt is an obligation to repay an amount you owe. Debt securities, such as bonds,  notes, and commercial paper, are all forms of debt that bind the issuing organization, such as a corporation, bank, government, or government agency, to repay the holder of the security.

Debt security

These interest-paying investments are issued by governments or corporations, and are held by investors who have lent money to the issuer. Debt securities generally pay a fixed rate of interest over a fixed time period in exchange for the use of the money. The principal, or amount that is loaned, is repaid at maturity. US Treasury bills, corporate bonds, commercial paper, and mortgage-backed bonds are examples of debt securities.

Debt-to-equity ratio

You find a company's debt-to-equity ratio by dividing its total long-term debt by its total assets minus its total debt. You can find these figures in the company's income statement provided in its annual report. The ratio indicates the extent to which a company is leveraged, or financed by credit. A higher ratio is a sign of greater leverage, which may mean a fast-growing company or one that is overextended.

Average ratios vary significantly from one industry to another, so what is high for one company may be normal for another company in a different industry. From an investor's perspective, the higher the ratio, the greater the risk you take in investing in the company. But your potential return may be greater as well.

Decimal pricing

In mid-2000, the US stock markets will convert from trading in dollars and sixteenths of dollars to trading in decimals, or dollars and cents. That is, a price that has been expressed as 57¼ will be stated as 57.25. This change marks the final stage of conversion from trading in eighths, a practice that originated in the 16th century, when North American settlers cut European coinage into eight pieces to use as currency.

Many investors and industry experts favor decimal pricing, which is already used everywhere else in the world, as a more efficient system because it allows for narrowing the spread between the highest price offered and the lowest price asked.

Decliner

Stocks that have dropped, or fallen, in value over a particular period are described as decliners. If more stocks decline than advance—or go up in value—over the course of a trading day, the financial press reports that decliners led advancers. The indexes that track the market may decline as well. If that situation persists for a period of time, the market may also be described as bearish.

Deep discount bond

Deep discount bonds are originally issued with a par value, or face value, of $1,000. But they decline in value by at least 20%, typical-  ly because interest rates have increased, or because people believe the company may have difficulty making the interest payment. As a result, investors will no longer pay full price for a smaller yield than they can get on newer bonds or ones they feel more secure about.

Deep discount bonds are different from original issue discount bonds, which are sold at less than par value and accumulate interest until maturity, when they can be redeemed for par value.

Deep discount brokerage firm

A financial services company that offers rock-bottom rates for large-volume securities transactions is sometimes described as a deep discount firm. However, online brokerage firms or electronic communications networks (ECNs) may offer individual investors even cheaper prices for smaller volume trades.

Default

A corporation or government is in default if it fails to meet the interest payments on debt securities it has issued or does not repay the principal at maturity. When the issuer defaults, the bondholders may try to recover what they're owed by making claims against the issuer's assets. There's an elaborate hierarchy for determining the order in which the claimants are paid.

Similarly, if you fail to pay principal and interest that you owe on a loan, you are in default. The lender may attempt to recover the loss by claiming any property of yours that was security for the loan or by taking other legal measures.

Defensive security

Defensive securities tend to remain more stable in value than the overall market—especially when prices in general are falling. Defensive securities include stocks in companies whose products or services are always in demand, such as food, pharmaceuticals, and utilities, and are not as price-sensitive to changes in the economy as other stocks.

Deferred annuity

Unlike an immediate annuity, which starts paying you income right after you buy it, a deferred annuity contract allows you to accumulate earnings on a tax-deferred basis and sometimes add assets to your contract over time. Your deferred annuity can be either fixed or variable, depending on the way your money is invested. Deferred annuities are designed primarily as retirement savings accounts, so you may owe a penalty if you withdraw earnings before you reach age 59½.

Defined benefit plan

A defined benefit plan—otherwise known as a pension—provides income for retired employees, and sometimes their spouses, for the rest of their lives. The amount you receive usually depends on your age when you retire, your final salary, and the number of years you worked for your employer. Many employers are replacing these traditional retirement plans, at least in part, with defined contribution and salary reduction plans.

Defined contribution plan

401(k), 403(b), 457, and profit-sharing plans are examples of defined contribution retirement plans offered by employers. The benefits—that is, what you can expect to accumulate and ultimately withdraw from the plan—are not predetermined, as they are with a conventional defined benefit pension, and vary according to the plan's investments.

One advantage of defined contribution plans is that you often have some control over how your retirement dollars are invested—usually in stock or bond mutual funds, annuities, guaranteed investment contracts (GICs), company stock, cash equivalents, or a combination of these choices.

An added benefit is that, if you switch jobs, you can often take your accumulated retirement assets with you. The downside is that there is no guarantee of the amount of retirement income you'll have available. The terms 401(k),

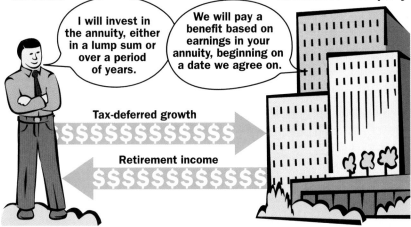

HOW A DEFERRED ANNUITY WORKS

Investor

Insurance Company

I will invest in the annuity, either in a lump sum or over a period of years.

We will pay a benefit based on earnings in your annuity, beginning on a date we agree on.

Tax-deferred growth
$$$$$$$$$$$$

Retirement income
$$$$$$$$$$$$$

TWO KINDS OF PENSION PLANS

COMPANY A

COMPANY B

THE COMPANY PUTS MONEY INTO A PENSION FUND IN YOUR NAME

DEFINED BENEFIT PLAN

"Company A guarantees you a yearly pension."

DEFINED CONTRIBUTION PLAN

"Company B invests an amount equal to a percentage of your salary."

403(b), and 457 refer to the sections of the Internal Revenue Code where the plans are described.

Deflation

The opposite of inflation, deflation is a gradual drop in the cost of goods and services, usually caused by a surplus of goods and a shortage of cash. Although deflation seems to increase your buying power in its early stages, it is generally considered a negative economic trend because it is typically accompanied by rising unemployment and falling production.

Delivery date

The delivery date is the day on which a stock or bond trade must be settled, or finalized. Normally, it is three business days after the trade date and is also known as T+3, or the settlement date. By the delivery date of a regular transaction, the seller must turn over the security, and the buyer must pay the purchase price.

Rather than literally handing over securities, most deliveries are done electronically, since an increasing number of securities are registered in street name and held by your broker. If you, as the buyer, do not have enough cash in your brokerage account to cover the transaction, you must send a check, arrange an electronic transfer, or ask your broker to sell investments already in your account by the delivery date.

Delta

The relationship between an option's price and the price of the underlying stock or futures contract is called its delta. If the delta is 1, for example, the relationship of the prices is 1:1. That means there's a $1 change in the option price for every $1 change in the price of the investment.

With a call option, an increase in the price of an underlying investment typically results in an increase in the price of the option. With a put option, however, an increase in the option's price is usually triggered by a decrease in the price of the underlying investment, since investors buy put options expecting their prices to fall.

Depository Trust and Clearing Corporation (DTCC)

The DTCC is the world's largest securities depository—holding more than $20 trillion in assets for the members of the financial industry that own the corporation. It is also a national clearinghouse for the settlement of corporate and municipal securities transactions. The DTCC, a member of the Federal Reserve System, was created in 1999 by the merger of the Depository Trust Company (DTC) and the National Securities Clearing Corporation (NSCC).

Depreciation

Certain assets, such as buildings and equipment, depreciate, or decline in value, over time. You can amortize, or write off, the cost of such an asset over its estimated useful life, thereby reducing your taxable income without reducing the cash you have on hand.

Depression

A depression is a severe and prolonged downturn in the economy. Prices fall, reducing purchasing power. There tends to be high unemployment, lower productivity, shrinking wages, and general economic pessimism. Since the Great Depression following the stock market crash of 1929, the governments and central banks of major industrialized countries have carefully monitored their economies and adjusted their economic policies to try to prevent another financial crisis of this magnitude.

Derivative

Derivatives are hybrid investments, such as futures contracts, options, and mortgage-backed securities, whose value is based on the value of an underlying investment. For example, the changing value of a crude oil futures contract depends on the upward or downward movement of oil prices. Certain investors, called hedgers, are interested

in the underlying investment. For example, a baking company might buy wheat futures to help estimate the cost of producing its bread in the months to come. Other investors, called speculators, are concerned with the profit to be made by buying and selling the contract at the most opportune time. Derivatives are traded on exchanges, over the counter (OTC), and in private transactions.

Devaluation

Devaluation is a deliberate decision by a government or central bank to reduce the value of its own currency in relation to the currencies of other countries. Governments often opt for devaluation when there is a large current account deficit, which may occur when a country is importing far more than it is exporting.

When a nation devalues its currency, the goods it imports, and the overseas debts it must repay, become more expensive. But its exports become less expensive, and thus more competitive abroad, which often stimulates higher sales and reduces the deficit. In 1998, for example, Brazil devalued its currency in a move to help stabilize the country's economy.

DIAMONDS

DIAMONDS are shares in a unit investment trust (UIT) called the DIAMONDS Trust, which holds the 30

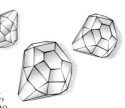

stocks in the Dow Jones Industrial Average (DJIA). The UIT is listed on the American Stock Exchange (AMEX) as DIA and trades the way stocks do, rather than being repriced at the end of each trading day, as is the case with mutual funds. However, the trust does resembles an open-end mutual fund in the sense that there isn't a fixed number of shares available for trading. The trust will sell as many shares as investors are interested in buying.

DIAMONDS trade at about $1/100$ the value of the DJIA. So, for example, if the Dow is at 10,600, shares in the trust will be priced around $106. Part of their appeal, like the appeal of Standard & Poor's Depositary Receipts (SPDRs), is that the trust mirrors the performance of the benchmark for dramatically less than it would cost to buy shares in all 30 stocks in the DJIA. In addition, you get monthly dividends based on the dividend yields of the stocks in the DJIA, which you can reinvest to buy additional shares.

Diluted earnings per share

In addition to reporting earnings per share, corporations must report diluted earnings per share to account for the possible, though unlikely, occurrence that all outstanding warrants and stock options are exercised, and all convertible bonds and preferred shares are exchanged for common stock. Diluted earnings actually report the smallest potential earnings per common share that a company could have. In theory, at least, knowing the diluted earnings could influence how much you would be willing to pay for the stock.

Dilution

If all the outstanding warrants and stock options on an individual stock were exercised, and all the convertible bonds and preferred stock the company had issued were converted to common stock, there would be a noticeable, negative effect on the earnings per share and the book value per share. That's because both of these measures are calculated by dividing by the number of outstanding shares—so the greater the number of such shares, the lower the value. Since 1998, companies have had to report the effect of potential dilution to their shareholders.

If two companies merge, or a company buys one or more other companies, earnings may be diluted if they don't increase proportionately with the total combined number of shares in the newly created company.

Disclosure

A disclosure document explains how a financial product or offering works, the terms to which you must agree in order to buy it or use it, and, in some cases, the risks you assume in making such a purchase.

For example, government regulatory agencies like the Securities and Exchange Commission (SEC) and self-regulating organizations like the National Association of Securities Dealers (NASD) require publicly traded corporations to provide all the information they have available that might influence your decision to invest in the stocks or bonds they issue. Mutual fund companies are required to disclose the risks associated with buying shares in the fund. Similarly, federal and local governments require lenders to explain the costs of credit, and banks to explain the costs of opening and maintaining an account.

Despite the consumer benefits, disclosure information isn't always accessible, because it is either expressed in confusing language, printed in tiny type, or so extensive that consumers choose to skip over it.

Discount

When bonds or preferred stocks sell below their face value, they are said to be selling at a discount. Certain bonds, called original issue discount bonds, are issued at a discount but are worth par, or their full face value, at maturity. Other bonds are discounted when they are traded in the secondary market after they are issued, usually because the interest they pay is lower than the current market rate, or because the issuer's rating has been downgraded. Closed-end mutual funds can also trade at a discount to their net asset value (NAV).

Discount brokerage firm

Discount brokerage firms charge lower commissions than full-service brokerage firms when they execute investors' buy and sell orders. Some discount firms provide fewer services—for example, they may not typically recommend stocks or maintain independent research departments. In return, they reduce commissions by as much as 50%.

Because of the extensive information now available on brokerage websites, as well as the increased attention to customer service, the traditional differences between full-service and discount brokerages are starting to blur.

Discount rate

The discount rate is the interest rate charged by the Federal Reserve on loans it makes to banks and other financial institutions. The discount rate becomes the base interest rate for most consumer borrowing as well, since a bank generally uses what it pays for money—the discount rate—as a benchmark for the interest it charges you on the loans you take. For example, when the discount rate is increased, the interest rate lenders charge on home mortgages and other loans increases as well.

Disinflation

Disinflation is a slowdown in the rate of price increases that historically occurs during a recession, when the supply of goods is greater than the demand for them. Unlike deflation, however, when prices for goods actually drop, with disinflation prices do not usually fall, but the rate of inflation becomes negligible.

Distribution

Each open- and closed-end mutual fund pays out the capital gains it realizes on the sale of securities in its portfolio to all existing shareholders. These distributions are typically paid annually, often in December. If the fund owned the security for more than a year before selling it, federal income tax on the distribution is figured at your long-term capital gains rate. But if the fund owned the security for a shorter time, you owe tax at your regular rate.

Diversification

Diversification is an investment strategy in which you spread your investment dollars among different markets, industries, and securities. The goal of the strategy is to protect your overall portfolio in case a single security, market sector, or market takes a serious downturn and loses value.

A well-diversified portfolio might include small-cap, medium-cap, and large-cap stocks, bonds, and cash and cash equivalents as well as investments in international markets.

Studies indicate that diversification can help insulate your investments against market volatility without sacrificing the level of return you want. Finding the diversification mix that's right for you depends on your age, your assets, your tolerance for risk, and your investment goals.

Dividend

Corporations may pay out part of their earnings as dividends to you and other shareholders as a return on your investment. These stock dividends are usually in the form of cash, stock, or scrip, and are typically paid quarterly.

Mutual fund companies also pay dividends to their investors, based on a fund's earnings. Dividends are ordinarily taxable unless you own the investment through an employer-sponsored retirement plan or individual retirement account (IRA).

Dividend payout ratio

You find payout ratio by dividing the dividend a company pays by the company's earnings. The normal range is 25% to 50% of earnings, though the average is higher in some sectors than in others. Some analysts think that an unusually high ratio may indicate that a company is in financial trouble but doesn't want to alarm shareholders by reducing its dividend.

Dividend reinvestment plan (DRIP)

Many publicly held companies allow shareholders to automatically reinvest dividends in the company's stock as well as make regular purchases of additional shares of the stock. These plans—called dividend reinvestment plans, or DRIPs—enable you to build your investment gradually, taking advantage of dollar cost averaging and usually paying only minimal sales charges for the additional stock you buy. Many DRIPs will also buy back shares at any time you want to sell, in most cases for a minimal sales charge.

Dividend yield

If you owe dividend-paying stocks, you figure the current yield on your investment by dividing the dividend being paid on each share by the share's current market price. The result is the dividend yield, or annual percentage return. For example, if a stock whose market price is $35 pays a dividend of 75 cents per share, the dividend yield is 2.14% ($0.75 ÷ $35 = .0214, or 2.14%).

Dividend yield, which rises as the price per share drops (and drops as the share price increases), does not tell you your return based on your original investment or the income you can expect to earn in the future. However, some investors seeking current income look for high-yielding stocks, and dividend yield is a key figure in the investment strategy known as Dogs of the Dow. Yields for all dividend-paying stocks are reported regularly in newspaper stock tables and on financial websites.

Dogs of the Dow

If you follow a Dogs of the Dow investment strategy, you buy the 10 highest-yielding stocks in the Dow Jones Industrial Average (DJIA) and hold them for a year. Then, on the anniversary of your purchase, you sell that

portfolio and buy the next batch of dogs. In most economic climates, the dogs are likely, over the year, to produce a total return that's higher than the return on the average as a whole.

Here's how it works: If you compare two stocks that are paying the same dividend but have a different price per share, the one with the lower price is potentially a dog because it has a higher yield. (You figure yield by dividing the current dividend per share by the current market price per share.) For example, a stock paying a dividend of 75 cents a share and selling at $35 a share has a yield of 2.14%. But a stock paying the same dividend and selling at $15 a share has a much higher yield of 5%.

According to this theory, when investors buy stock for its high yield, demand for that stock increases, so the price tends to rise. When the year is up, and the stock is no longer a dog, you sell it. When you do, you'll get a higher price than you paid, plus you will have collected the dividend payment as well.

Dollar cost averaging

Adding a fixed amount of money on a regular schedule to an investment, such as a mutual fund or a dividend reinvestment plan (DRIP), is called dollar cost averaging, or a constant dollar plan. Since the share price of the investment fluctuates, you buy fewer shares when the share price is higher and more shares when the price is lower.

The potential advantage of this type of formula investing, over time, is that the average cost you pay per share is lower than the average price per share. To get the most from this approach, you have to invest regularly, including during any market downturns. However, dollar cost averaging does not guarantee a profit.

DOLLAR COST AVERAGING

Suppose you invest $100 for four months

Month	1	2	3	4
Avg. price per share	$22	$17	$14	$18
Number of shares purchase	4.55	5.88	7.14	5.56

AVERAGE SHARE PRICE

$$\frac{\text{Total amount}}{\text{Number of months}} = \text{AVERAGE SHARE PRICE}$$

for example

$$\frac{(\$22+\$17+\$14+\$18)}{4} = \$17.75$$

AVERAGE SHARE COST

$$\frac{\text{Total amount invested}}{\text{Total shares purchased}} = \text{AVERAGE SHARE COST}$$

for example

$$\frac{\$400}{4.55+5.88+7.14+5.56} = \$17.29$$

Average share cost is generally less than average share price.

Domini Social Index 400

First published in 1990, the Domini Social Index 400 is a broad-based, market capitalization-weighted index that tracks the performance of companies that meet or exceed a wide range of social and environmental standards. For instance, the index screens out companies that manufacture or promote alcohol, tobacco, gambling, weapons, and nuclear power, and includes others that have outstanding records of social responsibility.

About half the stocks included in the Standard & Poor's 500-stock Index (S&P 500), on which the Domini Index is modeled, make the cut, including giants like Microsoft and Coca-Cola. The other stocks are selected based on the industries they represent and their reputations for socially conscience business practices. The index is considered a benchmark for measuring the effect that selecting socially responsible stocks—sometimes described as social screening—has on financial performance.

Dow Jones 65 Composite Average

This composite of three Dow Jones averages—the Dow Jones Industrial Average (DJIA), the Dow Jones Transportation Average, and the Dow Jones Utility Average—tracks the stock performance of 65 companies in three major market sectors.

Dow Jones Total Market Index

This benchmark index measures price changes in approximately 2,200 US stocks, representing more than 100 industries that trade on the New York Stock Exchange (NYSE), the American Stock Exchange (AMEX), and the Nasdaq Stock Market (Nasdaq). Representing approximately 80% of the US equity market, this index is market capitalization-weighted. That means a stock's influence on the movement of the index is in proportion to its current price multiplied by the total number of shares investors own.

Dow Jones Global Indexes

These global indexes are market capitalization-weighted indexes tracking the stock market performance of more than 3,000 companies in 34 countries (as of December 1999). Together they represent more than 80% of the equity capital on stock markets throughout the world.

Market capitalization weighting means that those companies with higher market capitalizations, figured by multiplying the current price per share by the number of outstanding shares, have a greater impact on the index. Eventually, these indexes will include every country where stocks can be purchased.

Market performance is also tracked in eight geographically defined regional indexes and in the Dow Jones World Stock Index, a composite of the global indexes.

Tracking the Markets

No single index or average gives you a complete picture of what's up—or down.

Indexes and averages track day-to-day changes in stock and bond prices and longer-term trends in financial markets. In fact, the best known US indicators, such as Standard & Poor's 500-stock Index (S&P 500) and the Dow Jones Industrial Average (DJIA), are sometimes used as snapshots of the country's economic health. They're also benchmarks against which to measure the performance of investment portfolios.

The catch is that each index or average measures something a little bit different.

Weight Limitations

Weighted indexes can give a skewed picture of the markets by suggesting that most prices are moving in a particular direction when in fact the change is being driven by a relatively small number of stocks.

For example, it's quite possible for the price-weighted DJIA to rise—even though the majority of its stocks are falling in value—provided a handful of its most expensive stocks are gaining. (Of course, the opposite could happen as well.)

Similarly, the upward trend of the S&P 500 in the late 1990s was driven by the market capitalization of some high-flying stocks. Their momentum overshadowed the fact that many other stocks remained flat or lost value during the same period.

On the other hand, equally weighted indexes don't always produce the same results, and may understate or overstate the combined performance of the stocks they track. The reason for this discrepancy is that indexes are calculated differently. For example, the Value Line Geometric

Weighting the Outcome

Some indexes and averages count all of their components equally. Others give more weight to some components than to others on the grounds that price changes in the stock of the biggest companies or in the prices of the most expensive stocks have a greater impact on the economy.

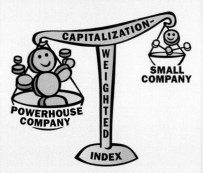

Capitalization-weighted indexes are designed to reflect the significant impact — economically and psychologically — of powerhouse companies: those with lots of stock selling at higher-than-average prices.

Index increases less in value during any one time period than the Value Line Arithmetic Index—despite the fact that the indexes include exactly the same stocks.

Index or Average?

Did you ever wonder why some stock market benchmarks are called indexes and others are called averages? Or why one well-known stock benchmark is at 10,600 while another is at 1,362 and a third at 3,055? The difference is based not only on what's included in the average or index, but how each is computed.

Basically, to find an average you add a series of numbers and divide the total by that number of items. For example, you could figure the average net asset value (NAV) of 25 mutual funds by adding their total returns for one year and dividing by 25.

To construct an index, on the other hand, you compare a current average to a baseline value, stating the difference as percentage change. For example, using January 1, 1990, as the starting point, you could track the way that average NAV changed each day or each month over a decade.

The best known financial average, the DJIA, is actually a hybrid. It's initially computed by adding the weighted closing prices of its 30 stocks and then dividing not by 30, but by a number that has been adjusted over the years to account for changes based on additions, deletions, and mergers, as well as stock splits. Then changes in the average are reported in the same way changes in an index would be reported, as a percentage change.

Price-weighted indexes emphasize changes in the value of higher-priced stocks more heavily than changes in the value of lower-priced stocks.

Equally weighted equity indexes count an increase in the value of one stock as much as an increase in the value of another stock, regardless of the opening price of the stocks or how many shares have been issued.

Defining Features

A key factor in assessing how much an index or average can tell you about the economy as a whole, or about the performance of your investment portfolio, is whether it's a broad or narrow measure.

Despite its enormous influence, the DJIA is a narrow measure, tracking only 30 large, mostly industrial stocks. In contrast, the Wilshire 5000 is the broadest of the US indexes and averages, and tracks all of the companies currently being traded on organized exchanges and markets.

Between the narrow DJIA and the broad Wilshire is the S&P 500, which tracks 500 large-company stocks. This index is frequently used as the benchmark for equity mutual fund performance, in large part because it includes so many of the stocks these funds hold in their portfolios.

Index Investing

If you buy shares in a mutual fund or unit investment trust (UIT) that tracks a particular market index, your investment's performance mirrors the performance of the index. In other words, it gains in value when the index goes up, and declines when the index drops.

Index investing is appealing for a number of reasons, especially when the securities markets are strong. For one thing, you get instant diversification at a much lower price than you'd have to pay to buy a diversified portfolio of individual investments. And the management fees for index mutual funds tend to be low, since the fund changes its holdings only when the index it is tracking changes. For the same reason, index funds are typically tax-efficient.

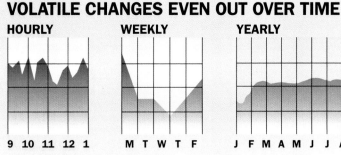

VOLATILE CHANGES EVEN OUT OVER TIME

Dow Jones Industrial Average (DJIA)

The Dow Jones Industrial Average, often referred to as the DJIA or the Dow, is the best-known and most widely followed market indicator in the world. It tracks 30 blue chip US stocks and is quoted in points, not dollars. Though it is called an average, it is actually a price-weighted index, which means it gives the greatest weight to stocks with the highest prices.

The DJIA is computed by totaling the prices of the 30 stocks and dividing by a number that is regularly adjusted for stock splits, spin-offs, and other changes in the stocks being tracked. The companies that make up the DJIA are changed from time to time—most recently in October, 1999, when Microsoft, Intel, SBC Communications, and Home Depot were added—to reflect shifts in the economy and the emerging or declining impact of a specific company or type of company.

Dow Jones Transportation Average

The Dow Jones Transportation Average tracks the performance of the stocks of 20 airlines, railroads, and trucking companies, and is one of the components of the Dow Jones 65 Composite Average.

Dow Jones Utility Average

The Dow Jones Utility Average tracks the performance of the stocks of 15 gas, electric, and power companies, and is one of the components of the Dow Jones 65 Composite Average.

Dow theory

Dow theory maintains that a major market trend—up or down—will continue only if both the Dow Jones Industrial Average (DJIA) and the Dow Jones Transportation Average move simultaneously in the same direction until they both hit a new high or a new low. Some experts discount this approach, arguing that waiting to invest until a trend is confirmed can mean losing out on potential growth.

Downtick

When a security sells at a lower price than its previous sale price, the drop in value is called a downtick. For example, if a stock that had been trading at 25 sells at $24\frac{15}{16}$ the next time it trades, that's a downtick.

Dutch auction

A Dutch auction opens at the highest price and gradually drops until a buyer is willing to pay the amount being asked. In contrast, a conventional commercial auction begins with the lowest price, which gradually increases as potential buyers bid against each other. Under this system, the selling price is determined when no bidder will top the offer on the table.

A double-action auction—the system in place on US stock exchanges—features many buyers and sellers bidding against each other to close a sale at a mutually agreed-upon price. The only securities auctions in US markets that are conducted as Dutch auctions are the competitive bids for US Treasury bills, notes and bonds.

Early withdrawal

If you withdraw your assets from a fixed-term investment, such as a certificate of deposit (CD), before it matures, or from an individual retirement account (IRA) or qualified retirement plan before you turn 59½, it is generally considered an early withdrawal.

If you withdraw early, you usually have to pay a penalty imposed by the issuer (in the case of a CD) or by the federal government (in the case of an IRA). However, you may be able to withdraw early without penalty under certain circumstances—for example, if you use IRA funds to pay for higher education or the purchase of a first home.

Earned income

Your earned income is the amount you get from salaries, wages, tips, professional fees, or pay for work you perform. You include your earned income when you figure your adjusted gross income (AGI), along with unearned income from interest, dividends, and capital gains. If you have earned income, you're eligible to contribute to an individual retirement account (IRA).

Earnings

From a corporate perspective, earnings are profits, or net income, after the company has paid income taxes and bond interest. In the case of an individual, earnings generally refers to money you receive from salary and other forms of compensation as well as interest, dividends, and other increases in the value of your investments.

Earnings estimate

Professional stock analysts use mathematical models that weigh the financial data of companies to predict their future earnings per share on a quarterly, annual, and long-term basis. Investment research companies, such as Zacks, publish averages of analysts' estimates, called consensus estimates, for stocks that are closely followed by market professionals.

When a company's earnings report either exceeds or fails to meet analysts' expectations, it's called an earnings surprise. An upside surprise occurs when a company reports higher earnings than analysts predicted and usually triggers a rise in the stock price. A negative surprise, on the other hand, occurs when a company fails to meet expectations and often causes the stock's price to fall. Companies try hard to avoid negative surprises since even a small difference can create a big stir.

Earnings momentum

When a company's earnings per share grow from year to year at an ever-increasing rate, that pattern is described as earnings momentum. One example might be a company whose earnings grew one year at 10%, the next year at 20%, and a third year at 38%. The outcome, usually, is that the stock's share price increases as well, since investors are willing to pay more to own a stock they expect to continue to increase in value.

Earnings per share

Earnings per share is a way to explain what a company has left of its revenue after paying taxes, bond holders, and owners of preferred stock. Earnings per share is calculated by dividing total company earnings by the number of outstanding shares.

For example, if a company earns $100 million in a year and has 50 million outstanding shares, the earnings per share is $2. Earnings and other financial measures are provided on a per-share basis to help investors analyze the information and make comparisons to other investments.

EARNINGS PER SHARE

$$\frac{\text{Total company earnings}}{\text{Number of outstanding shares}} = \text{EARNINGS PER SHARE}$$

for example

$$\frac{\$100,000,000}{50,000,000} = \$2\ \text{PER SHARE}$$

Earnings surprise

If a company's earnings are higher, or its profits are lower, than Wall Street financial analysts are expecting, it's a surprise. There's typically an impact—sometimes a dramatic one—on the price of the company's stock. That is, higher-than-expected earnings tend to send the price higher, and lower-than-expected profits tend to drive the price down. And the analysts, having been surprised once, generally anticipate similar surprises in the upcoming quarters.

Economic indicator

A number of regularly reported statistics are used to evaluate current business conditions and forecast economic trends. Each month The Conference Board, an independent research organization, releases its index of the 10 leading economic indicators, including those relating to employment and production, stock prices, the money supply, and consumer confidence. The index has successfully projected economic downturns in the past, though it has also predicted some that did not occur.

Education IRA

You can put up to $500 a year into Education IRAs established in the names of the minors you would like to benefit. (There is no limit on the number of minors you can establish these accounts for, but there is a $500 limit on the amount that can be added to any single account in one year.)

The contribution is not tax-deductible, but there's no tax on any earnings that accumulate in the account. What's more, withdrawals are tax-free if they're used to pay qualified higher-education expenses for a beneficiary until he or she reaches age 30.

There are some limitations, however, including an income cap for contributors and certain restrictions on using the money from the IRA in conjunction with other education tax breaks.

Efficient market

When the information that investors need to make investment decisions is widely available, thoroughly analyzed, and regularly used in making trading decisions—as is the case with securities traded on the major US stock markets—the result is an efficient market. Conversely, an inefficient market is one in which there is limited information available for making rational investment decisions.

Efficient market theory

Proponents of the efficient market theory believe that a stock's current price accurately reflects what investors know about the stock, and that you can't predict a stock's future price based on its past performance. Their conclusion, which is contested by other experts, is that it's not possible for an individual or institutional investor to outperform the market as a whole. Index funds, which are designed to match, rather than beat, a particular market and are not actively managed, are in part an outgrowth of efficient market theory.

Electronic communications network (ECN)

An ECN is an alternative securities trading system that allows institutional and individual investors to buy and sell outside the organized stock markets, such as the New York Stock Exchange (NYSE) and the Nasdaq Stock Market (Nasdaq).

Because an ECN automatically collects, displays, and executes orders without a middleman (such as a specialist or market maker), trades are faster and less expensive than trades on traditional markets. Further, ECNs facilitate extended, or after-hours, trading. The Securities and Exchange Commission (SEC) lets these alternative trading systems apply for status as official stock exchanges, which is spurring significant changes in the way stocks are traded, both nationally and globally.

Emerging market

Countries in the process of building market-based economies are broadly referred to as emerging markets, though there are major differences among the countries usually included in this category. Some emerging-market countries, including Russia, have only recently relaxed restrictions on a free-market economy. Others, including Indonesia, have opened their markets more widely to overseas investors, and still others, including Mexico, are expanding industrial production. Combined, they have stock market capitalization of less than 3% of the world's total.

Emerging-markets fund

These mutual funds invest primarily in the securities of emerging markets. Some funds specialize in the markets of a certain region, such as Latin America or Southeast Asia. Others invest in a global cross-section of countries and regions.

Employee stock ownership plan (ESOP)

These plans encourage employees to buy and own stock in the company they work for, often as part of a bonus arrangement. ESOPs give participants a greater stake in the company's financial success and can be an easy way to build a long-term investment. In some cases, ESOPs may also provide a way to participate in the company's management policies.

Employer-sponsored retirement plan

Tax-deferred retirement savings plans that employers establish for their employees are also described as qualified plans. As plan sponsors, employers may contribute to a pension, profit-sharing, or salary-reduction plan, such as a 401(k) or 403(b), get a tax deduction for the amount of their contribution, and enjoy other tax benefits.

Employees benefit by deferring tax on their own contributions and on those made by their employer, as well as on any earnings, until they withdraw assets from their accounts, usually after they retire or when they leave the job.

Enhanced index fund

Unlike an index fund, which strives to mirror the combined performance of all the stocks in a particular index by owning all of those stocks, an enhanced index fund chooses from among the stocks in a particular index selectively in order to produce a slightly higher return. The goal is to narrowly beat the index by anywhere from a fraction of a percent to two percentage points but not more, since a wider spread would classify the enhanced fund as a more traditional mutual fund.

Managers of enhanced funds seek higher returns by identifying under-valued stocks, adjusting holdings to reflect higher performing sectors, and using other investment strategies such as buying derivatives. While enhanced index funds are somewhat riskier than their plain-vanilla counterparts, there is also an opportunity for higher returns.

Equity

In the broadest sense, equity means ownership. If you own stock, you have equity in, or own a portion—however

House Valued at $300,000

$200,000 Outstanding mortgage

$100,000 Your equity

small—of the company that issued it. Having equity is the opposite of owning a bond or commercial paper, which is a debt the company must repay to you. Equity also means the difference between the amount an asset could be sold for—its current market value—and any claim or debt against it. For example, if you own a home currently valued at $300,000 but still owe $200,000 on your mortgage, your equity in the home is $100,000.

Equity fund

Equity mutual funds invest primarily in stocks. The type of stocks a fund buys—whether those of small, up-and-coming companies or large, well-established ones—depends on the fund's investment objectives. The objectives are described in the fund's prospectus and are often implied by the fund's name, such as large-cap growth fund or small-cap aggressive-growth fund. You can reasonably expect a blue chip fund, for example, to concentrate on high-profile, well-established companies.

Equivalent taxable yield

Although tax-exempt municipal bonds generally pay interest at a lower rate than taxable corporate bonds, agency bonds, and Treasurys, they may actually provide a greater yield, or rate of return on your investment, especially if you are in the higher federal income tax brackets. You can calculate the rate you'd have to get on a taxable bond to equal the yield on a tax-exempt bond using this formula:

EQUIVALENT TAXABLE YIELD

$$\frac{\text{Tax-exempt yield}}{100 - \text{your tax rate}} = \text{EQUIVALENT TAXABLE YIELD}$$

Escrow

When someone else holds assets of yours, such as money, securities, real estate, or even a deed, until the terms of a contract or an agreement are fulfilled, your assets are said to be held in escrow. The person or organization that holds the assets is the escrow agent, and the account in which they are held is an escrow account.

For example, if you make a down payment on a home, the money is held in escrow until the sale is completed or the deal falls through. Amounts you prepay for homeowner property taxes and insurance premiums as part of your regular mortgage payment are also held in escrow until those bills come due and are paid. In that case, you may earn interest on the amount in the escrow account.

Estate

Your estate is what you leave behind, financially speaking, when you die. To figure its worth, your assets are valued to determine your gross estate. The assets may include cash, investments, retirement accounts, business interests, real estate, precious objects and antiques, and personal effects. Then all of your outstanding debts, which may include income taxes, loans, or other obligations, are paid, and any costs of settling the estate are subtracted.

If the amount that's left, plus the value of any taxable gifts you have made during your lifetime, is larger than the amount you can leave to your heirs tax-free—in 2000 and 2001 that amount is $675,000, and it will increase gradually to $1 million in 2006—you have a taxable estate, and federal estate taxes will be due. Depending on the state where you live and the size of your taxable estate, there may be additional taxes as well.

After any taxes that may be due are paid, what remains is distributed among your heirs according to the

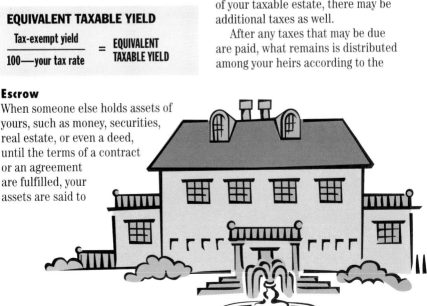

terms of your will or the rulings of a court, if you didn't leave a will.

Estate tax

You owe federal estate tax on the value of your taxable estate (your gross estate minus your liabilities and the cost of settling the estate) if the estate is larger than the amount you are permitted to leave your heirs tax-free. That amount, determined by the Federal Unified Gift and Estate Tax Credit, is $675,000 in 2000 and 2001 and will gradually increase to $1 million by 2006.

Federal estate tax rates range from 37% to 55%, depending on the size of your taxable estate, and some states impose estate taxes as well. If your estate could be vulnerable to these taxes, you may want to try to reduce its value by using a number of tax planning strategies, including making nontaxable gifts and creating irrevocable trusts.

If you're married to a US citizen and leave your entire estate to your spouse, neither federal nor state estate taxes apply, no matter how much the estate is worth. However, estate taxes may be due when your surviving spouse dies.

Euro

On January 1, 1999, the euro became the common currency of the European Union (EU). Eleven participating members—Austria, Belgium, Finland, France, Germany, Ireland, Italy, Luxembourg, Netherlands, Portugal, and Spain—share a central bank and have uniform currency policies.

Electronic transactions and check transfers are currently handled in euros, though the national currencies of the participating countries are being used as subdivisions of the euro until 2002, when they will be replaced with euro coins and bills. Supporters of the euro believe that it will contribute to Europe's economic stability and growth, and enable Europe to realize its potential as an economic and political superpower.

Eurobond

A eurobond is an international bond sold outside of the country in whose currency it is denominated, or issued. For example, an Italian automobile company might sell eurobonds issued in US dollars to investors living in European countries. Multinational companies and national governments, including governments of developing countries, use eurobonds to raise capital in international markets.

Eurocurrency

Eurocurrency is any major currency that is deposited in a bank—called a eurobank—by a national government or corporation from outside the country where the bank receiving the funds is located. For example, Japanese yen deposited in a British bank is called euroyen and is considered eurocurrency. Eurocurrency is used in international trade and for making international loans.

Eurodollar

A eurodollar is US currency deposited in banks outside the United States, usually—but not always—in Europe. Certain securities are issued in euro-dollars and pay interest in US dollars into foreign bank accounts. Eurodollars are a form of eurocurrency.

European Central Bank (ECB)

The European Central Bank is the central bank of the European Monetary Union (EMU), whose 11 member countries (Austria, Belgium, Finland, France, Germany, Ireland, Italy, Luxembourg, the Netherlands, Portugal, and Spain) use the euro as their currency. The ECB, which is based in Frankfurt, Germany, issues currency, sets interest rates, and over-sees other aspects of monetary policy for the EMU.

The EMU's 11 National Central Banks (such as the Banque de France and the Deutsche Bundesbank), together with the ECB, form the European System of Central Banks, and play an important role in imple-menting monetary policy, conducting foreign exchange operations, and maintaining the foreign reserves of member states.

Exchange

An exchange is a physical location for trading securities, typically by using what's known as an open outcry or auction system. In the US, for example, stocks are traded on the New York Stock Exchange (NYSE), the largest stock exchange in the world, on the American Stock Exchange (AMEX), a division of the Nasdaq-Amex Market Group, and on smaller regional ex-changes in Boston, Chicago, Cincinnati, and Philadelphia, and on the Pacific Exchange in California.

Futures contracts and options are traded on exchanges in Chicago, Kansas City, Minneapolis, New York, and Philadelphia. Increasingly, however, trading also takes place on electronic markets, including the Nasdaq Stock Market (Nasdaq), which

allow brokers to trade by computer from any location.

The term exchange also describes moving assets from one mutual fund to another in the same fund family, or from one variable annuity subaccount to another offered through the same contract.

Exchange rate

The exchange rate is the price at which the currency of one country can be converted to the currency of another. Although some exchange rates are fixed by agreement, most fluctuate or float from day to day. For example, on October 13, 1999, $1 could buy 106.54 Japanese yen. One week later, $1 was worth 106.63 yen. Daily ex-change rates are listed in the financial sections of newspapers and can also be found on financial websites.

Exchange-traded fund

Exchange-traded or closed-end funds behave like mutual funds in some ways and like stocks in others. Like other mu-tual funds, exchange-traded funds buy and sell individual investments in keep-ing with their investment objectives.

But the funds resemble stocks in the way they are traded, since they raise money by selling a fixed number of shares when the fund is first issued. Then the shares trade in the secondary market, either on a stock exchange or in an electronic market. The market price of shares of a closed-end fund fluctuates not only according to the value of its underlying investments but also in response to investor demand.

Ex-dividend

There is a period, called ex-dividend, between the announcement and pay-ment of a dividend on a stock or mutual fund. Any investors who buy in that pe-riod are not entitled to the dividend.

Generally, the price of a stock rises in relation to the amount of the antici-pated dividend as the ex-dividend date approaches. It then drops back on the first day of the ex-dividend period to reflect the amount that is being paid out. On the day the ex-dividend period begins, the stock is said to go ex-dividend and is marked with an x in the newspaper until the dividend has been paid.

Executor/Executrix

When you die, an executor (male) or executrix (female) administers your estate and carries out the terms of your will. Among the duties are collecting and valuing your assets, paying taxes and debts out of those assets, and distributing the remaining assets according to the terms of your will.

You may want to appoint a professional—often a bank trust officer or lawyer—as executor, or you may choose a family member or close friend. Or you may appoint a professional and a nonprofessional to work together.

Executors are entitled to be paid for the job, which ends when your estate is settled, usually in anywhere from one to three years. Professional executors always charge, while non-professional ones may or may not.

Exercise

When you act on a buying or selling opportunity—known as a right—that you have been granted under the terms of a contract, you are said to exercise that right. Typical rights contracts include exchanging stock options for stock or buying the underlying stock of a call option.

For example, if you buy a call option giving you the right to buy shares of a stock at $50 a share, and the market price jumps to $60 a share, you would be likely to exercise your option to buy at the lower price.

Exercise price

An option's exercise price, also called the strike price, is the price at which you can buy or sell the stock or commodity that underlies that option. While the exercise price is set by the exchange on which the option trades and remains constant for the life of the option, the market value of the underlying investment rises and falls continuously during the period in response to market demand.

Expense ratio

An expense ratio is the percentage of a mutual fund's or variable annuity's current value that you pay every year to cover the cost of management, customer service, and other expenses related to administering the fund or contract. For example, if you own shares in a fund with a 1.25% expense ratio, you're charged $1.25 for every $100 of fund value that you own.

The amounts you owe are subtracted directly from your account rather than charged separately. Expense ratios vary from one fund company to another and among different types of funds. Typically, international funds have among the highest expense ratios, and index funds among the lowest.

HOW EXPENSE RATIOS WORK

Value of your shares
x Expense ratio
_____
YEARLY FEES

for example

$150,000 Value
x 1.25% Expense ratio
_____
$1,875 YEARLY FEES

Expiration date

You must exercise an option before its expiration date, or it expires worthless. Options are available in three-, six- and nine-month contracts, and always expire on the third Friday of the month in which they come due. For example, if you buy a September option, you can exercise it any time until the third Friday in September.

Markets and Exchanges

Today's markets are a dynamic mixture of tradition and innovation.

Today a stock transaction may take place on the floor of a traditional exchange, in a telephone conversation between two market makers, or when one investor's electronic buy order is matched with another's sell order.

The fact that transactions can happen in all of these ways—not to mention that you can trade by computer—demonstrates how dramatically stock trading has changed.

Traditional Exchanges

The **New York Stock Exchange**, which was organized in 1789, and the **American Stock Exchange** (originally know as the New York Curb Exchange), established in 1842, are traditional brick-and-mortar exchanges. So are the exchanges in Boston, Chicago, Cincinnati, Philadelphia, and San Francisco.

Trading on these exchanges takes place **auction style**, with brokers and traders dealing with specialists—one specialist for each different stock—located in a particular place on the exchange floor.

Commodities futures contracts and options on stocks, stock indexes and a range of other underlying investments are also traded on exchange floors across the country, using a system called **open outcry**. Sellers in the pit where a particular contract is traded shout out the price they want and buyers respond with the price they will pay. When the prices correspond, a deal is struck.

posted and matched at a rapid pace, which is one reason that trading volume on the Nasdaq market is significantly greater than on traditional exchanges.

Electronic Markets

The Nasdaq Stock Market was founded in 1971 by the National Association of Securities Dealers (NASD) as the world's first electronic stock market. Instead of trading on a exchange floor as they would in traditional markets, buyers and sellers operate through a vast international computer and telecommunications network.

The Nasdaq is an open-market, multiple dealer system. That means many market makers compete with each other electronically to buy and sell a particular stock rather than going through a single specialist. Prices are

Over-the-Counter Markets

Both the Nasdaq and the traditional exchanges have listing requirements, which means that corporations have to meet specific size and other criteria to be traded there. Smaller companies, as well as many newer ones that don't make the cut, are traded over the counter (OTC), which these days actually means over the telephone or via computer.

Trading in OTC stocks may be thinner, or less frequent, than in listed stocks, and there is typically less information about them available in the financial press.

ECNs: A Gateway to the Future

In recent years, a revolution in electronic trading has followed in the footsteps of Nasdaq's innovations. One of the biggest changes has been the arrival of **electronic communication networks (ECNs)**. When an order is placed through an ECN, it's added to an electronic record of orders, and if a matching order exists, the ECN executes the deal automatically and anonymously, without involving specialists or market makers.

ECNs have introduced several innovations into stock trading. First, by keeping activity internal among their users, they function much like stock exchanges, revolutionizing the notion that an exchange is a physical place. (In fact, some ECNs have applied to become exchanges, which would allow them to trade securities listed on the NYSE, AMEX, and regional exchanges.)

By making all of the orders on their systems visible, ECNs provide investors a better sense of the current market value of a stock. And their computer- and network-based format facilitates trading after normal market hours.

One potential problem of multiple ECNs, however, is the impact of trading volume on pricing. Buy and sell orders executed after-hours, when fewer stocks are traded, might be settled at higher prices than transactions in those same stocks during exchange hours, when trading is more active.

The National Market System

Since 1975, all the major markets in the US have been linked, using an Intermarket Trading System (ITS) that displays bid and ask prices for stocks trading on a particular exchange and the best prices that are currently available anywhere in the country.

The Future of Futures

Futures and options exchanges have recently introduced technological and organizational innovations similar to those that are changing the stock markets. Trading still takes place primarily on traditional exchange floors, but electronic order-filling and trading across exchanges—and even across nations—are becoming increasingly common.

For example, both the **Chicago Board of Trade (CBOT)** and the **Chicago Board Options Exchange (CBOE)** have adopted networked electronic trading systems system similar to ECNs' order books.

The CBOT's **Project A** handles trading 22 hours a day, both during the hours when trading is being conducted by traditional open outcry and during hours when the exchange is closed. When the two overlap, most trading is still conducted by open outcry. But in the early morning hours, before the exchange opens, there is a brisk market in financial futures contracts.

> The French word for stock exchange — **la Bourse** — literally, the purse — is the term of choice in Europe and in various markets around the world. The eight major European exchanges — in Amsterdam, Brussels, Frankfurt, London, Madrid, Milan, Paris, and Switzerland — are planning for a single pan-European bourse by November 2000.

The CBOE executes about 25% of its orders electronically through its **Retail Automatic Execution System (RAES)** and **Electronic Book (EBOOK)**, which are both networked automatic execution systems like ECNs, but CBOE's traditional floor activity also still dominates the trading volume.

401(k)

This type of employer-sponsored retirement savings plan is funded with money deducted from your pretax salary, up to an annual cap established by Congress. In 2000, the cap is $10,500. Your employer may match some or all of your contribution, based on the terms of the plan you participate in.

With a 401(k), you are responsible for making your own investment decisions and choosing from among different offerings, typically mutual funds, annuities, and fixed-income investments, and sometimes company stock. 401(k) plans offer you the double benefit of current tax savings, because your contributions reduce your taxable salary, and tax-deferred growth on your investment.

In addition, 401(k) plans are usually portable, which means that you can move your accumulated assets to a new employer's plan or an IRA rollover. Amounts you withdraw are taxed at the same rate as other income you receive at the time of withdrawal, but you may owe an additional 10% federal tax penalty if you make those withdrawals before you reach age 59½.

401(k) plans are increasingly replacing traditional defined benefit pension plans in the workplace, largely because they are less expensive to administer and shift much of the responsibility for providing retirement income to the employee.

403(b)

This type of employer-sponsored retirement savings plan is designed for employees of not-for-profit organizations, such as colleges, hospitals, foundations, and cultural institutions.

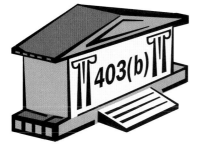

The more you contribute to your 401(k) plan...

the lower your taxable salary...

the less tax you owe...

the faster your investment may grow.

Contributions are tax-deductible, earnings are tax-deferred, and annual contribution limits are similar to those for 401(k) plans, though some of the regulations governing contributions are more complex. In some organizations, 403(b) plans may be set up as a supplement to—rather than a replacement for—defined benefit pensions.

457

This tax-deferred retirement savings plan was designed for state and municipal employees. Like 401(k) and 403(b) plans, the money you contribute is not taxed until you begin making withdrawals—usually at retirement. Unlike many employer-sponsored salary reduction plans, however, 457s are funded solely by the employee, and the annual contribution cap is somewhat lower than for 401(k) plans.

Face value

Face value, also known as par value, is the dollar value of a bond, generally $1,000. That is the amount to be repaid at maturity, provided the issuer doesn't default, and is frequently the amount you pay to buy the bond. However, bonds can be sold at a discount, or less than face value, when they are issued, and either at a discount or at a premium, which is more than face value, in the secondary market.

In any of those cases, however, face value is repaid at maturity. The death benefit of a life insurance policy, which is the amount the beneficiary receives when the insured person dies, is also known as the policy's face value.

Fair market value

Fair market value is the price you would have to pay to buy a particular asset or service on the open market. The concept of fair market value assumes that both buyer and seller are reasonably well informed of market conditions, that neither is under undue pressure to buy or sell, and that neither intends to defraud the other.

Fallen angel

These corporate or government bonds were investment-grade when they were issued but have been downgraded by a rating service, such as Moody's Investors Service or Standard & Poor's (S&P). Downgrading may occur if the issuer's financial situation weakens, or if the rating service anticipates financial problems that could lead to default.

The term is sometimes used more generically, too, to refer to stocks or other securities that are out of favor.

Family of funds

Many large mutual fund companies offer a variety of stock, bond, and money market funds with different investment strategies and objectives. Together, these funds make up a family of funds.

If you own one fund in a family, you can usually transfer assets to another without sales charges—a transaction also known as an exchange. (Unless you hold the funds in a tax-deferred retirement plan, though, you will owe capital gains taxes on any increase in share value of the fund you're moving out of.)

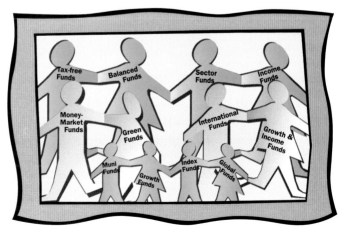

Investing in a family of funds can make diversification and asset allocation easier, provided there are funds within the family that meet your investment criteria. Investing in a family of funds can also simplify recordkeeping.

However, the advantages of consolidating your assets within one fund family are being challenged by the recent proliferation of fund networks, sometimes called fund supermarkets, which make it easy to spread your investments among several fund families.

Federal Deposit Insurance Corporation (FDIC)

Established by the federal government in 1933 after the bank failures of the Great Depression, the FDIC guarantees deposits in member banks and thrift institutions for up $100,000 per depositor per bank. If the bank fails, the government will make good on your money up to the established limits.

You can actually qualify for more than $100,000 coverage at a single bank, however, provided your assets are in different types of accounts. For example, you could be insured for $100,000 in an account registered in your own name, $100,000 in your individual retirement account (IRA), and another $100,000 representing your share of jointly held accounts.

FDIC

Federal funds

When banks have more cash available than they're required to hold in their reserve accounts, they can deposit the money in a Federal Reserve bank or lend it to another bank overnight. That money is called federal funds, and the interest rate at which the banks lend is called the federal funds rate.

The term also describes money the Federal Reserve uses to buy government securities when it wants to take money out of circulation to tighten the money supply and forestall an increase in inflation.

Federal Home Loan Mortgage Corporation (FHLMC)

Affectionately known as Freddie Mac, this shareholder-owned corporation buys mortgages from banks and other lenders, packages them as securities, and resells them to investors.

Freddie Mac provides the dual consumer benefit of providing funds for mortgage lending and offering the opportunity to invest in high-yielding investments backed by the federal government. Its shares are traded on the New York Stock Exchange (NYSE).

FreddieMac

Federal Insurance Contributions Act (FICA)

FICA is the federal law that requires employers to withhold wages from employee paychecks and deposit that money in designated government accounts. These accounts, or trust funds, provide a variety of benefits to US citizens through a program commonly known as Social Security. Retirement income is the largest benefit that FICA withholding supports, but it also funds disability and unemployment insurance.

FICA takes 6.2% of every paycheck you receive, up to an annual cap ($76,200 for 2000) set by Congress. Your employer is required to contribute an equal amount. If you're self-employed, you pay as both employer and employee, or 12.4%.

An additional 1.45% of your salary is also withheld, and matched by your employer, to pay for Medicare, a medical trust fund for people over 65. There's no salary cap for this part of your contribution.

Federal National Mortgage Association (FNMA)

The FNMA—otherwise known as Fannie Mae—is a shareholder-owned corporation that buys mortgages primarily from the US Federal Housing Administration (an agency that insures home mortgages to protect lenders from losing money) and repackages them to sell as securities on the open market.

Like Freddie Mac, Fannie Mae provides investment opportunities while also making money available for potential home buyers to borrow. Fannie Mae shares are traded on the New York Stock Exchange (NYSE).

FEDERAL RESERVE BANK LOCATIONS

Federal Open Market Committee (FOMC)

The 12-member Open Market Committee of the Federal Reserve Board makes policy decisions that influence the health of the American economy. The committee, whose decisions are closely watched by investors and market analysts, meets eight times a year to evaluate the threat of inflation or recession.

Based on its findings, the FOMC determines whether to change interest rates or alter credit policies to curb or stimulate economic growth. It may, for instance, raise the interest rate that the Federal Reserve charges member banks to borrow money. This move would be an effort to tighten the availability of credit in the economy and thereby limit growth. Or it may decide to buy government securities to increase the amount of money in circulation.

Federal Reserve

Established in 1913 to stabilize the country's financial system, the Federal Reserve System—known as the Fed—is the central bank of the US. The seven-member Federal Reserve Board oversees the banking system and sets national monetary policy, with the goal of keeping the US economy healthy and its currency stable.

Like the other members of the Board, the chairman is appointed by the president of the United States, and has emerged as one of the primary shapers of the American economy and economies throughout the world.

The Federal Reserve System includes 12 regional Federal Reserve banks, 25 Federal Reserve branch banks, all national banks, and some state banks. Member banks must meet the Fed's financial standards. The Fed's Open Market Committee sets interest rates and establishes credit policies, and the New York Federal Reserve Bank puts those policies into action by buying and selling government securities.

Fiduciary

A fiduciary is an individual or organization legally responsible for holding or investing assets on behalf of someone else, usually called the beneficiary. The assets must be managed in the best interests of the beneficiary and never for personal gain to the fiduciary.

However, acting responsibly can be broadly interpreted, and may mean preserving principal to some fiduciaries and producing reasonable growth to others. Fiduciaries include executors, trustees, guardians, and agents appointed in powers of attorney.

Fill or kill (FOK)

If an investor places an FOK order, it means the broker must cancel the order if it can't be filled immediately. Usually the designation applies when an investor wants to place a large trade at a particular price.

FINANCIAL FUTURES IN ACTION

THE HEDGERS

Mutual fund that owns US Treasury bonds	Hedges to protect against falling prices in bond market	• If prices stay strong, uses offsettting contract to get out of market • If prices drop, offsets losses with money from sale of contract
Mutual fund that plans future purchase of US Treasury bonds	Hedges to protect against rising prices in bond market	• If prices stay low, uses offsetting contract to get out of market • If prices increase, buys bonds at contract price

Finance charge

The interest you pay on money you borrow, plus certain fees for arranging the loan, is known as a finance charge. The term also refers to the interest you owe on outstanding balances on your credit cards.

A finance charge is expressed as an annual percentage rate (APR) of the amount you borrow, and it can be calculated in a number of different ways. The Truth-in-Lending Law requires your lender to disclose the APR you'll be paying and the way it is calculated before you agree to the terms of the loan.

Financial Accounting Standards Board (FASB)

FASB This independent, self-regulatory board establishes and interprets generally accepted accounting principles (GAAP). It operates under the principle that the economy in general and the financial services industry in particular work smoothly when credible, concise, and understandable financial information is available.

The FASB periodically revises its rules to make sure corporations fully account for different kinds of income, avoid shifting income from one period to another, and properly categorize their income.

Financial future

When the underlying investment of a futures contract is a financial product, such as certificates of deposit (CDs), US Treasurys, US agency bonds, or overseas currencies, the contract is described as a financial future.

Generally, the contract changes in value in response to changes in the interest rate. Increases in the rate produce falling contract prices, while drops in the rate produce rising contract prices. In most cases, the hedgers who use these contracts are banks and other financial institutions who want to protect their portfolios against sudden changes in value triggered by changing interest rates.

Financial institution

Any institution that collects money from the public and puts it into assets such as stocks, bonds, bank deposits, or loans, rather than into tangible property (such as real estate or an automobile), is considered to be a financial institution.

There are two types of financial institutions: Depository institutions, such as banks and credit unions, which pay you interest on your deposit and use the deposit to make loans, and nondepository institutions, such as insurance companies, brokerage firms, and mutual fund companies, which sell financial products. Many financial institutions provide services in both categories.

Financial planner

A professional financial planner evaluates your personal financial situation and helps you develop a plan to meet both your immediate needs and your long-term goals.

Fee-only planners charge you by the hour or sometimes charge a flat fee for a

specific service. They don't sell products or get sales commissions. Other planners don't charge a fee but earn commissions on the products you buy. Still others charge fees and get commissions but may offset part of their fee with commissions on products you buy.

Financial planning is not regulated, so while accountants, bankers, lawyers, brokers, insurance agents, and other professionals with special training and credentials act as planners, people without credentials may also work as planners.

Professional organizations, such as the International Association of Financial Planning, the Institute of Certified Financial Planners, and the National Association of Personal Financial Advisors, provide information on planners who meet their standards.

Financial pyramid

Many investors allocate their investments in what's described as a pyramid structure. A typical financial pyramid has four levels: The majority of assets are in safe, liquid investments that form the base of the pyramid. The next level is composed of securities that provide both income and longer-term capital growth.

At the third level, a smaller portion of resources is invested in more speculative investments with higher potential returns. And the top level, containing the smallest percentage of the overall portfolio, is invested in ventures that have the highest potential return but also the greatest investment risk. Using a financial pyramid to distribute your investments allows you to balance need for stability with your desire for a higher return.

Firm quote

A firm quote is a bid or ask price for a round lot of a security (stocks sold in multiples of 100, for example) that a market maker will honor without further negotiation. For example, if the market maker posts an ask price of 42½, an order to buy at that price will be filled from the market maker's inventory.

Fixed annuity

To guarantee you'll have regular income, particularly in retirement, you can buy a fixed annuity contract issued by a life insurance company. You pay the required premium, either in a lump sum or over a period of time.

The insurance company invests its assets, including your premium, so there will be money available to pay you a fixed rate of return beginning at a time you select. The issuer of the annuity contract assumes the risk that you could outlive your life expectancy and therefore collect income over a longer period than anticipated.

A fixed annuity differs from a variable annuity, which does not guarantee your rate of return or the amount of your future income but provides the possibility of earning a higher rate of return.

Fixed-income investment

Fixed-income investments, such as government, corporate, and municipal bonds, preferred stock, and guaranteed investment contracts (GICs), pay interest or dividends on a regular schedule. In addition, bonds promise return of your principal when the bond matures.

A portfolio heavy with fixed-income investments, however, may not provide the protection you

HIGH RISK

MORE RISK

SOME RISK

STABLE RISK

Financial Credentials

You can get confused stirring through the alphabet soup of financial credentials.

Are you looking for a CPA or an RR or a CFP? As the world of financial services changes, you may encounter a barrage of financial credentials. But you may not be sure how someone with one or more sets of initials after his or her name might help you manage your finances or make investment decisions.

One of the major distinctions these credentials can make is between people who sell investments and those who provide advice. In some cases, they can also designate professionals who have passed certain nationally recognized exams. Of course, what they can't tell you is what working with these advisors will be like

RIA...Not RIP

Any person or investment firm that sells stocks, bonds, mutual funds or any other publicly traded investments registered with the Securities and Exchange Commission (SEC) must be listed as a registered investment advisor (RIA). Individuals and firms managing over $25 million must register with the SEC, while those who manage less must register with the securities agencies of the states in which they do business.

CFP, ChFC

Financial planners can help you formulate your long-term financial goals. They consider the big picture of your finances, including investing, insurance, taxes, and retirement planning, and suggest how the various parts could fit together.

Almost all financial professionals, from accountants to stockbrokers, can advertise their services as financial planners, though only those who meet other criteria can sell investments. The federal government doesn't regulate financial planners, and only some states oversee them.

There are several independent, non-governmental organizations that grant

CPAs

Certified public accountants (CPAs) wear many financial hats. Most commonly, they help you do tax planning and provide tax preparation services. But they can also serve as financial planners and investment advisors, and some of them may sell investments as well. In that case, they may also use an APFS after their names,

RR, AE, FC, Etc.

Investment advisors who act as agents for brokerage firms and who take orders from individual investors to buy and sell stocks must pass a series of state and national exams that test their command of the field. Qualified agents are licensed as registered representatives (RRs) by the SEC. They must also belong to the NASD.

Brokerage firms use different names for these agents, including stockbroker and registered representative, but also account executive (AE), financial consultant (FC), investment executive (IE), and so on. While the names for these professionals may vary, what they have in common is that they have all mastered a body of information about the investment industry.

RIAs must file information on their education, experience, and fees when they register, and must make this information available if you request it. There is also a record of disciplinary actions taken against any registered advisor. You can get this information from the SEC for advisors registered with the commission or through the National Association of Securities Dealers (NASD) for advisors registered with the various states.

credentials to financial planners. Their endorsement can be useful as an initial gauge of a planner's experience and knowledge.

The Certified Financial Planner Board of Standards, established in 1985, grants certified financial planner (CFP) status. CFPs must have three years of financial counseling experience, in addition to completing a course of study and passing an examination, to earn their certification. In addition, they must attend re-certification classes every two years. To check whether a planner is certified, check with the Board at 888-CFP-MARK or www.CFP-Board.org.

Insurance agents who offer financial planning services can earn the designation of chartered financial consultant (ChFC). The ChFC accreditation process consists of a three-year, ten-course program administered by the American College. You can get more information by contacting the college at www.amercoll.edu or 888-AMERCOL.

You can also contact the International Association for Financial Planning for referral to financial planners in your area who meet IAFP standards by calling 800-945-4237 or checking www.IAFP.org.

which stands for accredited personal financial specialist.

In most states there aren't any prerequisites for simply calling yourself an accountant. But to become a CPA, you must pass a national examination. Boards of Accountancy in most states also impose additional experience and education requirements.

Public accountants are people who were practicing their profession before CPA certification was required. They can legally perform all of the services a CPA is entitled to offer.

need against the effects of inflation, since the rates of return on these securities are generally lower over the long term than the return on more volatile investments, such as common stock. Nonetheless, fixed-income securities provide diversification in a well-balanced investment portfolio and can be a useful source of income.

Flexible spending account

Some employers offer flexible spending accounts, sometimes called cafeteria plans, as part of their employee benefits package. You contribute a percentage of your pretax salary, up to the limit your plan allows, which you can then use to pay for qualifying expenses, including medical costs that aren't covered by your health insurance, child care and care for your elderly or disabled dependents.

The amount you put into the plan is not reported to the IRS as income, which means your taxable income is less. However, you have to estimate the amount you'll spend before the tax year begins. And if you don't spend it all, you forfeit any amount that's still in your account at the end of the year.

Float

In investment terms, a float is the number of outstanding shares a corporation has available for trading. If there is a small float, stock prices tend to be volatile, since one large trade could significantly affect the availability—and therefore the price—of these stocks. If there is a large float, stock prices tend to be more stable.

In banking, the float is the time that elapses from the time you write a check until it clears your account. The same term also refers to the time lag between your depositing a check in the bank and the day the funds become available for use. For example, if you deposit a check on Monday, and you can withdraw the cash on Friday, the float is four days. When you write a check, the float works to your advantage. When you deposit a check, the float works to the bank's advantage.

Floating an issue

When a corporation or public agency offers new stocks or bonds to the public, making the offering is called floating an issue. The securities may be the first public issues of a company that was previously private, or an initial public offering (IPO). The securities may also be new issues of companies that have already gone public, in which case they're called secondary offerings. All issues must be registered with the Securities and Exchange Commission (SEC).

Floor broker

Floor brokers are members of a stock or commodities exchange who handle client orders that are sent to the floor of the exchange from the trading department or order room of the brokerage firms they work for. When a transaction is completed, the broker relays  that information back to the firm, and the client is notified.

Floor trader

Unlike floor brokers who fill client orders, floor traders buy and sell stocks or commodities for their own accounts on the floor of an exchange.

Floor traders don't pay commissions, which means they can make a profit on even small changes in price. But they must still abide by trading rules established by the exchange. One of those rules is that client orders take precedence over floor traders' orders.

Foreign exchange (FOREX)

Any type of financial instrument—from electronic transactions to paper currency, checks, and signed, written orders called bills of exchange—that's used to make payments between countries is considered foreign exchange.

Large-scale currency trading, with minimums of $1 million, is also considered foreign exchange and can be handled as spot price transactions, forward contract transactions, or swap contracts. Spot transactions are closed within two days, and the others are set

US dollars

German marks

Australian dollars

for an agreed-upon price at an agreed-upon date in the future.

Formula investing
When you invest on a schedule—as you might with dollar cost averaging—or make investments to maintain a pre-determined asset allocation, you're using a technique known as formula investing. The appeal of this approach, for investors who follow it, is that it eliminates having to agonize over when to buy or sell. But it does not guarantee your portfolio will grow in value.

Forward contract
Buying foreign currency, government securities, or other commodities to be delivered and paid for on a specific future date is called a forward contract. Such a contract specifies that the price to be paid is the spot price, or the market price, on the day the contract was arranged, rather than the price on the delivery date, which is the day the contract is settled.

Forward price-to-earnings (forward P/E)
Stock analysts calculate a forward price-to-earnings ratio by dividing a stock's current price by what they estimate its future earnings per share will

be. Some forward P/Es use estimated earnings for the next four quarters. Others combine actual earnings in the past two quarters with estimated earnings for the next two.

Unlike a P/E figure based exclusively on past performance—sometimes described as a trailing P/E—a forward P/E may help you evaluate the current price of a stock in relation to what you can reasonably expect to happen to it in the near future. For example, a stock whose current price seems high in relation to last year's earnings may seem more reasonably priced if earnings estimates are higher for the next year. (Of course, the exact opposite could be true as well, which would make the current price seem even higher.)

Fourth market
Institutional investors, including mutual fund companies and pension funds, who trade large blocks of securities among themselves rather than on one of the traditional exchanges or the Nasdaq Stock Market (Nasdaq), are operating in what's called the fourth market. The trades are handled through electronic communications networks (ECNs).

Among the appeals of the ECNs are the reduced cost to trade without going through market makers, the ability to trade after hours, and the fact that offers to buy and sell are matched anonymously.

Fractional share
If you reinvest your dividends or invest a fixed dollar amount—for example, $100 a quarter—in a stock dividend reinvestment plan (DRIP) or mutual fund, the amount may not be enough to buy a full share, or there may be money left over after buying one or more full shares. The excess amount buys a fractional share, a unit that is less than one whole share.

In a DRIP, a fractional share gives you credit toward the purchase of a full share. With a mutual fund, in contrast, the fractional share is included in your account value.

Front-end load

When you purchase shares of a mutual fund or annuity, you may have to pay a load, or sales charge. If you pay the charge when you make the purchase, it's called a front-end load. Some mutual funds identify shares purchased with a front-end load as Class A shares.

Full faith and credit

Federal and municipal governments can promise repayment of the debt securities they issue because they are able to raise the money they need through taxes, borrowing, and other sources of revenue. That power is described as full faith and credit.

Full-service brokerage firm

Full-service brokerage firms usually offer their clients a range of services in addition to executing buy and sell orders. For example, they may provide investment advice, help in developing a financial plan, or strategies for meeting financial goals. They usually have access to full-time research departments and investment analysts to provide information they share with clients. However, in exchange for providing these services, these firms tend to charge higher commissions and fees than discount or online brokerage firms.

Fundamental analysis

One of two primary methods for analyzing a stock's potential return, fundamental analysis involves assessing a corporation's financial history to predict its future performance. Analysts consider internal factors, such as earnings, sales, and management, as well as the strength of the corporation's product in the marketplace.

A fundamental analysis might indicate whether the stock is likely to increase or decrease in value in the short- and long-term, and whether its current price is an accurate reflection of its value.

Fungible

When two or more things are interchangeable, can be substituted for each other, or are of equal value, they are described as fungible. For example, shares of common stock issued by the same company are fungible at any point in time since they have the same value no matter who owns them.

Forms of money, such as dollar bills or euros, are fungible since they can be exchanged or substituted for each other. Similarly, put and call futures contracts on the same commodity that expire on the same date are fungible since a futures contract to buy (a call) can offset, or neutralize, a futures contract to sell (a put).

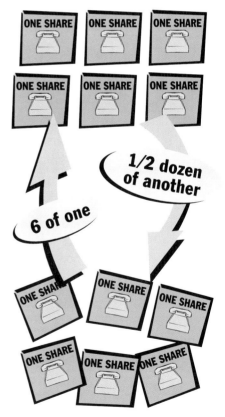

WINNING AND LOSING WITH A FUTURES CONTRACT

JULY 1	OCTOBER 14	DECEMBER 14
You buy one March orange juice contract. Market price: $12,975	Orange juice prices rise 10%. Contract is now worth $14,272.50	Orange juice prices drop 7% since July 1. Contract is now worth $11,917.50
$12,975 Initial value	$1,297.50 Profit	
		$1,057.50 Loss
	Exchange credits your account—this is profit if you sell now	You must add money now to your account to meet the required margin

On the other hand, multiple classes of the same stock may not be fungible. For example, this may occur in markets where citizens of the country are eligible to buy one class of stock and noncitizens a different class. Typically, the shares have different prices and may not be exchanged for each other.

Futures contract

A futures contract obligates you to buy or sell a specified quantity of the underlying investment, which can be a commodity, a stock or bond index, or a currency, for a specific price at a specific date in the future. But you can usually sell the contract to another trader or offset your contract with an opposing contract before the settlement date.

Futures contracts provide some investors, called hedgers, a measure of protection from the volatility of prices on the open market. For example, wine manufacturers are protected when a bad crop pushes grape prices up on the spot market, provided they have a futures contract to buy the grapes at a set price. Similarly, grape growers are protected if prices drop dramatically—if, for example, there's a surplus caused by a bumper crop—provided they have a contract that sets the price at a higher level.

Unlike hedgers, speculators use futures contracts to seek profit on price changes. For example, speculators can make (or lose) money, no matter what happens to the grapes, depending on what they paid for the futures contract and what they can sell it for.

Futures exchange

Traditionally, futures contracts and options on those contracts have been bought and sold on a futures exchange, or trading floor, in a defined physical space. In the US, for example, there are currently futures exchanges in Chicago, Kansas City, Minneapolis, New York, and Philadelphia.

As electronic trading of these products expands, however, buying and selling doesn't always occur on the floor of an exchange, so the term is also being used to describe the activity of trading futures contacts.

Gainer

Stocks that increase in value over the course of the trading day are described as gainers or advancers. More specifically, stocks that increase the most in value in relation to their opening price are called percentage gainers (or percentage winners), while stocks that go up the greatest number of points are called net gainers (or dollar winners).

Percentage gainers and net gainers tend not to be the same stocks. For example, a $1 increase in market price would be a significant percentage gain—50%—for a stock trading at $2, whereas for a stock trading at $100, $1 would be a moderate 1% gain. The number of gainers during the trading day is usually compared to the number of losers or laggards—the stocks that lose the most value over the trading day.

General Agreement on Tariffs and Trade (GATT)

The GATT pact was ratified by Congress  in 1994 to foster trade among nations by cutting international trade tariffs, standardizing copyright and patent protection, and liberalizing trade legislation.

General obligation (GO) bond

Because municipal GO bonds are repaid out of general revenues, they are considered somewhat less risky—and therefore pay slightly lower rates—than the same municipality's revenue bonds, which are backed by income from a specific project or agency. A municipality's general revenues come from the taxes it raises and money it borrows—sometimes described as its full faith and credit.

Gift tax

A gift you make to anybody other than your spouse is taxable if it's worth more than $10,000, and you, rather than the recipient, are responsible for the tax that may be due.

However, you can postpone actually paying the tax until the total combined value of all of your lifetime taxable gifts (or the value of your taxable gifts plus your taxable estate) reaches the tax-free limit set by the Federal Unified Gift and Estate Tax Credit. In 2000 and 2001, that amount is $675,000, and it will gradually increase to $1 million in 2006.

When the combined total exceeds the limit, you (or your estate) owe federal gift and estate tax on the amount that's over the limit, and you may owe state taxes as well. However, you can avoid gift tax entirely if you make individual gifts that are valued at $10,000 or less. In fact, you can make as many of these nontaxable gifts to as many different people as you wish each year, as long as the combined total value of your gifts to any one person stays below the tax-free limit. (The $10,000 limit is indexed to the inflation rate but will increase only in $1,000 increments, or in any year when inflation hits 10%.)

If you want to be even more generous, you and your spouse can give a joint gift of up to $20,000 to as many

Form **709**	**United States Gift Tax Return**			
	(Section 6019 of the Internal Revenue Code) (For gifts made after December 31)		OMB No. 1545-0020 Expires 5-31-96	
Department of the Treasury Inte	**Calendar year 19**			
Form 709 (Rev.				Page **2**
SCHEDULE A	**Computation of Taxable Gifts**			
Part 1—Gifts Subject Only to Gift Tax. *Gifts less political organization, medical, and educational exclusions—see instructions*				
A Item number	B • Donee's name and address • Relationship to donor (if any) • Description of gift	C Donor's adjusted basis of gift	D Date of gift	E Value at date of gift

people as you choose each year without owing gift taxes. And you can give your spouse gifts of any value at any time. These gifts are always tax-free, provided your spouse is a US citizen.

Gilt-edged security

When applied to bonds, the term gilt-edged is the equivalent of describing a stock as a blue chip. Both terms mean that the issuing corporation has a long, strong record for meeting its financial obligations to its investors, including making interest and dividend payments on time and redeeming bonds on schedule.

Global depositary receipt (GDR)

In order to raise money in several markets, some corporations offer shares of their stock on markets in countries other than the one where they have their headquarters. To do it, they issue global depositary receipts in the currency of the country where the stock is trading.

For example, a Mexican company might offer GDRs priced in pounds in London and in yen in Tokyo. Individual investors in the countries where the GDRs are issued buy them to diversify into international markets without having to deal with currency conversion and other complications of overseas investing. However, GDR prices are often volatile and the stocks may be thinly traded, which makes buying them riskier than buying domestic stocks.

Global fund

Global, or world, mutual funds invest in US securities as well as those of other countries. Global funds differ from international

funds, which invest only in overseas—non-US—markets. Although global funds typically keep approximately 75% of their assets invested in the US, fund managers are able to take advantage of opportunities they see in a variety of overseas markets.

Go long

When you go long, you buy an investment that you intend to hold for a period of time or one that you expect to increase in value so that you can sell it at a profit. Going long is the opposite of going short, or selling short, which means you sell an investment you don't own because you expect it to decline in value in the near future.

Go public

A corporation goes public when it issues shares of its stock in the open market for the first time, in what is known as an initial public offering (IPO). That means that at least some of the shares are held by members of the public rather than exclusively by the investors who founded and funded the corporation initially.

Go short

When you go short, you borrow shares of stock from your broker, sell the borrowed shares at their current market price, and pocket the money, minus commission. The reason you go short, which is also known as selling short, is because you expect the stock's price to decline in the near future. If it does, you can buy shares at the lower price and return the number you borrowed, plus interest, to your broker.

The amount you make on the transaction depends on the difference between the price at which you sold and the price at which you can repurchase the shares, plus the amount of time you have to wait for the price to drop. However, there is always the risk that the price will remain stable or even increase, which could mean losing money on the transaction.

Gold standard

The gold standard is a monetary system that measures the relative value of a currency against a specific amount of gold. Developed in England in the early 18th century, when the scientist Sir Isaac Newton was Master of the English Mint, the gold standard was used through-

out the world by the late 19th century. The US was on the gold standard until 1971, when it stopped redeeming its paper currency for gold.

Good 'til canceled (GTC)

If you want to buy or sell a security at a specific price, you can ask your broker to issue a good 'til canceled order. When the security reaches the price you've indicated, the broker will execute the trade. This order stays in effect until it is filled or you cancel it.

A GTC, also called an open order, is the opposite of a day order, which is automatically canceled at the end of the trading day if it isn't filled.

Good will

When analysts estimate the value of a corporation, they look first at the value of its tangible assets, or what it owns. But they also look at its good will, a term that covers the intangible value of its reputation, its satisfied clients, and its productive work force—factors that are considered evidence of the corporation's potential to produce strong earnings.

Government bond

The term government bond is used to describe all types of debt securities issued by the federal government, such as US Treasury bills, notes, bonds, and zero-coupon STRIPS. You can buy these bonds directly using a Treasury Direct account that you set up through a Federal Reserve Bank or through a broker.

Treasurys are backed by the full faith and credit of

the US government, and the interest they pay is exempt from state and local—though not federal—taxes. The cash raised by the sale of Treasurys is used to finance a variety of government activities. Trading in the bonds also helps regulate the money supply and pay off the national debt. The main difference between bills, notes, and bonds is the length of their terms and their rates of return.

Government National Mortgage Association (GNMA)

GNMA—better known as Ginnie Mae—is an agency of the US Department of Housing and Urban Development. The agency guarantees, backed by the full faith and credit of the US government, mortgage-backed

securities issued by private institutions. The agency's dual mission is to provide affordable mortgage funding for all Americans while creating high-quality investment securities that offer safety, liquidity, and an attractive yield.

Since Ginnie Maes are mortgage securities, they pay interest as well as return of principal with each payment. GNMA securities are sold in large denominations—usually $25,000. But you can buy Ginnie Mae mutual funds, which allow you to invest more modest amounts.

Green fund

A mutual fund that makes investments based on a commitment to social, environmental, or political principles may be described as a green fund, a conscience fund, or a socially responsible fund. Although the returns on green funds have sometimes trailed the performance of those buying more widely to meet their investment objectives, many green funds have strong records, and some have led their sectors in recent years.

Not all green funds stress the same values, however. A fund that shuns the defense industry may buy tobacco company stocks, or one that seeks environmentally friendly businesses may not be concerned about what those businesses manufacture.

If you have strong feelings about how your money in mutual funds is invested, you need to do some research about any fund you're considering and take a look at its portfolio to see what the fund is purchasing.

Gross domestic product (GDP)

The total value of all the goods and services produced within a country's borders are described as its gross domestic product. When that figure is adjusted for inflation, it is called the real gross domestic product, and it's generally used to measure the growth of the country's economy. In the US, the GDP is calculated and released quarterly by the Department of Commerce.

Growth

Investment growth is an increase in the value of an investment over time. Unlike investments that produce income, those that are designed for growth don't necessarily provide you with a regular source of cash. A growth company is more likely to reinvest its profits to build its business. If the company prospers, however, its stock typically increases in value.

Stocks, stock mutual funds, and real estate are typical growth investments, but some stocks and mutual funds emphasize growth more than others.

Growth and income fund

These mutual funds invest in securities that provide a combination of growth and income. These funds generally funnel most of their assets into common stocks of well-established companies that pay regular dividends and increase in value at a regular, if modest, rate. Some or all of the balance may be in high-rated bonds.

Guaranteed investment contract (GIC)

A GIC (pronounced *gick*) is a promise to preserve your principal and to provide a fixed rate of return when you begin to withdraw from the contract, typically after you retire. You can invest in a GIC through a salary-reduction plan, such as a 401(k) or 403(b) sponsored by your employer, provided that investment option is offered.

Because of their fixed rates, GICs are vulnerable to inflation. And you may have to pay a penalty if you decide to change from a GIC to a different investment. Insurance companies that offer GICs assume the risk that the rate they earn on their investments will outperform the rates they've guaranteed on the GICs.

GROWTH AND INCOME FUNDS

FUND TYPE	INVESTMENT OBJECTIVE	WHAT THE FUND BUYS
Balanced	Income and growth	Part common and preferred stocks (usually 60%) and part bonds (40%)
Equity income	Income and growth	Blue chip stocks and utilities that pay high dividends
Growth and income	Growth plus some current income	Stocks that pay high dividends and provide some growth
Income	Primarily income	Primarily bonds, but some dividend-paying stocks

Hedge fund

Hedge funds are private investment partnerships open to institutions and wealthy individual investors. These funds pursue returns through a number of alternative investment strategies, including hedging against market downturns by holding both long and short positions, investing in derivatives, using arbitrage, and speculating on mergers and acquisitions.

Some hedge funds use leverage, which means investing borrowed money, to boost returns. Because of the substantial risks associated with hedge funds, securities laws limit participation to individuals with incomes of at least $200,000 a year ($300,000 for couples) or those who have a net worth of at least $1 million.

Hedger

Hedgers in the futures market try to offset potential price changes in the spot market by buying or selling a futures contract. For example, a cereal manufacturer may want to hedge against rising wheat prices by buying a futures contract that promises delivery of September wheat at a specified price.

If, in August, the crop is destroyed, and the spot price increases, the manufacturer can take delivery of the wheat at the contract price, which will probably be lower than the market price. Or the manufacturer can trade the contract for more than the purchase price and use the extra cash to offset the higher spot price of wheat.

Hedging

Hedging is an investment technique designed to offset, or neutralize, a potential loss on one investment by purchasing a second investment that you expect to perform in the opposite way. For example, you might sell short one stock, expecting its price to drop. At the same time, you would buy a call option on the same stock as insurance against a large increase in value.

High-yield bond

Low-rated bonds pose greater risk of default than higher-rated bonds. As a result, their issuers must pay investors a higher rate of interest to offset that risk, which, in turn, produces a higher yield. These high-yield bonds are also described, somewhat more graphically, as junk bonds.

Hot issue

If a newly issued security rises steeply in price after its initial public offering (IPO) because of intense investor demand, it is considered a hot issue.

HOW HEDGING CAN WORK

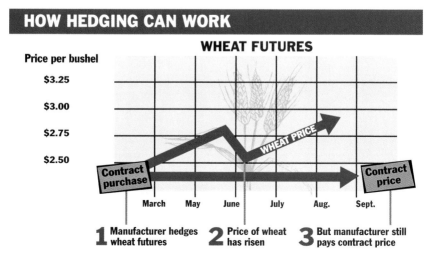

WHEAT FUTURES

Price per bushel

$3.25
$3.00
$2.75
$2.50

Contract purchase

WHEAT PRICE

Contract price

March   May   June   July   Aug.   Sept.

1 Manufacturer hedges wheat futures
2 Price of wheat has risen
3 But manufacturer still pays contract price

Immediate annuity

You buy an immediate annuity by paying the full cost of the annuity contract at the time of purchase. The annuity then begins paying income right away or within a year at the latest. Immediate annuities appeal to

people who want to convert a large sum of money to a source of regular income, either for their own retirement or for a beneficiary.

You can choose a fixed immediate annuity, which guarantees the amount of income as well as the terms of the contract, or a variable immediate annuity, where the income generated is based on the performance of the investment portfolios, or subaccounts, that underlie the contract.

In the money

You are in the money when you own a stock option with a strike price that's close enough to the current market price to allow you to exercise the option at a profit. If it's a put option, giving you the right to sell, the current market price must be below the strike price. If it's a call option, giving you the right to buy, the current price must be above the strike price.

For example, if you have a call option with a strike price of $50, and the current market price of the stock is $52, you're in the money, since you could buy the stock at $50 and sell it at $52. In-the-money options are generally among the most actively traded, especially as the expiration date approaches.

Incentive stock option (ISO)

This compensation plan, created by the Economic Recovery Tax Act of 1981 (ERTA), lets executives receive options to purchase company stock at a deep discount and exercise those options free of income tax until they sell the shares.

If, after exercising the options, participating executives keep the shares they receive for the required period, any earnings on these shares are taxed at the capital gains rate. However, stock option transactions may make sellers vulnerable to the alternative minimum tax (AMT).

Income fund

Income funds are mutual funds whose investment objective is to produce current income rather than long-term growth, typically by investing in bonds. The amount of income a fund may generate is related to the risk posed by the investments that the fund makes.

A fund that buys lower-grade bonds will often pay more income than a fund buying investment-

grade bonds. But under certain market conditions, the riskier fund may pay less or put your principal, or investment amount, at risk.

Index

An index reports changes, usually expressed as a percentage, in a specific financial market, in a number of related markets, or in the economy as a whole. Each index—and there are a large number of them—measures the

STOCK MARKET INDEXES

Index	Exchange	Net Chg	Pct Chg
Nikkei Average	Tokyo	−32.0	−0.16
Topix Index	Tokyo	+6.55	+0.40
FT 30-share	London	−6.3	−0.28
100-share	London	−2.4	−0.08
Gold Mines	London	−9.8	−4.10
DAX	Frankfurt	+63.94	+3.72
Swiss Market	Zurich	+24.9	+1.05
CAC 40	Paris	+36.64	+1.89
Stock Index	Milan	+22.0	+1.87
ANP-CBS General	Amsterdam	+2.2	+0.96
Affarsvarlden	Stockholm	+8.7	+0.79
Bel-20 Index	Brussels	+8.89	+0.70
All Ordinaries	Australia	+8.7	+0.49
Hang Seng	Hong Kong	−18.72	−0.26
Straits Times	Singapore	−0.21	−0.01
J'burg Gold	Johannesburg	−121.0	−5.78
General Index	Madrid	+1.11	+0.43
I.P.C.	Mexico	+37.11	+2.24
300 Composite	Toronto	−51.86	−1.81
MCSI	Euro, Aust, Far East	−2.5	−0.28

market or markets it tracks from a specific starting point, which might be as recent as the previous day or many years in the past. That's one reason two indexes tracking similar markets may report different numbers.

Another reason two indexes seem to produce different results is that some indexes are weighted and others are not. Weighting means giving more significance to some elements in the index than to others. For example, a market capitalization index weighs larger companies more than smaller companies.

Index fund

An index mutual fund is designed to mirror the performance of one of the major stock or bond indexes, such as Standard & Poor's 500-stock Index (S&P 500) or the Russell 2000, by purchasing all of the securities included in the index, or a representative sample of them.

Each index fund aims to keep pace with an index, not to outperform it. This strategy can be successful during a bull market, when an index reflects increasing prices. But it may produce disappointing returns during economic downturns, when an actively managed fund might take advantage of invest-

ment opportunities where and when they arise.

Because the typical index fund's broadbased portfolio is not actively managed, most index funds have lower-than-average management costs and smaller expense ratios. That means less of the fund's growth goes to pay expenses, and more can be returned to the fund's investors. However, not all index funds provide the same level of performance.

Index of Leading Economic Indicators

This monthly composite of 10 economic measurements was developed to track and help forecast changing patterns in the economy. It is compiled by The Conference Board, a business research group. The components are adjusted from time to time to help improve the accuracy of the index, which in the past has successfully predicted major downturns (although it has also warned of some that did not materialize).

The current components are the average work week, average initial claims for unemployment benefits, manufacturers' new orders for consumer goods and materials, vendor performance (how quickly companies receive deliveries from suppliers), plant and equipment orders, building permits, stock prices of 500 common stocks, the M2 money supply, the interest rate spread, and the index of consumer expectations.

LEADING INDICATORS

Index option

Index options give investors the chance to make (or lose) money by anticipating the gains or losses in an industry group or a broader segment of the market. For example, an investor who thinks technology stocks are going to fall can buy a put option on a technology index rather than selling short a number of different technology stocks.

However, since changes in an index are difficult to predict, index options tend to be very volatile. And the further out the expiration date for exercising an index option, the more volatile the option tends to be. Most trading in index options takes place on the New York Stock Exchange (NYSE), the American Stock Exchange (AMEX), and the Chicago Board Options Exchange (CBOE).

Individual retirement account (IRA)

These tax-deferred retirement accounts are designed to encourage working people to invest for the long term. If you earn income from work, or are married to someone who does, you can put up to $2,000 per year in an IRA and postpone paying tax on any earnings. However, you must be at least 59½, or qualify for an exception, to withdraw without owing a 10% penalty, in addition to taxes due on the amount you take out.

There are two types of retirement IRAs, traditional and Roth, which have different qualification, contribution, and withdrawal rules. For example, you can contribute to a traditional IRA regardless of your income, and some people, depending on their income and participation in an employer-sponsored retirement plan, can deduct all or part of their annual contribution on their tax returns as well.

Withdrawals from traditional IRAs must begin by age 70½, and all earnings (plus any deductible contributions) are taxed at your current tax rate as they are withdrawn. Withdrawals from Roth IRAs are tax-free after you reach age 59½, provided the account has been open at least five years. In addition, Roth IRAs have no required withdrawals.

WEIGHING THE CHOICE

If you have a choice of which IRA to open, you'll want to weigh the pros and cons:

| | ROTH | TRADITIONAL IRA | |
		Nondeductible	Deductible
PROS	• Tax-free income • No required withdrawals	• Tax-deferred earnings	• Immediate tax savings on tax-deferred investment • Tax-deferred earnings
CONS	• Not deductible • Account must be open five years to qualify for tax-free provision	• Not deductible • Tax paid at regular rates at withdrawal • Required withdrawals beginning at age 70½	• Tax paid at regular rates at withdrawal • Required withdrawals beginning at age 70½

Inefficient market

When a market is described as inefficient, it means that investors do not
know enough about the securities in
that market to make informed decisions
about what to buy or the price to pay.
Markets in emerging nations may be
inefficient, since few analysts follow the
securities being traded there. Similarly,
there can be inefficient markets for
stocks in new companies, particularly
those in new industries.

An inefficient market is the opposite
of an efficient one, where it's assumed
that investors know everything there
is to know about the securities they
are buying.

Inflation

Inflation is a persistent increase in
prices, triggered when demand for
goods is greater than the available
supply. Moderate inflation often
accompanies economic growth, but
the Federal Reserve Bank and central
banks in other nations try to keep inflation in check, usually by decreasing the
money supply when inflation heats up,
making it more difficult to borrow.

Among the more obvious methods
used by the Fed are raising the federal
discount rate (the rate the Fed charges
member banks on loans) and/or the
federal funds rate (the rate that banks
charge to lend money to other banks

THE INFLATION CYCLE

1.
**Increasing
demand
boosts
prices**

3.
**Lower prices
increase
demand,
and cycle
begins again**

2.
**Rising prices
decrease
demand, so
prices drop**

overnight). That reduces the money
available for investment and spending,
since the banks, in turn, raise the rates
they charge borrowers.

Hyperinflation, when prices rise by
100% or more annually, can destroy
economic, and sometimes political,
stability by driving the price of necessities higher than people can afford.

Inflation-adjusted return

Inflation-adjusted return is what you
earn on an investment after accounting
for the impact of inflation. For example, if you earn 7% on a bond during a
period when the inflation rate averages
3%, your inflation-adjusted return is 4%.

Since inflation diminishes the
buying power of your
money, it's important
that the rate of re-
turn on your overall
investment portfolio
be greater than the
rate of inflation.
That way, your money
grows rather than
shrinks in value
over time.

Inflation-indexed security

Bonds and notes that promise your return will beat inflation if you hold them
until maturity are known as inflation-
indexed securities. Mutual funds that
invest in these bonds and notes are
described as inflation-indexed funds.

For example, inflation-indexed
Treasury notes, which were introduced
in 1997, pay a fixed interest rate but
offset the effects of inflation by adjusting your principal periodically, based
on the Consumer Price Index for all
Urban Consumers (CPI-U). If you buy
a $1,000 inflation-indexed Treasury,
the interest will be calculated and paid
twice a year on the inflation-adjusted
principal, which will increase over
time. These inflation adjustments are
federally taxable each year, as is the
interest, even though you don't receive
the increases until the security matures. These securities also provide a
safeguard against deflation since they
guarantee that you'll get back no less
than par, or face value, at maturity.

Initial public offering (IPO)

When a company reaches a certain
stage in its growth, it may decide to

issue stock to the public. The goal may be to raise capital, to provide liquidity for the existing shareholders, or a number of other reasons.

If a small company experiencing rapid growth goes public, it usually means good news for the company's original investors, since the market value of their holdings tends to increase substantially. Any company planning an IPO must register with the Securities and Exchange Commission (SEC).

Insider trading

When the management of a publicly held company, or members of its board of directors, or anyone else who holds more than 10% of the company, buys or sells its shares, the transaction is considered insider trading.

This type of trading is perfectly legal, provided it's based on information available to the public. But insider trading is illegal if the buy or sell decision is based on knowledge of corporate developments—such as an executive change, an earnings report, or an acquisition or a takeover—that has not yet been made public.

It is also illegal for people who are not part of the company, but who gain access to private corporate information—such as lawyers, investment bankers, or relatives of company officials—to trade the company's stock based on this inside information.

Instinet

Instinet, a division of Reuters Group PLC, is the world's largest agency brokerage firm. As an agency firm, it doesn't trade stock for its own account as traditional brokerage houses do, so it doesn't bid against the mutual funds, insurance companies, pension funds, and other institutional investors who are its primary clients.

Using Instinet's sophisticated electronic network, these investors can trade directly and anonymously with each other in more than 40 global markets. Or, using Instinet brokers, the investors can place orders on all US exchanges and many overseas exchanges, including those that aren't automated.

Institutional investor

Institutional investors buy and sell securities in large volume, typically 10,000 or more shares of stock, or $200,000 or more worth of bonds, in a single transaction. In most cases, the investors are organizations with large portfolios, such as mutual funds, banks, universities, insurance companies, pension funds, and labor unions. Institutional investors may trade their individual assets, or assets that they are managing for other people.

Interest

The term interest is used in several different ways. Interest is the cost of using the money provided by a loan, credit card, or line of credit, usually expressed as a percentage of the amount borrowed and pegged to a specific period of time. For example, the interest on your mortgage may be 8.25% annually, or you may pay 1.2% interest monthly on the unpaid balance of your credit card purchases.

Interest also refers to the income, figured as a percentage of your principal, that you receive for buying a bond, putting money into a bank, or making other fixed-income investments. Interest is also a share or right in a property or asset. For example, if you are part-owner of a vacation home, you have an interest in it.

Interest rate

The percentage of the face value of a bond or other debt security that you receive as payment on your investment is the security's interest rate. If you multiply that rate by the face value, you get the annual amount you receive as interest. For example, if you buy a bond with a face value of $1,000 that's paying 6% interest, you'll receive $60 a year. If you pay the face value of the investment, the interest rate will be the same as the yield on your investment.

But if you paid either more or less than the face value, the rate and the yield will be different. For example,

Rules of Thumb

Time-tested rules of thumb can help you get a grip on your finances.

You can use some simple guidelines to help you decide what you can afford to spend and how much you should be investing. These rules of thumb, and others like them, may make handling your finances a little less daunting.

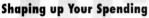

Shaping up Your Spending

In figuring how to get your spending in shape, you could follow the **70-20-10 rule**. This means allocating 70% of your take-home pay to cover major living expenses, such as housing and food, and capping the amount you're using to pay off debts, such as car payments and credit card bills, at 20%. That leaves the remaining 10% for investing, which should give you a headstart on meeting your financial goals, especially if you start early enough.

Of course, what's missing in this approach is any recreation, something you might want to factor into your budget—even if there's no official category for fun and games.

100
– Your age

Amount you should invest in stocks

107
– Your age

Amount you should invest in stocks

Taking Stock of Your Future

One rule of thumb to help you invest suggests that you figure the percentage of your portfolio to be invested in stocks by subtracting your age from 100 if you're a man and from 107 if you're a woman. (The difference accounts for the fact that women, on average, live seven years longer than men.) So, for example, if you're in your 20s, you would invest about 80% of your portfolio in stocks, but by the time you're 40, you might cut back to between 50% and 60%. You'd put the difference, in each case, into bonds or cash. The idea is to emphasize long-term growth in the early years and more fixed income later on in life.

But rules of thumb aren't universal, or without controversy. Many experts feel that this approach is too conserva-tive, especially as you get older. In a bull market, they argue, it's wiser to put a greater percentage in stocks—maybe as much as 95% for a 20-year-old and closer to 70% for someone who is 40.

The Rule of 5 — Or Is It 7?

Insurance is a key part of financial planning, since nobody wants to leave his or her dependents at risk finan-cially. One rule of thumb suggests that people with children need enough insurance to provide a lump sum equal to at least five to seven times the household's take-home pay. While you may want some expert advice before actually deciding how much coverage you need, you can begin by calculating whether your current coverage comes close to those guidelines, and then determining how much more you can afford.

Thumbs Up...And Down

The **rule of 72** can give you a sense of how long it will take for an investment you make today to double your money—or how long it will take for money you don't invest to shrink to half its value.

To find how long doubling will take, you divide 72 by the rate of return you're currently earning.

And to find out how quickly loss of value will occur, you divide 72 by the current inflation rate.

For example, if your return on an investment is 10%, you'll double your money in just over seven years (72 ÷ 10), provided you don't withdraw from the account and you earn at the same rate each year. Similarly, if the inflation rate is 3%, the buying power of money that you don't invest will be worth just half of what it's worth today in 24 years (72 ÷ 3).

The catch is, if you're earning 3%, it will also take 24 years to double your money. But if inflation is 10%, the value of your money will be halved in just over seven years.

Rules of Two

Two **rules of two** are popular guidelines for home financing. One suggests that you can afford to buy a house whose price is about two and a half times your annual income. So if you're earning $75,000, you might look in the $187,000 range. While it's a good starting place, the amount you have for a down payment, the current mortgage interest rate, and the amount you'll owe for property taxes and homeowner's insurance may mean that in reality you can actually afford more—or less.

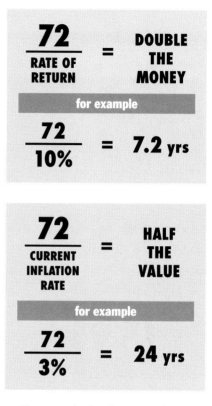

$$\frac{72}{\text{RATE OF RETURN}} = \text{DOUBLE THE MONEY}$$

for example

$$\frac{72}{10\%} = 7.2 \text{ yrs}$$

$$\frac{72}{\text{CURRENT INFLATION RATE}} = \text{HALF THE VALUE}$$

for example

$$\frac{72}{3\%} = 24 \text{ yrs}$$

The second rule of two says that you should refinance your mortgage if

- You can find a rate at least 2% lower than your current rate
- You don't plan to move for at least two years

But you have to look at several factors closely before you refinance. If you compare your current and future property tax and mortgage interest deductions and the changing value of money over time, you may find that it takes closer to five years to reap the benefits of refinancing, even if you're paying 2% less in interest.

YOUR INCOME

MORTGAGE RATE

A rule of thumb that's been nibbled away by rising rents in urban areas is that you should spend no more than 25% of your income on housing (before real estate taxes and insurance).

if you paid $1,100 for a bond with a face value of $1,000 paying 6% interest, you'd receive an annual yield of 5.45% ($60 ÷ $1,100 = .0545, or 5.45%).

Similarly, the percentage of the principal you pay on a loan is also called the interest rate. For example, if you had a $100,000 fixed-rate home mortgage at 7.9%, the interest rate on the loan is 7.9%.

INTEREST RATE	
Rate	6%
x Face value	x $1,000
ANNUAL INTEREST	**$60 PER YEAR**

Interest-rate risk

Interest-rate risk describes the impact that a change in current interest rates is likely to have on the value of your investment portfolio. You face interest-rate risk when you buy long-term bonds or bond mutual funds whose market value will drop if interest rates increase. That happens because other  investors will be able to buy bonds paying the new, higher rate, so they'll be unwilling to pay full price for a bond paying a lower rate of interest.

Intermarket Trading System (ITS)

The ITS is a video-computer link between members of the National Market System (NMS), which was created in 1975 to carry out a congressional mandate to increase competition in securities trading.

It connects National Association of Securities Dealers (NASD) market makers, and New York Stock Exchange (NYSE), American Stock Exchange (AMEX), and regional exchange specialists who make a market in the same security. The electronic system displays bid and ask prices for securities in each of the markets so that brokers are able to trade in the market where they can get the best price.

Intermediate-term bond

Intermediate-term bonds mature in two to ten years from the date of issue. Typically, the interest on these bonds is greater than that on short-term bonds of similar quality but less than that on comparable long-term bonds. The rule of thumb on bond interest is that the longer the term, the higher the interest paid.

Intermediate bonds work well in an investment strategy known as laddering, which involves buying bonds with staggered maturity dates so that portions of your total investment mature in different years.

International fund

This type of mutual fund invests in stocks or bonds that are traded in overseas markets, or in indexes that track international markets. Like other funds, an international fund has an investment objective and strategy, and poses some level of risk, including the risk that fluctuations in currency can significantly affect the value of the fund.

Some international funds focus on countries with established economies, some on emerging markets, and some on a mix of the two. US investors, for example, buy funds that invest in other markets to diversify their portfolios, since owning a fund is usually simpler than investing in individual securities abroad. A different group of funds, called global or world funds, also invest in overseas markets but typically keep a substantial portion of their portfolios in US securities.

International Monetary Fund (IMF)

The IMF was set up as a result of the United Nations Bretton Woods Agreement of 1944 to help stabilize world currencies, lower trade barriers, and help developing nations pay their debts. The IMF's activities are funded by developed nations and are sometimes the subject of intense criticism, either by the nations the IMF is designed to help, the nations footing the bill, or both.

Investment bank

An investment bank is a financial institution that helps companies take new bond or stock issues to market, usually acting as the intermediary between the issuer and investors. Investment banks may underwrite the securities, for example, by buying all the available shares at a set price and then reselling them to the public. Or they may act as agents for the issuer and take a commission on the securities they sell.

Investment banks are also responsible for preparing the company prospectus, which presents important data about the company to potential investors. In addition, investment banks handle the sales of large blocks of previously issued securities, including sales to institutional investors, such as mutual fund companies. Unlike a commercial bank or a savings and loan company, an investment bank doesn't provide retail banking services to individuals.

Investment club

If you're part of an investment club, you and the other members jointly choose the investments the club

makes and decide on the amount each of you will contribute to the club's account. Among the reasons that clubs are popular is that they allow investors to invest only modest amounts, share in a diversified portfolio, and benefit from each other's research.

In addition, clubs may pay lower commissions than individual investors, as a result of arrangements they make with a brokerage firm or through the National Association of Investors

Corporation (NAIC). NAIC also provides information on how to get an investment club started and supplies support services to existing groups.

Investment company

An investment company is a firm that offers either open-end funds, called mutual funds, or closed-end funds, sometimes called investment trusts. Each fund that a company offers has a specific investment objective, and money that individuals and institutions put into the fund is pooled and invested by a manager employed by the investment company to meet that objective.

For example, an open-end investment company might offer an aggressive-growth fund, a growth and income fund, a US Treasury bond fund, and a money market fund. Or a closed-end investment company might offer an international fund focused on a single country, such as Ireland, or a region, such as Latin America. The term investment company is often used to describe a mutual fund company to distinguish the company from the funds that it offers.

Investment-grade

Most US corporate and municipal bonds are rated by independent services such as Moody's Investors Service and Standard & Poor's (S&P). The ratings are based on a number of criteria, including the likelihood that the corporation or agency issuing the bond will be able to make interest payments and repay the principal in full and on time.

The highest-quality bonds—rated BBB and higher by S&P or Baa and higher by Moody's—are considered investment-grade. That means their issuers are likely to meet their obligations by paying the interest due and paying off the bonds when they mature.

Investment objective

An investment objective is a financial goal and helps determine the type of investments you make. For example, if you want to provide a source of regular income, you might select a portfolio of high-rated bonds and dividend-paying stocks. Each mutual fund describes its investment objective in its prospectus, along with the strategy the manager follows to meet that objective. Mutual fund investors often look for funds whose stated objectives are compatible with their own.

IRA rollover

If you take a lump sum out of an employer-sponsored retirement plan and put it into an individual retirement account (IRA), the new account is called an IRA rollover. Any earnings in your IRA continue to grow tax-deferred, and you owe no income tax on the money you move, provided that you deposit the full amount into the new IRA within 60 days.

If you don't, you risk owing tax on any amounts you haven't deposited, as well as owing a penalty for making an early withdrawal. You can generally avoid this problem by arranging a direct transfer from your plan to the IRA.

If you're moving the money in an employer's retirement plan to an IRA yourself, the plan administrator is required to withhold 20% of the total. That amount is refunded after you file your income tax return, provided you've deposited the full amount into the new account on time, including the 20% that's been withheld.

In this case, too, any amount you don't deposit is considered a withdrawal, and you'll have to pay tax on it, and possibly a penalty for early withdrawal as well. Again, you can avoid this problem by arranging a direct transfer from your old plan to the new IRA rollover. That way, nothing is withheld.

Issue

When a government or corporation issues a new stock or bond, it offers it for sale for the first time. The stock or bond is known as an issue, and the company is the issuer.

Issuer

An issuer is a corporation, government, agency, or investment trust that sells securities, such as stocks and bonds, to investors, either through an underwriter as part of a public offering or as a private placement.

IRA ROLLOVER

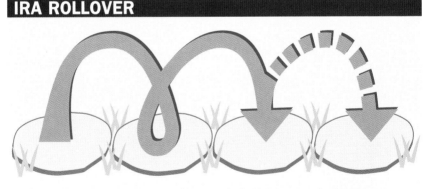

| Tax-protected IRA in savings account | Can use money from account during 60-day period | Tax-protected IRA in broker account | Pay tax if not reinvested |

J-K

Junior security

In the world of bonds, the term junior means having less claim to repayment. If you own a junior security, as such bonds are known, and the issuing company goes out of business, you have less claim on the company's assets than an investor who owns a senior security issued by the same company. But all bondholders, whether they own junior or senior securities, are senior to, or have a greater claim than, holders of preferred stock, who in turn are senior to holders of common stock.

Junk bond

Junk bonds carry a higher-than-average risk of default, which means that the bond issuer may not be able to meet interest payments or repay the loan when it matures. Except for bonds that are already in default, junk bonds have the lowest ratings, usually Caa or CCC, assigned by rating services such as Moody's Investors Service and Standard & Poor's (S&P).

Issuers offset the higher risk of default on junk bonds by offering substantially higher interest rates than are being paid on investment-grade bonds. That's why junk bonds are also known, more positively, as high-yield bonds.

Keogh plan

Named after Eugene Keogh, a US representative from Brooklyn, NY, Keoghs are qualified retirement plans for self-employed people, small-business owners, and others in similar work situations. Keoghs offer the double benefit of salary reduction and

Eugene Keogh

tax-deferred earnings, plus control over how your money is invested.

When you withdraw from a Keogh, typically after you retire, you owe income tax on the withdrawal amounts at whatever tax rate you are currently paying. There may be penalties for withdrawals before you reach age 59½, and you may be required to begin withdrawals by age 70½.

There are several ways to set up a Keogh using profit sharing, money purchase, or a combination plan. Since the contribution and reporting requirements are complex, it's wise to have professional help in setting up a Keogh plan.

JUNK BOND RATINGS

MOODY'S	S&P'S	MEANING
Caa	CCC	Poor quality
Ca	CC	Highly speculative quality
C	C	Lowest-rated
•	D	In default

Laddering

By laddering, or staggering, the maturities on fixed-income investments, such as certificates of deposit (CDs) and bonds, you can set up a schedule for

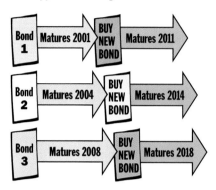

when various investments come due. That way, you can avoid having to reinvest all your money at one time, when interest rates may be low, and you can take advantage of new investment opportunities, including those with higher returns, as they become available.

As each investment matures, you can reinvest that amount, use it for a preplanned purchase, or have it available to cover unexpected expenses. For example, instead of one $15,000, five-year CD yielding 5%, you can buy three $5,000 CDs maturing one year apart. Laddering is sometimes used in planning to pay for college expenses, with each investment coming due in time to pay tuition for that year.

Large-capitalization (large-cap) stock

This is the stock of large, established companies, with market capitalizations in the billions of dollars. (Market capitalization is figured by multiplying the number of outstanding shares by the current share price.) Large-cap stocks, such as those tracked by Standard & Poor's 500-stock Index (S&P 500), are generally considered less volatile than mid-cap or small-cap stocks. Mutual funds that invest in this type of stock are known as large-cap funds.

Recently, however, several Internet stocks have enjoyed large market capitalizations as their stock prices have soared, though as new issues they would not ordinarily be thought of as large-cap stocks.

Level load

Some mutual funds impose a recurring sales charge, called a level load, each year you own the fund rather than charging either a front- or back-end load.

The level-load rate is generally less, usually 1% to 2% annually, than the rate that's charged on a front- or back-end load fund. But the total sales charge you pay over time with a level load can be substantially more than other types of loads, especially if you own the fund for a number of years. Level-load funds are frequently identified by mutual fund companies as Class C shares to distinguish them from front-end loads (Class A shares) and back-end loads (Class B shares).

Leverage

Using leverage is an investment technique in which you borrow money to increase the size of your investment. The expectation is that you'll realize a much greater return than you could by investing your own money alone. In addition, using leverage lets you wield greater financial power without putting your own money at stake. For example, if you borrow money to buy a home, you are using the leverage of the mortgage to buy a much more expensive home that you could have afforded by paying cash.

A $3,700 investment buys a $37,000 contract

100 oz. GOLD

Leverage of 10 to 1

Buying on margin is a type of leveraging, as is buying a futures contract or an option. Leveraging can be very risky, however, if the investment doesn't perform as you anticipate, since you risk losing your own money as well as the borrowed money you will have to repay.

Leveraged buyout

A leveraged buyout occurs when a small group of investors, using borrowed money, often raised with junk bonds or other kinds of debt, takes over a company.

Liability

In personal finance, liabilities are the amounts you owe to creditors, or the people and organizations that lend you money. Typical liabilities include your mortgage, car and educational loans, and credit card debt. When you figure your net worth, you subtract your liabilities, or what you owe, from your assets. The result is your net worth, or the cash value of what you own.

In business, liabilities also refer to the claims against the assets of a corporation, and may include accounts payable, wages and salaries, dividends, taxes, and debt obligations, such as bonds and bank loans.

Limit order

When you give your broker an order to buy or sell a stock when it reaches a certain price or better, it is called a limit order. For example, if you place a limit order to buy a certain stock at $25 a share when its current market price is $28, your broker will not buy the stock until its share price is at $25 or lower.

Limited partnership

A limited partnership is a financial affiliation, including a general partner and a number of limited partners, that usually invests in real estate or some other venture.

The arrangement can be public, which means you can buy into the partnership through a brokerage firm. Or it can be private, which generally means you have to know the people involved to participate. What makes the partnership limited is that everyone but the general partner has limited liability. The most they can lose is the amount they invest.

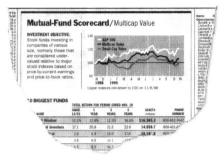

Lipper Inc.

Lipper Inc. provides financial data and performance analysis for more than 30,000 open- and closed-end mutual funds and variable annuities worldwide. Lipper fund ratings are closely watched, and its mutual fund indexes are considered benchmarks for the 29 categories of funds Lipper defines.

LIPPER INDEXES

Thursday, November 11, 1999

			Percentage chg. since	
Equity Indexes	Prelim. Close	Prev.	Wk ago	Dec. 31
Large-Cap Growth	4755.78	+ 1.15	+ 2.93	+ 20.18
Large-Cap Core	2560.02	+ 0.56	+ 1.68	+ 11.13
Large-Cap Value	9521.55	+ 0.21	+ 0.73	+ 7.59
Multi-Cap Growth	3459	+ 0.64	+ 3.54	+ 24.01
Multi-Cap Core	7053.72	+ 0.63	+ 1.85	+ 11.68
Multi-Cap Value	3240.11	+ 0.05	+ 0.40	+ 3.94
Mid-Cap Growth	770.91	+ 0.09	+ 4.57	+ 38.33
Mid-Cap Core	474.82	+ 0.72	+ 3.25	+ 11.37
Mid-Cap Value	618.72	− 0.20	+ 1.13	+ 4.23
Small-Cap Growth	498.16	− 0.31	+ 4.09	+ 29.23
Small-Cap Core	252.84	+ 0.11	+ 1.63	+ 6.11
Small-Cap Value	318.01	− 0.30	− 0.13	− 3.16
Equity Income Fd	3758.63	+ 0.05	+ 0.45	+ 3.47
Science and Tech Fd	1235.88	+ 1.25	+ 6.48	+ 67.93
Gold Fund	75.25	− 0.98	+ 1.83	+ 5.95
International Fund	815.94	+ 1.05	+ 2.70	+ 19.49
Emerging Markets	84.56	+ 0.83	+ 3.15	+ 39.31
Balanced Fund	4494.02	+ 0.23	+ 0.95	+ 5.88
Bond Indexes				
Short Inv Grade	204.36	+ 0.02	+ 0.01	+ 2.78
Intmdt Inv Grade	221.59	+ 0.03	+ 0.07	− 0.14
US Government	300.88	+ 0.04	+ 0.06	− 1.44
GNMA	330.58	+ 0.04	+ 0.01	+ 1.36
Corp A-Rated Debt	795.03	0.00	+ 0.05	− 1.14
High Current Yield	788.76	0.00	+ 0.46	+ 2.84
Global Income	207.8	− 0.01	+ 0.27	− 2.16
International Income	137.3	− 0.10	+ 0.21	− 3.69
Short Municipal	123.63	+ 0.02	+ 0.11	+ 1.86
General Muni Debt	557.16	+ 0.02	+ 0.50	− 3.05
High Yield Municipal	272.24	+ 0.03	+ 0.40	2.2

Indexes are based on the largest funds within investment objective and do not include multiple sh es of similar funds. The Yardsticks Friday's listings, includes all funds Source: Lip ed with Lip

Liquid asset

Liquid assets include cash, money in bank accounts, and investments that can be converted readily to cash with little loss of value. Money market mutual funds and US Treasury bills are often described as liquid assets. Most stocks, bonds, and stock and bond mutual funds are also liquid in the sense that they can be sold easily for cash. But since their prices fluctuate, there is always the chance of having to sell at a loss if you need the money quickly.

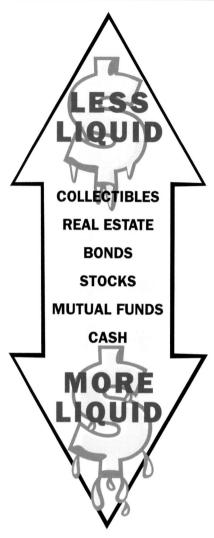

LESS LIQUID

COLLECTIBLES

REAL ESTATE

BONDS

STOCKS

MUTUAL FUNDS

CASH

MORE LIQUID

Liquidity

If you can convert an investment easily and quickly to cash, with little or no loss of value, you have liquidity. For example, you can typically redeem shares in a money market mutual fund at $1 a share. Similarly, you can cash in a certificate of deposit (CD) and get back at least the amount you put into it (though you may forfeit some or all of the interest you had expected to earn if you liquidate before the end of the CD's term).

In a related way, investments have liquidity if you can buy or sell them quickly. For example, you could sell several hundred shares of a blue chip stock by simply calling your broker, something that might not be possible if you wanted to sell stock in a small, thinly traded company.

The difference between cash-equivalent investments and securities like stocks and bonds, however, is that securities constantly fluctuate in value. So while you may be able to sell them quickly, you might get back less than you paid if you have to sell when the price is down.

Listed security

A listed security is a stock or bond that is traded on an organized exchange, such as the New York Stock Exchange (NYSE), or on a stock market, such as the Nasdaq Stock Market (Nasdaq). Being listed has advantages, including being part of an orderly and widely reported trading process that helps insure fairness and liquidity.

Listing requirement

Each organized securities exchange and stock market—including the New York Stock Exchange (NYSE) and the Nasdaq-Amex Market Group—has its own listing requirements, which a corporation must meet in order to have its stocks or bonds traded there.

Among the criteria used for listing are a corporation's pretax earnings, number of outstanding shares, and minimum market value. For example, the NYSE, which has the most stringent requirements, requires pretax earnings of $2.5 million, a minimum of 1.1 million outstanding shares, and a minimum market value of $100 million.

Load

If you buy mutual funds through a broker or other sales representative, you often pay a sales charge or commission, also called a load. If the charge is levied when you purchase the shares, it's called a front-end load. If you pay when you sell shares, it's called a back-end load. And with a level load, you pay a percentage of your investment amount each year you own the fund.

Load fund

Some mutual funds charge a load, or sales commission, when you buy or sell shares or, in some cases, each year you own the fund. The charge is generally figured as a percentage of your investment amount. Most load funds are sold by brokers, financial planners, and other advisors, while no-load funds, which don't have sales charges (but may levy other fees), are usually sold directly to the public by the fund company.

There's no evidence that load funds outperform no-loads, or that funds with higher loads outperform those with lower ones, so the added cost of load funds should be considered in choosing one fund rather than another.

Long bond

The long bond is the 30-year bond issued by the US Treasury. The yield, or what you earn, on a long-term bond is usually higher than the yield on shorter-term bonds. That's because the long bonds have to pay higher interest rates to attract investors who are willing to tie up their money for an extended period of time. The yield on the long bond is considered a benchmark, or key indicator, of long-term interest rates.

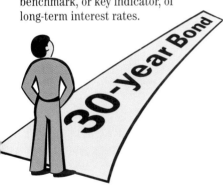

Long position

Having a long position when you own a stock or bond means you have the right to collect the dividends or interest it pays, the right to sell it or give it away when you wish, and the right to keep any profits if you do sell.

It's the opposite of having a short position, which means you have borrowed shares from your broker, sold them, and must return them at some point in the future. The term long position is also used to describe stocks or bonds you own that are held by your brokerage firm in street name.

Long-term equity anticipation security (LEAPS)

These long-term stock options expire in two to five years rather than within a year, as most stock options do. The advantage, from an investment perspective, is that you have more time for the price movement you anticipate to actually occur. However, stocks on which LEAPS are available are more limited than those on which there are standard options.

Long-term gain (or loss)

When you sell an asset, such as a security or real estate, that you have held 12 months or longer, any money you make on the sale is considered a long-term capital gain. If you lose money on the sale, you have a long-term capital loss.

Long-term gains are taxed at 20% for people in the 28% tax bracket and higher, and at 10% for those in the 15% bracket. Long-term losses are deductible against long-term gains. Each year, you can also usually deduct up to $3,000 of your long-term losses against your ordinary income.

Loose credit

In order to combat a sluggish economy, the Federal Reserve Board (the Fed) sometimes institutes a loose credit policy. The Fed buys large quantities of Treasury securities, which gives banks additional money to lend at lower interest rates. This abundance, or looseness, of credit tends to stimulate borrowing, which in turn is designed to stimulate the economy as a whole.

Tight money is the opposite of loose credit. It's the result of the Fed's selling securities, which makes borrowing—and therefore spending— harder. A tight money policy is designed to slow down a rapidly accelerating economy.

Loser

Stocks whose market price drops the most during the trading day are described, rather bluntly, as losers. The stocks that lose the most value relative to their opening price are called percentage losers, and stocks that lose the most points are called net losers or dollar losers.

The number of losers in a trading day is usually compared to the number of gainers, or stocks that have risen the most in value during the day. If there are more losers than gainers over a period of days, the market as a whole is in a slump.

Lump sum

A lump sum is money you pay or receive all at once rather than in increments over a period of time. For example, you buy an immediate annuity with a single lump-sum payment. Similarly, if you receive the face value of a life insurance policy when the insured person dies, or get a check for the full value of the assets in your retirement account, those payments are also lump sums.

Lump-sum distribution

When you retire, you may have the option of taking the value of your pension, salary reduction, or profit-sharing plan in a series of regular payments, generally described as an annuity, or all at once, in what is known as a lump-sum distribution.

If you take the lump sum from a pension, your employer calculates how much you would have received over your estimated lifespan if you'd taken the pension as an annuity and then subtracts the amount the pension fund estimates it would have earned in interest on that amount during the years of payout.

When you take a lump-sum distribution from a salary reduction or profit-sharing plan, you receive the amount that has accumulated in the plan. You may also take a lump-sum distribution from these plans when you change

jobs. However, that is usually not the case with a traditional pension plan.

Whether you're retiring or changing jobs, you can take a lump-sum distribution as cash, or you can roll over the distribution into an individual retirement account (IRA). If you take the cash, you owe income tax on the full amount of the distribution, and you may owe an additional 10% penalty if you're younger than 59½. If you roll over the lump sum into an IRA, the full amount continues to be tax-deferred, and you can postpone paying income tax until you withdraw from the account.

LUMP SUM

CASH DISTRIBUTION

PROS
- Can use money immediately
- Can make your own investment decisions

CONS
- Taxes due immediately
- Owe additional taxes on investment gains
- Must make initial investment decisions quickly
- Easy to spend too fast

IRA ROLLOVER

PROS
- Defer taxes until you withdraw funds
- Make investment decisions at your own pace
- Enjoy tax-deferred or tax-free growth

CONS
- May pay more taxes in the long run
- Responsible for your investment decisions
- May have to begin withdrawls by 70½

Make a market

A dealer who specializes in a specific security, such as a bond or stock, is said to make a market in the security. That means the dealer is ready to buy or sell the bond, or at least one round lot of the stock, at its publicly quoted price. Other dealers regularly turn to a market maker when they want to buy or sell that particular security.

The overall effect of having multiple market makers in a particular security, which is typical of electronic markets such as the Nasdaq Stock Market (Nasdaq), is greater liquidity in the marketplace and, ideally, more competitive prices.

Margin

If you buy on margin, you borrow from your broker to buy stocks. The margin is the value of the cash or securities that you must deposit as collateral in your margin account. That initial margin requirement is set by the Federal Reserve Board under Regulation T, also known as Reg T. It says that to initiate a purchase, you need a margin of at least 50% of the total price of the stock you're buying.

In addition, there's a maintenance requirement of at least 25% of the purchase price, a figure set by the New York Stock Exchange (NYSE) and the National Association of Securities Dealers (NASD). Individual firms may set their maintenance requirement higher—at 30%, for example. If you're buying futures contracts, the good-faith deposit you put up to buy the contract, typically around 10% of the cost, is your margin.

In either case, if the value of the margin account drops below the maintenance requirement, you must, in most cases, add cash or securities to the account to bring its value back to the minimum.

Margin account

Margin accounts are brokerage accounts that allow you to pay for part of the cost of buying stock with money that you, in effect, borrow from your broker. You use the account to buy on margin, sell short, or day trade. To open the account, you must make a minimum deposit of at least $2,000. To use the account to buy on margin, you must have a balance of cash and

HOW MARGIN WORKS

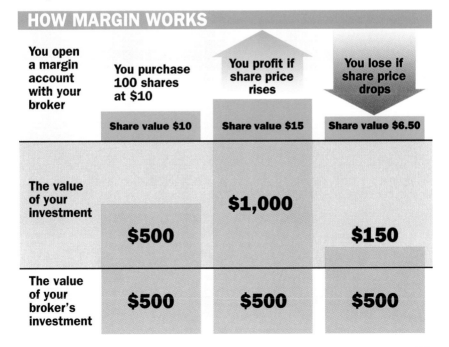

You open a margin account with your broker	You purchase 100 shares at $10	You profit if share price rises	You lose if share price drops
	Share value $10	Share value $15	Share value $6.50
The value of your investment	$500	$1,000	$150
The value of your broker's investment	$500	$500	$500

securities equal to 50% of the purchase you wish to make.

If you use a margin account to buy on margin or sell short, you pay interest on what you borrow but don't have to repay the loan until you sell the stock—ideally, at a large enough profit to cover the interest. If the value of the stock that you bought on margin or sold short declines, and you don't have enough assets in your account to cover the margin requirement, you may get a margin call from your broker.

Margin call

Buying on margin or selling short can be potentially profitable but also potentially risky. To protect themselves, brokers issue a margin call if your margin account falls below the required maintenance level or a specific percentage of its original value. The New York Stock Exchange (NYSE) and the National Association of Securities Dealers (NASD) set that requirement at 25%, and some brokerage firms make it 30%.

You could get a margin call, for example, if the market price of the stock you bought on margin drops significantly. If you get a margin call, you must deposit additional money to meet the call, bringing the balance of the account back up to the margin required. Otherwise, your stock may be sold at a loss, and your broker repaid in full.

For example, if you buy 200 shares at $80 a share on margin, their value is $16,000. If the price drops to $20 a share, their value will be $4,000, which is below 30% of the original value. To meet your margin call, you would have to deposit an additional $800 to bring your account value up to $4,800, or 30% of $16,000.

You might get a margin call in other situations as well, such as when you sell stock short or when you day trade, if the value of your account drops below the required maintenance. If you purchase a futures contract with a percentage of the value of the contract, and the value of the contract drops, you will also get a margin call to add enough cash or securities to your account to bring it back to the required level.

Margin requirement

The margin requirement is the minimum amount the Federal Reserve Board, in Regulation T, requires you to deposit in a margin account before you can trade through that account. Currently this minimum, or initial margin, is $2,000, or 50% of the purchase price of securities you buy on margin, or 50% of the amount that you receive for selling securities short.

In addition, there's a minimum maintenance requirement, typically 25% to 30% of the market value of the securities in the account, set by the New York Stock Exchange (NYSE), the National Association of Securities Dealers (NASD), and the individual brokerage firms.

Mark to the market

When an investment is marked to the market, its value is adjusted to reflect the current market price. In the case of mutual funds, for example, marking to the market means that a fund's net asset value (NAV) is recalculated each day based on the closing prices of the fund's underlying investments.

With a margin account, the value of the investments in the account is recalculated continuously to determine whether it meets margin requirements. If that value falls below the minimum specified, you get a margin call and must add assets to your account to return it to the required level.

Markdown

A markdown is the difference between the market price of a security and the price you receive if you sell that security to a broker/dealer in the over-the-counter (OTC) market.

A markdown is comparable to the commission you would pay for selling the security through your broker, though the cost of the markdown, unlike a broker's commission, is not stated separately on a confirmation statement. A markdown is determined, in part, by the demand for securities of a certain type in the marketplace, since a broker/dealer may charge a smaller

MARKDOWN

Market price
− Markdown
―――――――
PRICE YOU GET

markdown if the security can be resold at a favorable markup.

The term markdown also refers more generally to a price reduction on retail products and certain securities that a seller wants to unload and will sell at less than the original offering price.

Market

Traditionally, a securities market has been a place—such as the New York Stock Exchange (NYSE)—where securities are bought and sold. But in the age of electronic trading, the term market is also used to describe the organized activity of buying and selling securities, even if those transactions do not occur at a specific location. In that sense, the Nasdaq National Market (Nasdaq), the Nasdaq Small-Cap Market, and electronic communications networks (ECNs) are considered stock markets.

Market capitalization

Market capitalization is a measure of the value of a company, calculated by multiplying the number of outstanding shares in the company by the current stock price.

For example, a company with 100 million shares of outstanding stock at a current market value of $25 a share would have a market capitalization of $2.5 billion.

Market capitalization, or cap, is one of the criteria investors use to choose stocks, which are often categorized as small-cap, mid-cap, and large-cap. Generally, large-cap stocks are considered the least volatile, and small caps the most volatile. The term market capitalization is sometimes used interchangeably with market value.

Market maker

A dealer in an electronic market, such as the Nasdaq Stock Market (Nasdaq), who is prepared to buy or sell a specific security—such as a bond or at least one round lot of a stock—at its publicly

quoted price, is called a market maker. Typically, there are several market makers in each security. On the floor of an exchange, such as the New York Stock Exchange (NYSE), however, the dealer who handles buying and selling a particular stock is called a specialist, and there is only one specialist in each stock. Brokerage firms that maintain an inventory of a particular security to sell to their own clients, or to brokers at other firms for resale, are also called market makers.

Market order

When you tell your broker to buy or sell a security at the current market price, you are giving a market order. The broker initiates the trade immediately, and the transaction is usually completed within minutes. Market orders, which account for the majority of trades, differ from limit orders to buy or sell, in which a price is specified.

Market price

A security's market price is the price at which it is currently selling on the exchange, market, or electronic communications network (ECN) where it is traded. A good indication of the market price of a stock selling on the New York Stock Exchange (NYSE) or the Nasdaq Stock Market (Nasdaq) is the last transaction price that's been reported.

For bonds and over-the-counter (OTC) stocks, the market price is the combined bid and ask price—for example, 14⅛/15—currently being quoted by people making a market in the security.

Market timing

This trading strategy aims for quick profits by taking advantage of short-term changes in securities prices. Market timers, sometimes known as day traders, try to buy

low and sell high by taking advantage of minute-to-minute changes in the financial marketplace, such as a forecast on interest rates or a sell-off in a particular market sector.

Most experts agree that market timing is a risky approach because there is no way to predict changes accurately, and a small miscalculation can result in large losses. With the increasing popularity of online trading, the number of day traders has increased dramatically. So have concerns about the risks inexperienced investors take when trying to time the market. For one thing, there's no guarantee that an online transaction can be made quickly enough to lock in gains or prevent losses, especially in a volatile market.

Market value

The market value of a stock or bond is the current price at which that security is trading. In a more general sense, if an item has not been priced for sale, its fair market value is the amount a buyer and seller agree upon, assuming that both know what the item is worth and neither is being forced to complete the transaction.

Markup

When you buy securities over the counter (OTC) from a broker/dealer's inventory, you pay a markup, typically a percentage of the selling price, over and above the amount it cost the broker/dealer to purchase  the security. The amount of this markup, or spread, depends in part on the demand for that security or others like it. For example, if investors are buying up certain types of bonds, a broker/dealer may increase the markup for bonds in that category.

To determine the markup you're paying, and whether it is in line with the 5% guideline set by the National Association of Securities Dealers (NASD), you must either ask the broker/dealer about the markup amount or compare the prices (including the markups) that a number of broker/dealers quote you for the same security. The differences in price generally reflect the differences in markups.

Matching funds

When your employer contributes a percentage of the amount you put into an employer-sponsored retirement savings plan, the amount of the employer's contribution is described as matching funds. The advantage of matching funds is that the added amounts increase the base on which your earnings accumulate tax-deferred, helping to build your account more quickly.

Employers aren't required to provide matching funds, and they can set their own contribution rules. For example, some employers match 50% of your contribution, up to a cap of 6% of your salary, while others may offer larger or smaller matches. Unlike the money you contribute, which is yours from the start, you must be vested before you can withdraw or roll over the matching funds your employer contributes to your account.

Maturity date

A bond comes due on its maturity date.

 On that date, the full face value of the bond (and sometimes the final interest payment) must be paid in full to the investor.

Merger

Two or more independent companies can consolidate or pool their businesses in a number of different ways. These consolidations are often described as mergers, partly to distinguish them from acquisitions in which one company purchases, or takes over, the assets of another.

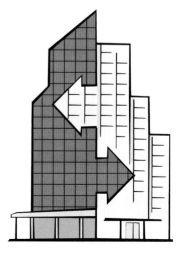

Technically, a merger occurs when two or more companies pool their interests, exchange their common stock, and one of them survives and continues to function. A merger is typically a tax-free transaction—meaning that shareholders owe no taxes on the stock that is pooled or merged, while an acquisition usually means that the owners or stockholders of the acquired company realize capital gains for the sale of their stock.

Despite their differences, mergers and acquisitions are invariably linked together, often simply described as M&A.

Micro-cap stock

A micro-cap stock is one with a smaller market capitalization—sometimes much smaller—than stocks described as small-caps. (Market capitalization is figured by multiplying the current market value by the number of outstanding shares.) The cut-off for deciding that a stock belongs in one category or the other is arbitrary, though the capitalization thresholds currently being suggested for micro-caps range from $50 million to $150 million.

Micro-caps are not only the smallest of the publicly traded corporations, but they are also the most volatile, in part because they lack the reserves of a larger company to weather rough periods. And, because there are generally fewer shares of a micro-cap company in the market, a large transaction may affect the stock price more noticeably than a similar transaction would affect the stock price of a larger company that had many more shares in the market.

Mid-capitalization (mid-cap) stock

A mid-cap stock is issued by a corporation whose market capitalization is between $500 million and $5 billion, making it smaller than the large-caps tracked by Standard & Poor's 500-stock Index (S&P 500) but larger than small-caps.

Investors buy mid-cap stocks for their growth potential and their prices, which are typically lower than for large-caps. At the same time, these companies tend to be less volatile than small-caps, in part because they have more resources with which to weather an economic downturn. Mutual funds that invest in this type of stock are known as mid-cap funds.

Minority interest

All shareholders whose combined shares represent less than half of the total outstanding shares issued by a corporation have a minority interest in that corporation. In fact, in many cases, the combined holdings of the minority shareholders are considerably less than half. In either case, it is difficult for minority shareholders, under normal circumstances, to have any real influence on corporate policy.

Modern portfolio theory

This approach to making investment decisions focuses on potential return in relation to potential risk. The strategy is to evaluate and select individual securities as part of an overall portfolio rather than strictly for their own investment qualities.

Asset allocation is a primary tactic, according to theory practitioners, because it allows investors to create portfolios to get the strongest possible return without assuming a greater level of risk than they are comfortable with. Another tenet of portfolio theory is that investors must be rewarded (in terms of a greater return) for assuming greater risk. Otherwise, there would be little motivation to make investments that might result in a loss of principal.

Momentum investing

Momentum investing is essentially the opposite of contrarian investing. A momentum investor focuses on stocks that are rising in price, and avoids stocks that are falling in price or that are

perceived to be undervalued. The logic is that when a pattern of growth has been established, the growth will continue.

Money market

The money market isn't a place. It's the continual buying and selling of short-term liquid investments, including Treasury bills, certificates of deposit (CDs), commercial paper, and other debt issued by corporations and governments. These investments are also known as money market instruments.

Money market account

These bank savings accounts normally pay interest at rates comparable to those offered by money market mutual funds. One appeal of money market accounts is that they have the added safety of Federal Deposit Insurance Corporation (FDIC) protection, up to a limit of $100,000 per depositor. One drawback may be that some banks reduce the interest they pay or impose fees if your balance falls below a specific amount. Money market accounts offer check-writing privileges, although there are usually limits on the number of withdrawals you can make each month.

Money market fund

Money market mutual funds invest in stable, short-term debt securities, such as commercial paper, government bonds, and certificates of deposit (CDs), and try to maintain the value of each share in the fund at $1. Most

MONEY MARKET FUNDS
TAXABLE OR TAX-FREE
LOW RISK

SHORT-TERM MUNICI

COMMERCIAL PAPER

13-WEEK T-BILLS

SHORT-TERM CORPORATE DEBT

funds offer check-writing privileges that do not trigger gains or losses, as writing a check against the value of a bond fund would.

Tax-free money market funds invest in short-term municipal bonds and other tax-exempt debt. With a single-state fund, investors who reside in the state that issues the bonds the fund buys can enjoy triple tax-free earnings, which means they owe no local, state, or federal income tax. While taxable funds offer a slightly higher yield than those that are tax-free, you must pay income tax on all earnings distributions.

Unlike bank money market accounts, money market funds are not insured by the Federal Deposit Insurance Corporation (FDIC). However, since they are considered securities at most brokerage firms, they may be insured by the Securities Investor Protection Corporation (SIPC) against the bankruptcy of the firm.

Money purchase plan

A money purchase plan is a defined contribution retirement plan that requires the employer to contribute a fixed percentage of each employee's salary every year the plan is in effect, regardless of how well the company does in a given year. In that sense, money purchase plans are the opposite of profit-sharing plans, where the employer's contribution is more flexible because it is based on annual profits.

However, some small-company employers or self-employed people create a paired plan—as part of a Keogh, for example—which combines money purchase with profit-sharing, requiring them to add at least a minimum percentage of each employee's salary to the plan each year.

Money supply

The money supply is the total amount of liquid or near-liquid assets in the economy. The Federal Reserve Board, or the Fed, manages the money supply, trying to prevent either recession or inflation by changing the amount of money in circulation. The Fed increases the money supply by buying government bonds in the open market, and decreases the supply by selling these securities.

In addition, the Fed can adjust the reserves that banks must maintain,

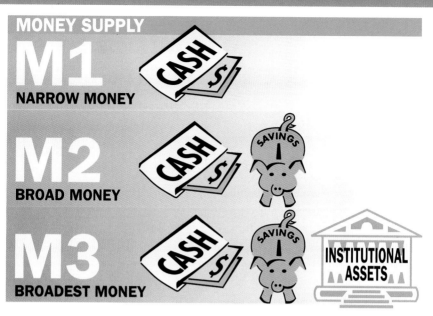

and increase or decrease the rate at which banks can borrow money. This fluctuation in rates gets passed along to consumers and investors as changes in interest rates.

The money supply is grouped into four classes of assets, called money aggregates. The narrowest, called M1, includes currency and checking deposits. M2 includes M1 plus assets in money market accounts and small time deposits. M3, also called broad money, includes M2 plus assets in large time deposits, eurodollars, and institution-only money market funds. L includes M3 plus assets such as private holdings of US savings bonds, short-term US Treasury bills, and commercial paper.

Monte Carlo

When used to analyze the return an investment portfolio is capable of producing, a Monte Carlo simulation generates thousands of probable investment performance outcomes, called scenarios, that might occur in the future. A simulation uses economic data such as a range of potential interest rates, inflation rates, tax rates, and so on, combined in random order. As a result, it can account for the uncertainty and performance variation that's always present in financial markets.

Specifically, financial analysts can use Monte Carlo simulations to project whether or not the investments you are making in your retirement accounts are likely to produce the return you need to meet your long-term goals.

Moody's Investors Service, Inc.

Moody's is a financial services company best known for rating bonds, common stocks, and other investments, including commercial paper, municipal short-term bonds, preferred stocks, and annuity contracts. Its bond rating system, which assigns a grade from Aaa through C3 based on the financial condition of the issuer, has become a world standard.

Moody's Investors Service

Morgan Stanley Capital International Indexes

These indexes, computed by the investment firm Morgan Stanley's Capital International group (MSCI), track stocks traded in 45 international stock markets, and are considered the benchmarks for international stock investments and mutual fund portfolios. The strong performance of the Europe and Australasia Far East Equity Index (EAFE) between 1982 and 1996 in relation to Standard & Poor's 500-stock Index (S&P 500) is often credited with generating increased US interest in investing in overseas markets.

Morningstar, Inc.

Morningstar, Inc., offers a broad range of investment information, research, and analysis online, in software products, and in print. For example, the company rates open- and closed-end mutual funds using a system of one to five stars, with five being the highest rating. The star rating is a risk-adjusted rating that brings performance, or return, and risk together into one evaluation. In addition, Morningstar produces analytical reports on the funds it rates, as well as on stocks sold in US and international markets, and on variable annuities.

M◯RNINGSTAR

Mortgage-backed security

These bonds are backed by real estate mortgages and are guaranteed by a government agency such as the Government National Mortgage Association (GNMA) or backed by publicly held corporations such as the Federal National Mortgage Association (FNMA).

These securities are described as self-amortizing because your earnings are part interest and part repayment of principal on the underlying mortgages. You can buy individual securities (often at a minimum of $25,000) or buy mutual funds that invest in mortgage-backed securities.

Moving average

A moving average of securities prices is an average that is recomputed regularly by adding the most recent price and dropping the oldest one. For example, if you looked at a 365-day moving average on the morning of June 30, the most recent price to be included would be for June 29, and the oldest one would be for June 30 of the previous year. The next day, the most recent price would be for June 30, and the oldest one for the previous July 1.

Multiple

A stock's multiple is its price-to-earnings ratio (P/E). It's figured by dividing the market price of the stock by its earnings—either the actual earnings for the past four quarters

(called a trailing P/E) or actual figures for the past two quarters plus an analyst's projection for the next two (called a forward P/E).

Investors use the multiple as a way to assess whether the price they are paying for the stock is justified by its earnings potential. The higher the multiple they are willing to accept, the higher their expectations for the stock. What's considered high, however, has changed dramatically in recent years as Internet stocks with low earnings (and very high multiples) or no earnings (and therefore no way to compute a multiple) have commanded high prices.

Municipal bond (muni)

Munis are debt securities issued by state or local governments or their agencies to finance general governmental activities or special projects, such as the construction of highways or hospitals. The interest on a muni is usually exempt from federal income taxes, and is also exempt from state and local income taxes, provided you live in the state where it was issued.

However, any capital gains you realize from selling a muni are taxable. Although munis generally pay interest at a lower rate than do commercial or Treasury bonds having similar maturity periods, they appeal to investors in the highest tax brackets, who benefit most from their tax-exempt status.

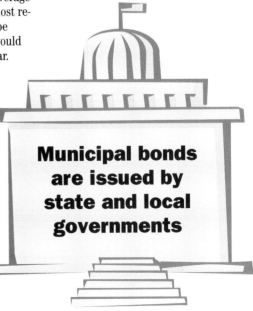

Municipal bonds are issued by state and local governments

Municipal bond fund

Municipal bond mutual funds invest in municipal bonds. Earnings from these funds are always free of federal income tax for all shareholders in the fund.

In addition, some mutual fund companies offer funds that invest exclusively in municipal bonds offered by a single state. In that case, the earnings are also free of state and local tax for residents of that state. For example, New Yorkers can buy shares of triple tax-free New York municipal bond funds and keep all of their earnings.

One advantage of muni bond funds is that buyers can invest a much smaller amount of money than they would need to buy a municipal bond on their own. Another advantage of these funds is that they pay income monthly rather than semi-annually.

Mutual fund

A mutual fund is a professionally managed investment that pools the capital of thousands of investors to trade in stocks, bonds, options, futures, currencies, or money market securities, depending on the investment objectives of the fund. The fund will also buy back any shares an investor wishes to redeem, or sell back.

Funds may vary from very aggressive and volatile, such as those specializing in the markets of developing countries, to conservative, such as those that buy only investment-grade bonds or blue chip stock. Because most mutual funds hold a large number of securities, they offer investors the opportunity to diversify, as well as the benefits of portfolio management.

Load funds—those that charge sales fees—are sold through brokers or other financial advisors. No-load funds, which don't charge sales fees (but may pass on other marketing expenses to share-holders through 12b-1 fees) are sold directly to investors.

All mutual funds charge management fees, though at different rates, and they may also levy other fees and charges. Details of a fund's objective, management, and expenses are spelled out in its prospectus.

INVESTORS

MUTUAL FUND COMPANY

FUND MANAGER

THE INVESTMENTS

Naked option

When you write, or sell, a call option but don't own the underlying security, the option you're writing is described as naked. You can make a profit if the underlying investment performs as you expect, and no one exercises the option, because you collect a premium when you sell it.

The risk you run, however, is that someone will exercise the option, and you'll have to buy the investment at market price in order to meet your obligation to sell. If that price has moved in the opposite direction from the one you expected—gone up instead of down—buying the investment could cost you a substantial amount of money, and you'd have an overall loss.

Nasdaq Composite Index

This index tracks the prices of all of the securities traded on the Nasdaq Stock Market (Nasdaq), which makes it a broader measure of market activity than the Dow Jones Industrial Average (DJIA) or Standard & Poor's 500-stock Index (S&P 500). The index is market capitalization-weighted, which means that companies whose market values are higher exert greater influence on the movement of the index.

Market value, or capitalization, is computed by multiplying the most recent sales price times the total number of outstanding shares. So, for example, if a stock with 1 million outstanding shares increased $3 in value, it would have a greater impact on the index than a stock that also increased $3 in value but had only 500,000 outstanding shares. The index is updated throughout the trading day.

Nasdaq National Market (Nasdaq)

The Nasdaq National Market is part of the electronic Nasdaq Stock Market administered by the National Association of Securities Dealers (NASD). Stocks traded on this market must meet specific listing criteria for market capitalization and trading activity.

One of the most important and active markets in the nation, the Nasdaq specializes in emerging companies, and is especially strong in technology and telecommunications. With the soaring value of many Internet stocks, however, many of which are traded on the Nasdaq, a growing number of Nasdaq companies have large market capitalizations. The Nasdaq Small-Cap Market lists smaller, emerging companies.

National Association of Securities Dealers (NASD)

NASD, a nonprofit, self-regulating association supervised by the Securities and Exchange Commission (SEC), sets standards and establishes rules for the way that its members, including brokerage firms active in the over-the-counter (OTC) market and investment banks, operate.

NASD also has the authority to discipline members who violate those standards. Among NASD's other responsibilities are reviewing and approving sales and marketing literature that its members use to promote their products. The goal is to protect investors from misleading information on the risks and rewards of investing.

National Association of Securities Dealers Automated Quotation System (NASDAQ)

NASDAQ is a computerized stock trading network that allows brokers to get price quotations for stocks being traded electronically or sold on the floor of a stock exchange.

National bank

All banks in the US are chartered by either a state government or the federal government. Federally chartered banks, or national banks, are overseen by the Comptroller of the Currency of the US Treasury. All national banks are members of the Federal Reserve System and are insured by the Federal Deposit Insurance Corporation (FDIC).

The US's dual banking system of federally- and state-chartered banks was established by the National Banking Act of 1863, which created the new system of federally chartered banks in an attempt to put state-chartered banks out of business. State banks have survived, however, and the two banking systems co-exist.

National debt

The total value of all outstanding Treasury bills, notes, and bonds that the federal government owes investors is referred to as the national debt. Some of this debt is held by the government itself, in accounts such as the Social Security, Medicare, Unemployment Insurance, and Highway, Airport and Airway Trust Funds. The rest is held by individual and institutional investors, both domestic and foreign, or by foreign governments.

In 1999, the national debt, or gross federal debt, was more than $5.5 trillion, and the interest on this debt is one of the federal government's largest expenditures. The national debt is not the same as the federal budget deficit, which is any federal spending that exceeds federal income in a fiscal year.

National Market System (NMS)

The NMS links all the major stock markets in the US and was developed to foster competition among them. Its electronic Intermarket Trading System (ITS) displays current bid and ask prices for stocks on each of those markets so that brokers can execute trades on any market where a stock is listed. Brokers can often get a better price or a faster turnaround on one market than on another, depending on the volume of trading or the size of the trade.

National Quotation Bureau

Every trading day, this subscription service publishes bid and ask prices for over-the-counter (OTC) stocks and bonds that don't meet the listing requirements of the Nasdaq National Market (Nasdaq) or the Nasdaq Small-Cap Market.

The Bureau gathers its information from market makers in these securities and prints the stock data on distinctively colored paper: pink sheets for stocks and yellow sheets for bonds. The same information, updated continuously throughout the trading day, is available electronically on the NQB website.

Net asset value (NAV)

The NAV is the dollar value of one share of a mutual fund. It is calculated by totaling the value of all the fund's holdings and dividing by the number of

Market Regulation

From the SEC to SROs, regulatory agencies help keep the markets safe for investors.

The financial markets are among the most heavily regulated aspects of the American economy. But it isn't always clear who is regulating whom, or what the relationship between the different regulators is.

Market Watchdogs

When the foundation of the federal regulatory system was put in place in the 1930s, the goal was to help prevent the kinds of abuses that were widely believed to have contributed to the stock market crash of 1929 and the depression that followed.

Today, market regulators play two important roles: First, they ensure that accurate information about publicly traded companies is available to all investors. For example, every company offering stocks, bonds, or mutual funds has to disclose detailed information about its economic situation and business practices, including its financial statements, fiscal relationships with board members, and the salaries of key players in the company.

Second, the regulators oversee the operation of the financial markets to make sure that trading practices are as fair and efficient as possible. That means not only enforcing existing trading rules, but also creating new ones to police evolving markets effectively.

Simple Goal, Complex System

The US regulatory system has two levels: the federal oversight agencies in Washington and the self-regulating organizations of every exchange and market. In addition, all of the states have their own regulatory agencies to oversee securities and commodities transactions that occur within the state, as well as sales of insurance and insurance company products.

Top Cops

The Securities and Exchange Commission (SEC) supervises all the nation's securities exchanges, the over-the-counter (OTC) markets, and investment companies. It requires most organizations or individuals issuing,

selling or trading investments, or handling the details of those trades, to register with the agency.

The Commodity Futures Trading Commission (CFTC) oversees all the commodity futures and options markets in the US. It plays the same role for these markets as the SEC does for the securities markets, keeping close tabs on how each exchange complies with CFTC trading rules.

Keeping Teeth in the Rules

The biggest challenge facing the SEC is how to adapt securities laws and regulatory structures created in the 1930s to fast-changing, technologically sophisticated, increasingly decentralized markets.

As electronic trading systems supplant centralized exchanges, and the barriers between banks, insurance companies, and securities firms dissolve, there is growing concern about competitive pricing, since a particular security may trade in many markets simultaneously. In response, the SEC is pushing development of a centralized system for displaying all stock orders across all markets.

The SROs

Every securities and commodities market in the US is designated a self-regulatory organization (SRO). For example, the National Association of Securities Dealers Regulation, Inc. (NASDR), a subsidiary of the National Association of Securities Dealers (NASD), is the SRO for the Nasdaq Stock Market and the over-the-counter markets. Through its Investment Companies Department, the NASD is

A Difference of Opinion

There's a continuing debate on how extensive and vigorous regulation of investment markets should be. To some market analysts and politicians, tight regulations threaten to undermine the vitality of the economy. To others, regulation helps foster economic growth because it builds investor confidence in the soundness of the nation's financial markets.

Despite the debate at home, the SEC is generally agreed to have done such a conscientious job that the US stock markets have become the standard for openness, accessibility, and fair play the world over.

Closer to Home

State regulators oversee virtually every aspect of the securities industry that operates within their borders. They license and monitor people and firms that trade stocks and bonds and manage investment portfolios, review all prospectuses and other information that must be filed before a security is offered for sale in the state, and follow up on reported violations.

While it may sound as if there's a lot of duplicated effort, it's probably more accurate to see the state systems as a second safety net. And state regulators are often the investor's first line of defense, both for information and resolving problems.

also responsible for overseeing the activities of investment companies, which sell mutual funds.

Each SRO is responsible for keeping close tabs on member firms and market activity, and for disciplining violations of trading rules. For example, an exchange SRO might use a sophisticated computer system to track the market continuously and alert regulators to unusual trading patterns.

Member firms are periodically audited to make sure their accounting and sales practices are on the up-and-up. When an irregularity is detected, regulators alert the Security Investor Protection Corporation (SIPC), the SEC, and other SROs, and assemble evidence to build a case. Disciplinary action may range from an informal warning to permanent suspension, fines, and imprisonment.

Net change

outstanding shares. That means the NAV changes regularly, though day-to-day changes are usually small.

With no-load funds, the NAV and the offering price, or what you pay to buy a share, are the same. With front-load funds, the offering price is the sum of the NAV and the sales charge per share. The NAV is also the price per share the fund pays when you sell back, or redeem, your shares.

NET ASSET VALUE (NAV)

$$\frac{\text{Value of funds holdings}}{\text{Outstanding shares}} = \text{NET ASSET VALUE}$$

Net change

Each trading day, the difference between the closing price of a stock, bond, or mutual fund, or the last price of a commodity contract, and the closing price on the previous day is reported as net change, sometimes simply as change. When a stock has gained in value, it has a positive net change—expressed with a plus sign and a number, such as $+\frac{1}{2}$, meaning that the price was up 50 cents from the previous trading day. On days that a stock falls, it has a negative change—expressed with a minus sign and a number, such as –1, meaning that the price was a dollar lower. You can find net change information in the financial pages of newspapers and on financial websites.

Net worth

A corporation's net worth, also known as stockholder's equity, is figured by adding its retained earnings, which is the amount left after dividends are paid, to the money in its capital accounts, and then subtracting all of its short- and long-term debt. Net worth figures are included in the corporation's annual report.

To figure your own net worth, you first add up the value of the things, or assets, you own (securities, personal property, real estate) and then subtract your liabilities, or what you owe in loans and other obligations. If your as-

NET WORTH

Value of assets
− Liabilities
―――――――
NET WORTH

sets are larger than your liabilities, you have a positive net worth. But if your liabilities outweigh your assets, you have a negative net worth.

New issue

When a stock or bond is offered for sale for the first time, it's considered a new issue. New issues can be the result of an initial public offering (IPO), when a private company goes public, or they can be additional, or secondary, offerings from a company that's already public. For example, a public company may sell bonds from time to time to raise capital. Each time a new bond is offered, it's considered a new issue.

New York Stock Exchange (NYSE)

The NYSE is the largest equity exchange in the world. Founded in 1789, it has a global market capitalization of over $15 trillion. Common and preferred stock, bonds, warrants, and rights are all traded on the NYSE, which is also known as the Big Board.

New York Stock Exchange Composite Index

This index tracks the market value of all the common stocks listed on the New York Stock Exchange (NYSE). The index is market capitalization-weighted, which means that companies with the greatest market value, based on their most recent market prices multiplied by the number of their outstanding shares, have a greater impact on the index than companies with fewer shares or lower prices.

No-load mutual fund

You can buy a no-load mutual fund directly from the investment company that sponsors the fund. You pay no sales charge, or load, on the fund when you buy or sell shares (though some no-load funds charge a redemption fee if you sell before a certain time has elapsed in order to limit short-term turnover). However, some companies charge an annual fee, called a 12b-1 fee, to offset their marketing costs. This fee is figured as a percentage of the value of your holdings in the fund.

You may also be able to buy no-load funds through a mutual fund network, sometimes known as a mutual fund supermarket, typically sponsored by a discount brokerage firm. If you have an account with the firm, you can choose among no-load funds sponsored by a number of different investment companies.

While load funds and no-load funds with similar investments tend to produce almost equivalent total returns over the long term—say 10 years or more—it can take that long to offset the higher cost of buying load funds.

Nonbank banks

Nonbank banks, also called limited-service banks, can offer some but not all of the services of a traditional commercial bank. They are typically owned by companies, including banking holding companies, insurance companies, brokerage firms, and retail stores, that want to provide financial services without being limited by the regulations that govern traditional banks, such as restrictions on interstate and branch banking.

Many of the nonbanks themselves, however, are insured by the Federal Deposit Insurance Corporation (FDIC) and are subject to the same reserve requirements and examinations as regular banks. Opponents of nonbanks believe they drain financial resources away from small towns to big cities in other states and undermine the nation's decentralized banking system.

In a more general way, the term nonbank bank is also sometimes applied to online banks, which don't operate from brick-and-mortar branches.

Noncallable

When a bond is noncallable, the issuer cannot redeem it before the stated maturity date. Some bonds have call protection for their full term, and others for a fixed period—often 10 years.

The appeal of a noncallable bond is that the issuer will pay interest at the stated coupon rate for the bond's full term. That means you won't unexpectedly find yourself with a lump-sum payment when the bond is called and suddenly have to find another way to invest your principal.

Noncompetitive bid

Investors who can't or don't wish to meet the minimum purchase requirements of $500,000 for competitive bidding on Treasury bills, notes, or bonds can enter a noncompetitive bid, also known as a noncompetitive tender.

You can invest as little as $1,000 or as much as $1 million through Treasury Direct, a system offered through the Federal Reserve banks that allows you to buy government securities without going through a bank or a brokerage firm. The Treasury sells T-bills, for example, to all buyers whose bids arrive by the weekly deadline, for a price equal to the average of all competitive bids for that week's issue.

Note

A note is a debt security that promises to pay interest during the term that the issuer has use of the money, and to repay the principal on or before the maturity date. In the case of US Treasury securities, a note is an intermediate-term obligation—as opposed to a short-term bill or a long-term bond—which matures somewhere between two and 10 years from its issue date.

Odd lot

The purchase or sale of stocks in quantities of fewer than 100 shares is considered an odd lot. If you buy or sell odd lots, you typically pay a slightly higher commission than someone trading round lots, or multiples of 100.

Offering price

When a security, such as a stock, is offered for sale to the public for the first time, or a publicly traded company issues new shares, the initial price per share is set by the underwriter. That's known as the offering price or the public offering price. When the stock begins to trade, its market price may be higher or lower than the offering price.

In the case of open-end mutual funds, the offering price is the price per share of the fund that you pay when you buy. If it's a no-load fund, a back-end or Class B fund, or a level-load or Class C fund, the offering price and the net asset value (NAV) are the same. If it's a front-load or Class A fund, the sales charge is added to the NAV to arrive at the offering price.

Online brokerage firm

To buy and sell securities over the Internet, you can set up an account with an online brokerage firm. The firm executes your orders and confirms them electronically, though you may have to mail the firm a check to settle your transaction.

Some online firms are divisions of traditional brokerage firms, while others operate exclusively in cyberspace. Most of them charge much smaller commissions than conventional firms, and most provide extensive investment information, including regularly updated market news, on their websites.

Online trading

If you trade online, you use a computer and an Internet connection to place your buy and sell orders. Some online traders are day traders, buying securi-ties and selling them within a few hours—or less—to take advantage of price changes as they occur. Others use online trading to place orders outside of normal trading hours.

While online trading may become the norm in the future, especially as after-hours trading and electronic communications networks (ECNs) gain popularity, there are a number of issues to be resolved. These include, for example, the responsibility of online brokerage firms to monitor trades by inexpe-rienced or over-  zealous investors to prevent major loss-es resulting from inappropriate buy and sell decisions, and the need to keep and provide accurate records of all trades.

Opening

The first trans-action in each security or commodity when trading begins for the day occurs at what's known  as its opening, or opening price. Sometimes the opening price on one day is the same as the closing price the night before. But that's not always the case, especially with stocks or contracts that are actively traded in the after-hours markets.

Open market

In an open market, any investor with the money to pay for securities is able to buy those securities. US markets, for example, are open to all buyers. In contrast, a closed market may restrict investment to citizens of the country where the market is located. Closed markets may also limit the sale of securities to overseas investors, or forbid the sale of securities in specific industries to those investors. In some countries, for example, overseas investors may not own more than 49% of any company, while in others, overseas investors may not invest in banks or other financial services companies.

The term open market is also used to describe an environment in which interest rates move up and down in response to supply and demand in contrast to those rates that are set by the Federal Reserve Board. The Fed's Open Market Committee assesses the state of the US economy on a regular schedule and instructs the Federal Reserve Bank of New York to buy or sell Treasury securities on the open market to help control the money supply.

Open outcry

Exchange-based commodities traders shout out their buy and sell orders. When someone who shouts an offer to buy and someone who shouts an order to sell name the same price, a deal is struck, and the trade is recorded. This potentially rowdy interaction is described as open outcry.

Open-end mutual fund

Most mutual funds are open-end funds, which issue and redeem shares on a continuous basis, and therefore grow in response to investor demand. An open-end fund is the opposite of a closed-end fund, which issues shares only once. After that, shares in the closed-end fund are traded like stock among investors. The sponsor of the fund is not involved in those transactions.

However, an open-end fund may be closed to new investors at the discretion of the management, usually because the fund has grown very large. Large funds may have difficulty investing their assets nimbly enough.

Option

Buying an option gives you the right to buy or sell a specific investment at a specific price, called the strike price, during a preset period of time.

If you buy an option to buy, which is known as a call, you pay a one-time premium that's a fraction of the cost of the actual transaction. For example, you might buy a call option giving you the right to buy 100 shares of a particular stock at a strike price of $80 a share when that stock is trading at $75 a share. If the price goes higher than the strike price, you can exercise the option and buy the stock, or trade the option to someone else at a profit.

If the stock price doesn't go higher than the strike price, you don't exercise

the option, and it expires. Your only cost is the money that you paid for the premium. Similarly, you buy a put option, which gives you the right to sell the underlying investment to the person who sold the option. In this case, you exercise the option if the market pricedrops below the strike price.

In contrast, if you sell a put or call option, you collect a premium and must be prepared to buy or sell the underlying investment if the investor who bought the option decides to exercise it. You can buy or sell individual stock options, stock index options, and options on futures contracts, currency, and Treasury securities interest rates.

Option chain

Option chains are charts showing the latest price quotes for all of the contracts on a particular stock option as well as the most recent quote for the underlying stock. Because all of this information is available in one place, option chains allow you to assess the market for a particular option quickly and easily. They're a popular feature of online trading and financial information sites.

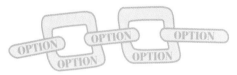

Option premium

When you buy an option, you pay the seller a non-refundable amount per share, known as the option premium, for the right to exercise that option before it expires. If you sell an option, you receive a premium from the buyer. In fact, collecting the premium is one motive for selling options, including those you anticipate will expire without being exercised.

An option premium is not a fixed amount, and typically increases as the demand for the option increases and decreases as demand shrinks. However, factors such as the price and volatility of the underlying investment, current interest rates, and the amount of time left before the option expires also affect the premium price.

You can get a sense of the current range of premium prices by looking at the Options Quotations tables in the financial pages of your newspaper. The figures you see there, expressed in numbers and fractions, represent the per-share price. You multiply by 100 to find the option premium. So, for example, 10 means a premium of $1,000 and ½ (or 0.5) means a $50 premium.

Options Clearing Corporation (OCC)

The Options Clearing Corporation issues all exchange-listed securities options and handles the processing, delivery, and settlement of all options transactions. The OCC, which is responsible for maintaining a fair and orderly market in options, is overseen by the Securities and Exchange Commission (SEC) and is jointly owned by each of the four exchanges that trade options: The American Stock Exchange, the Chicago Board Options Exchange, the Pacific Exchange, and the Philadelphia Stock Exchange.

The OCC is also a valuable source for investor information. For an overview of what you should know about options trading, check their publication *Characteristics and Risks of Standardized Options.*

Original issue discount

A bond or other debt security that is issued at less than par value but redeemed for full par value at maturity is an original issue discount.

The appeal, from an investor's perspective, is being able to invest less up front while anticipating full repayment later on. Issuers like these securities as well because they don't have to pay periodic interest. Instead, the interest accrues during the term of the bond so that the total interest when combined with the principal equals the full par value at maturity. Zero-coupon bonds are a popular type of original issue discount security.

OTC Bulletin Board

During the trading day, this electronic bulletin board provides continuously updated bid and ask prices for unlisted stocks being traded over the counter (OTC). Since the information is more timely than the data reported in the daily pink sheets covering this sector of the market, potential investors can make more informed trading decisions about these stocks, most of which are

too small to qualify for listing on an organized exchange or market.

Out of the money

In the options market, you are out of the money when the market price of a stock is not close to the strike price. In the case of call options—which you buy when you think the price is going up—you're out of the money when the stock price is below the strike price. And in the case of put options—which you buy when you think the price of the underlying investment is going down—you're out of the money when the stock price is higher than the strike price.

For example, a call option on a stock with a strike price of $50 would be out of the money if the current market price were $45. And a put option on the same stock would be out of the money if its market price were $55. When an option is out of the money, you don't exercise it but let it expire.

Outstanding shares

The number of shares of stock that a corporation has issued are described as its outstanding shares. A corporation's market capitalization is figured by multiplying its outstanding shares by the market price of a share.

The number of outstanding shares is also used to derive all of the financial information that's provided on a per-share basis, such as earnings per share or sales per share.

Overbought

When a stock, or a securities market as a whole, rises so steeply in price that technical analysts think that buyers are unlikely to push the price up further, the analysts consider the stock or the market to be overbought. For these analysts, an overbought market is a warning sign that a correction—or steep drop in stock prices—is likely to occur.

Oversold

A stock, a market sector, or an entire market may be described as oversold if it drops suddenly and dramatically in price, despite the fact that the country's economic outlook remains positive. For technical analysts, an oversold market is poised for a price rise, since there would be few sellers left to push the price down further.

Over the counter (OTC)

The majority of stocks in the US are traded over the counter, rather than on the floor of an organized stock exchange. That number includes more than 5,000 stocks that are listed on the Nasdaq Stock Market (Nasdaq) and are part of the National Market System (NMS), as well as stock in companies too small to meet stock market listing requirements.

In actual practice, OTC trading is done through a telephone and computer network. A number of companies that qualify for exchange listing have chosen to continue to trade OTC because they prefer the network of dealers to the centralized system typical of a large exchange. Government and municipal bonds (munis) are also traded OTC.

Overvaluation

A stock whose price seems unjustifiably high based on standard measures, such as its earnings history, is considered overvalued. One indication of overvaluation is a price-to-earnings ratio (P/E) significantly higher than average for the market as a whole and for the industry to which the corporation belongs.

The consequence of overvaluation is usually a drop in the stock's price—sometimes a rather dramatic one. However, in the current market, the high stock prices commanded by some Internet-based companies seem to defy conventional valuation standards.

Paper profit (or loss)
If you own a security or other invest-ment that increases in value, but you don't sell it, the gain is your paper profit, or unrealized gain. But if you sell at the higher value, your paper profit becomes an actual profit, or realized gain. The same relationship applies if the security has lost value. Your paper loss isn't realized until you sell.

Par value
Par value is the face value, or named value, of a stock or bond. With stocks, the par value, which is frequently set at $1, is used as an accounting device but has no relationship to the actual market value of the stock.

But with bonds, par value, usually $1,000, is the amount you receive when the bond is redeemed at maturity. It is also the basis on which the interest you earn on the bond is figured. For example, if you are earning 6% annual interest, that means you receive 6% of $1,000, or $60.

While the par value of a bond re-mains constant through its term, its market value does not. That is, a bond may trade at a premium (more than par) or at a discount (less than par) in the secondary market, based on changes in the interest rate.

Pass-through security
When agencies like the Federal National Mortgage Association (FNMA) or the Student Loan Marketing Association (SLMA) buy various types of debt—such as mortgages or student loans—from lenders and package them as securities for resale to investors, they create pass-through securities. The regular payments of interest and return of principal on the original loans are funneled, or passed through, the bank that made the loan and the agency that packaged it for sale to the investors.

Payout ratio
A payout ratio is the percentage of a company's net earnings that is distrib-uted to its shareholders as dividends. Normally the range is 25% to 50% of those earnings, though companies may pay a higher percentage to keep their dividends at a certain level. That's because reducing the dividend may cause the stock price to fall if investors believe that the company's future earnings are in doubt. Some types of companies that generally pay higher dividends than others are sometimes described as income stocks.

Penny stock
Stocks that trade for less than $1 a share are often described as penny stocks. Penny stocks change hands

PAR VALUE OF A BOND
The price of a bond, called its PAR VALUE, is usually $1,000 at issue and at redemption.

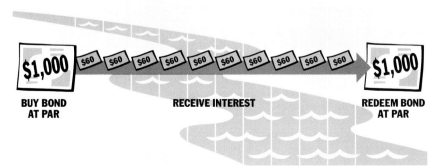

over the counter (OTC) and tend to be extremely volatile. Their prices may spike up one day and drop dramatically the next, reflecting the unsettled nature of the companies that issue them.

While some penny stocks may produce big returns over the long term, many turn out to be worthless. Institutional investors tend to avoid penny stocks, and brokerage firms typically warn individual investors of the risks involved before handling transactions in these stocks. However, penny stocks are sometimes marketed aggressively over the Internet to unsuspecting investors.

Pink sheet

Every trading day, the National Quotation Bureau publishes the bid and ask prices for unlisted stocks that trade over the counter (OTC) on distinctively colored pink sheets and also on a pink screen online. Pink sheets include the names of dealers making a market in each stock so it's easier for those interested in any of those stocks to execute a trade.

Portfolio

If you own more than one security, you have an investment portfolio. You build the portfolio by buying additional stocks, bonds, mutual funds, or other investments. Your goal is to increase

the portfolio's value by selecting investments that you believe will go up in price.

According to modern portfolio theory, you can reduce your investment risk by creating a diversified portfolio that includes enough different types, or classes, of securities so that at least some of them may produce strong returns in any economic climate.

Portfolio turnover

Portfolio turnover is the rate at which a mutual fund manager buys or sells securities in a fund, or an individual investor buys and sells securities in a brokerage account. A rapid turnover rate, which frequently signals a strategy of capitalizing on opportunities to sell at a profit, has the potential downside of generating short-term capital gains. That means the gains are usually taxable as ordinary income rather than at the lower long-term capital gains rate.

Rapid turnover may also generate higher trading costs, which can reduce the total return on a fund or brokerage account. As a result, you may want to weigh the potential gains of rapid turnover against the costs, both in your own buy and sell decisions and in your selection of mutual funds. You can find information on a fund's turnover rate in the fund's prospectus.

HOW A PORTFOLIO GROWS

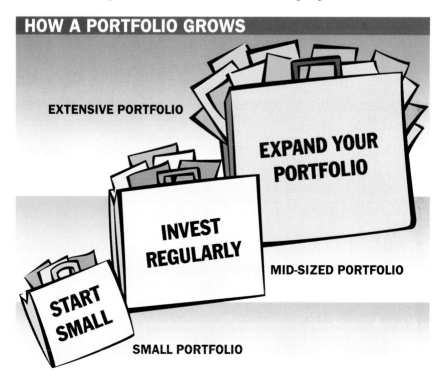

EXTENSIVE PORTFOLIO

EXPAND YOUR PORTFOLIO

INVEST REGULARLY

MID-SIZED PORTFOLIO

START SMALL

SMALL PORTFOLIO

Positive yield curve

When the interest rate on a long-term bond is higher than the interest rate on a shorter-term bond of the same quality, the relationship between the two, called the yield curve, is positive. That's the norm, since if you're tying up your money for an extended period, you want to earn more than someone who is investing for just a few months.

When the reverse is true, and interest rates on short-term investments are higher than the rates on long-term investments, the yield is negative, or inverted. That typically occurs if inflation spikes after a period of relatively stable growth.

Preferred stock

Some corporations issue preferred as well as common stock. Preferred stocks can be attractive because they pay a fixed dividend on a regular schedule, and their share prices tend to remain stable. They also take precedence over common stocks if the issuing corporation liquidates, or sells, its assets to repay its creditors and investors.

What preferred stock doesn't generally offer is the opportunity to share in the corporation's potential for increased profits, which are reflected in higher prices for the common stock and sometimes an increase in its dividend payment.

One category of preferred shares, called convertible preferred shares, can be exchanged for a specific number of common shares at an agreed-upon price, similar to the way that a convertible bond can be exchanged for common stock.

Premium

When used in connection with investments, the term premium usually describes the amount you pay for a security over its stated value, or the amount you collect over the stated value when you sell.

For example, if you pay $60 for a newly issued stock with an offering price of $40, you are paying a premium of $20. But if you sell a bond with a face value of $1,000 for $1,200, you collect a premium of $200.

In a more general sense, a security or group of securities that command higher prices than others are said to sell at a premium, either to comparable securities or to the market as a whole. Internet stocks, for example, sold at a premium to the market in the spring of 1999. A premium is also the amount you pay to purchase certain financial products, such as options, annuities, or insurance policies.

Prerefunding

When a corporation plans to redeem a callable bond on the first date the bond can be called, it typically issues a second bond and invests the income it receives from that sale in safe investments, such as US Treasury notes or bonds. The specific securities are chosen because their maturity dates correspond to the date on which the company will need the money to redeem the first bond. This process is called prerefunding, and the bond to be called is identified as a prerefunded bond.

Present value

The present value of a future payment, sometimes called the time value of money, is what the money is worth now in relation to what you anticipate it will be worth in the future based on the interest you expect it to earn. For example, if you're earning 10% annual interest, $1,000 is the present value of the $1,100 you expect to have a year from now.

The concept of present value is useful in calculating how much you need to invest now in order to meet a certain future goal, such as buying a home or paying college tuition. Many personal

investment handbooks and online financial services sites provide tables and other tools to help you calculate these amounts based on different interest rates.

Inflation has the opposite effect from interest on the present value of money, accounting for loss of value rather than increase in value. For example, in an economy with 5% annual inflation, $100 is the present value of $95 next year.

Price-to-book

Some financial analysts use price-to-book ratios to identify stocks they consider to be overvalued or under-valued. You figure this ratio by dividing a stock's market price per share by its book value per share. Other analysts argue that book value reveals very little about a company's financial situation or its prospects for future performance.

Price-to-cash flow

You find a company's price-to-cash flow ratio by dividing the market price of its stock by its cash receipts minus its cash payments over a given period of time, such as a year. Some institutional investors prefer price-to-cash flow over price-to-earnings as a gauge of a company's value. They believe that by focusing on cash flow, they can better assess the risks that may result from the company's use of leverage, or borrowed money.

Price-to-earnings (P/E)

The P/E is the relationship between a company's earnings and its share price, and is calculated by dividing the current price per share by the earnings per share.

A stock's P/E, also known as its multiple, gives you a sense of what you are paying for a stock in relation to its earning power. For example, a stock with a P/E of 30 is trading at a price 30 times higher than its earnings, while one with a P/E of 15 is trading at 15 times its earnings.

If earnings falter, there is usually a sell-off, which drives the price down. But if the company is successful, the share price and the P/E can climb even higher. Similarly, a low P/E can be the sign of an undervalued company whose price hasn't caught up with its earnings potential or a clue that the

market considers the company a poor investment risk.

Stocks with higher P/Es, which are typical of companies that are expected to grow rapidly in value, such as Internet and other emerging technology stocks, are often more volatile than stocks with lower P/Es because it can be more difficult for the company's earnings to satisfy the expectations of investors.

The P/E can be calculated two ways. A trailing P/E, the figure reported in newspaper stock tables, uses earnings for the last four quarters. A forward P/E generally uses earnings for the past two quarters and an analyst's projection for the coming two.

PRICE TO EARNINGS RATIO

$$\frac{\text{Current price share}}{\text{Earnings per share}} = \text{PRICE TO EARNINGS RATIO}$$

Price-to-growth flow (P/GF)

Price-to-growth flow is a method of stock evaluation that considers money spent on research and development (R&D) as an important factor in assessing a technology company's value and potential for growth. Proponents of this view, particularly analysts at the California Technology Stock Letter, maintain that a company's potential for growth through research and development can compensate for its having low (or no, or negative) earnings per share because R&D can lead to profits in the future.

According to these analysts, P/GF can be a more appropriate gauge for assessing whether to invest in technology companies than traditional measures such as price-to-earnings ratio (P/E). To calculate a company's growth flow, you add its R&D spending per share to its earnings per share, and then divide its current stock price by this sum.

Price-to-sales

A price-to-sales ratio, or a stock's market price per share divided by the revenue generated by sales of the company's products and services per share, may sometimes identify companies that are undervalued or overvalued within a particular industry or market sector. For example, a corporation with sales per share of $28 and a share price of $92 would have a price-to-sales ratio of 3.29, while a different stock with the same sales per share but a share price of $45 would have a ratio of 1.61.

Some financial analysts and money managers suggest that, since sales figures are less easy to manipulate than either earnings or book value, the price-to-sales ratio is a more reliable indicator of how the company is doing and whether you are likely to profit from buying its shares. Other analysts believe that steady growth in sales over the past several years is a more valuable indicator of a good investment than the current price-to-sales ratio.

Primary market

If you buy stocks, bonds, futures contracts, or options when they are initially offered for sale, and the money you spend goes to the issuer, you are buying in the primary market. In contrast, if you buy a security that's already on the market, and the amount you pay goes to an investor who is selling the security, you're buying in the secondary market.

Prime rate

The prime rate is frequently described as the interest rate banks charge their best and most credit-worthy commercial customers, such as blue chip companies. However, the discount rate, which is the rate the Federal Reserve charges member banks to borrow, has more influence than the prime rate on what banks actually charge to lend money.

The prime rate is often used, though, as a benchmark for interest rates on consumer loans. For example, a bank may charge you the prime rate plus two percentage points on a car loan or home equity loan.

Principal

Principal can refer to an amount of money you invest, the face amount of a bond, or the balance you owe on a debt, aside from the interest. The principal is also a person for whom a broker carries out a trade, or a person who executes a trade on his or her own behalf.

Private placement

If securities are sold directly to an institutional investor, such as a corporation or bank, the transaction is called a private placement. Unlike a public offering, a private placement does not have to be registered with the Securities and Exchange Commission (SEC), provided the securities are bought for investment and not for resale.

Privatization

Privatization is the conversion of a government-run enterprise to one that is privately owned and operated. The conversion is made by selling shares to individual or institutional investors.

The theory behind privatization is that privately run enterprises, such as utility companies, airlines, and telecommunications systems, are more efficient and provide better service than government-run

companies. But in many cases, privatization is a way for the government to raise cash and to reduce its role as service provider.

Profit

Also called net income or earnings, profit is the money a business has left after it pays its operating expenses, taxes, and other current bills. In regard to investments, profit is the amount you make when you sell an asset for a higher price than you paid for it. For example, if you buy a stock at $20 a share and sell it at $30 a share, your profit is $10 a share (minus sales commission and capital gains tax).

Profit margin

A company's profit margin is a ratio derived by dividing its net earnings, after taxes, by its gross earnings minus certain expenses. Profit margin is a way of measuring how well a company is doing, regardless of size. For example, a $50 million company with net earnings of $10 million, and a $5 billion company with net earnings of $1 billion, both have profit margins of 20%.

Profit margins can vary greatly from one industry to another, so it can be difficult to make valid comparisons among companies unless they are in the same sector of the economy.

Profit taking

Profit taking is the sale of securities after a rapid price increase to cash in on gains. Profit taking sometimes causes a temporary market downturn after a period of rising prices as investors sell off shares to lock in their gains.

Profit sharing

A profit-sharing plan is a type of defined contribution retirement plan that employers can establish for their workers. The employer may add up to $22,500 or 15% of salary, which-ever is less, to each employee's  profit-sharing account in any year the company has a profit to share. Employees owe no income tax on the contributions or on any of the earnings in their accounts until they withdraw money. In some cases, employees in the plan may also be able to borrow from the account to pay for expenses such as buying a home or paying for college.

Profit-sharing plans offer employers certain flexibility. For example, in a year without profits, they don't have to contribute at all. And they can vary the amount of each year's contribution to reflect the company's profitability for that year. However, each employee in the plan must be treated equally. This means that if an employer contributes 10% of one employee's salary to the plan, the employer must also contribute 10% of the salaries of all other employees in the plan.

Program trading

Normally used by institutional investors and arbitrageurs, program trading is the purchase or sale of large quantities of stock triggered by computer programs. These programs are designed to buy or sell stocks automatically when prices hit predetermined levels.

Such large and sudden trades can have a dramatic effect on the overall market. According to one theory, the stock market crash of 1987 was caused in part by program trading triggered by falling stock prices. Circuit breakers, which halt trading for a period of time when prices fall dramatically, have since  been instituted by the major stock exchanges to help prevent another crash of that type.

Proprietary fund

Proprietary mutual funds are managed by the financial institution—such as a bank or brokerage firm—that sells the funds. Characteristically, the funds' names include the name of the institution. For example, a hypothetical bank called Last Bank might offer a Last Bank Growth Fund or a Last Bank Capital Appreciation Fund. However, no mutual funds, whether or not they carry a bank brand, are insured by the Federal Deposit Insurance Corporation (FDIC). Some institutions market only their proprietary funds, while others offer both their own funds as well as funds managed by others.

Prospectus

A prospectus is a formal written offer to sell stock to the public. It is created by an investment bank that agrees to underwrite the stock offering. The prospectus sets forth the business strategies, financial background, products, services, and management of the issuing company, and information about how the proceeds from the sale of the securities will be used.

The prospectus must be filed with the Securities and Exchange Commission (SEC) and is designed to

Public and Private

What's public may be private—and the other way around.

Perhaps you've heard that the company you work for might be going public. Or maybe you've read that a major insurance company is being privatized. At the same time, you may see a report on different pay scales in the public and private sectors. So what's public and what's private, anyway?

Financially speaking, the terms public and private have a range of meanings. To begin with, there's the public sector—or government enterprises—as opposed to enterprises run by individuals—or the private sector.

To confuse matters, there are two types of private-sector companies: Those that are owned by an individual or a small group of entrepreneurs and venture capitalists are said to be privately held, and those whose stock trades in the open market are said to be publicly held.

PUBLIC SECTOR

The Public Sector

Virtually every democratic nation has a public sector and a private sector. The public sector consists of departments, offices, agencies, and sometimes corporations run by municipal, state, and federal governments. For the most part, they provide citizens with services, such as education, transportation, law enforcement, social welfare programs, and a system of national defense.

For example, in the US, local school systems, fire and police departments, and interstate highway agencies are part of the public sector, as are the Social Security Administration and the Federal Reserve Bank. State and national parkland is public property, as are government buildings. The US president is a public employee. So are your county's district attorney, the clerk in the motor vehicle office, and the librarian at your municipal library.

NATIONAL-IZATION

Mutual Companies

Some insurance companies and certain savings banks aren't really publicly held, but they're not completely privately held either. Rather, they are mutual companies, which means that they are owned by their policyholders (in the case of insurance companies) or their depositors (in the case of banks). Any profit the companies make is shared by these owners, as it might be in a publicly held company. But the company's stock isn't sold to investors on the open market.

Some mutual insurance companies convert to public ownership and sell shares to outside investors, though in some states they may have to use any profits to benefit their policyholders before they pay dividends to their shareholders.

PRIVATE SECTOR

The Private Sector

The private sector includes corporations, businesses, and institutions that are run by individuals rather than governments. Private sector institutions are often, though not always, profit-making enterprises—from enormous multi-national corporations to the local mom-and-pop grocery store. However, when large private-sector corporations issue stock that investors can buy and sell, those corporations are considered to be publicly held, since they are owned by their shareholders, including individual members of the public.

To sell shares in the marketplace, a corporation must register with the Securities and Exchange Commission (SEC)—a public, or government, institution—and disclose important information about its financial circumstances and activities, business model, and operations.

Public Offering vs. Private Placement

The first time a company issues stock that the public can buy, it's called an initial public offering (IPO), and the company is said to be going public. The company gets the revenue from the sale, but from then on when the stock is traded on the open market any profit (or loss) from a change in the stock's price goes to the investor, not the company.

PRIVATIZATION

GOING PUBLIC

Privatization vs. Nationalization

Privatization, sometimes called denationalization, is the process of shifting the ownership and operation of government-run enterprises to the private sector. The opposite process, when private companies are taken over by the government, is called nationalization.

Privatization is often seen as an effort to stimulate the economy, reduce the financial burden of providing expensive services, promote greater efficiency, or provide a one-time cash infusion to a revenue-starved government. For example, a government may privatize its railroad system, its telecommunications company, or, somewhat more controversially, schools and prison systems. In the US, the postal system has been privatized as has Fannie Mae, formerly known as the Federal National Mortgage Association.

In contrast, governments may nationalize companies to reduce economic exploitation, subsidize a struggling industry or sector, or as a matter of their economic and political philosophy.

Sometimes, however, a private company sells some or all of its shares directly to investors rather than offering shares to the public. This transaction or series of transactions is called private placement. A private placement may be designed either to raise capital for further development or to allow the owner or owners to cash in on the value of the company they have built. A private placement doesn't have to be registered with the SEC or meet strict criteria for disclosure since the shares can't be traded among investors.

help investors make informed investment decisions.

Each mutual fund provides a prospectus to potential investors, explaining its objectives, policies, investment strategy, and performance. The prospectus also summarizes the fees the fund charges and analyzes the risks you take in investing in the fund.

Proxy

If you own common stock in a US corporation, you have the right to vote on company policies and to elect the company's board of directors. You may vote in person at the annual meeting or authorize the board to vote on your behalf using an absentee ballot, or proxy, which you can submit by mail or, increasingly often, by telephone or over the Internet.

The Securities and Exchange Commission (SEC) requires each company to provide a proxy statement, which describes the issues being voted on and introduces the candidates for director. The proxy also reports the total compensation of the company's top five executives, as well as the company's stock performance in relation to Standard & Poor's 500-stock Index (S&P 500) and to comparable companies in the industry.

Public company

The stock of a public company is owned and traded by individual and institutional investors. In contrast, in a privately held company, the stock is held by company founders, employees, and sometimes venture capitalists.

Many privately held companies eventually go public to help raise capital to finance growth.

Put option

A put option gives the buyer of the option the right to sell a fixed number of shares (typically 100) of a specific stock at a specific price (called the exercise or strike price) to the writer, or seller, of the option before it expires.

The person who buys the put option pays a premium to the seller for the right to sell those shares. If the buyer exercises the put, the seller must buy the shares.

Not surprisingly, buyers and sellers have different goals. Buyers hope that the price of the underlying stock drops so they can sell shares at the exercise price, which would presumably be higher than the market price. This way, the buyer could offset the price of the premium, and hopefully make a profit as well. Sellers, on the other hand, hope that stock stays the same, or goes up in value, so they can keep the premium they've collected and not have to lay out any money.

Put-call ratio

Since investors buy put options when they expect the market to fall, and call options when they expect the market to rise, the relationship of puts to calls, called the put-call ratio, gives analysts a way to measure the relative optimism or pessimism of the marketplace.

The customary interpretation is that when puts predominate, and the mood is bearish, stock prices are headed for a tumble. The reverse is assumed to be true when calls are more numerous. The contrarian investor, however, holds just the opposite view—that by the time investors are concentrating on puts, the worst is already over, and the market is poised to rebound.

Qualified retirement plan

Qualified retirement plans are employer-sponsored, tax-deferred plans to which you and your employer both contribute, or to which you (but not your employer) contribute. Most qualified plans have a limit, or cap, on how much you and your employer can put into the account each year.

When you withdraw, you owe federal income tax on the amount of the withdrawal at your ordinary tax rate. And, if you withdraw from any of these plans before you reach age 59½, you'll owe a penalty as well as the income tax that's due, unless you qualify for one of the exceptions spelled out in the federal income tax code. (However, you may be able to borrow from some plans without penalty.)

To be classified as qualified, a plan must provide for all eligible employees equivalently. That means the plan can't treat highly paid employees more generously than it does the least well paid.

In contrast, a nonqualified plan may be available to some employees and not others. Nonqualified contributions are made with post-tax dollars, although any earnings in the plan accumulate on a tax-deferred basis. While you must postpone withdrawals to age 59½ to avoid penalty, the federal government does not require you to begin withdrawals at age 70½.

Qualitative analysis

When a securities analyst evaluates intangible factors, such as the integrity and experience of a company's management, the positioning of its products and services, or the appeal of its marketing campaign, that seem likely to influence future performance, the approach is described as qualitative analysis.

While this type of evaluation is more subjective than quantitative analysis—which looks at statistical data—advocates believe that success or failure in the corporate world is often driven as much by qualitative factors as by financial data.

Quantitative analysis

When a securities analyst focuses on a corporation's financial data in order to project potential future performance, the process is called quantitative analysis. This methodology involves looking at profit-and-loss statements, sales and earnings histories, and the statistical state of the economy rather than at more subjective factors such as

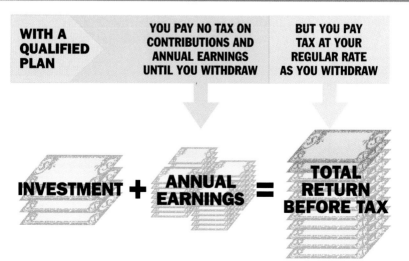

QUALIFIED PLANS

WITH A QUALIFIED PLAN	YOU PAY NO TAX ON CONTRIBUTIONS AND ANNUAL EARNINGS UNTIL YOU WITHDRAW	BUT YOU PAY TAX AT YOUR REGULAR RATE AS YOU WITHDRAW

INVESTMENT + ANNUAL EARNINGS = TOTAL RETURN BEFORE TAX

management experience, employee attitudes, and brand recognition. While some people feel that quantitative analysis by itself gives an incomplete picture of a company's prospects, advocates tend to believe that numbers tell the whole story.

Quarter

The financial world splits up its calendar into four quarters, each three months long. If January to March is the first quarter, April to June is the second quarter, and so on, though a company's first quarter does not have to begin in January.

The Securities and Exchange Commission (SEC) requires all publicly held US companies to publish a quarterly report, officially known as Form 10-Q, describing their financial results for the quarter. These reports—and the predictions that market analysts make for them—often have an impact on a company's stock price.

For example, if analysts predict that a certain company will have earnings of 55 cents a share in a quarter, and the results beat those expectations, the price of the company's stock may increase. But if the earnings are less than expected, even by a penny or two, the stock price characteristically drops, at least for a time.

Quarter is often abbreviated as Q in financial reports. For example, 3Q01 would mean the third quarter, or July to September, 2001.

Quasi-public corporation

In the US, quasi-public corporations have links to the federal government although they are technically in the private sector. That means that their managers and executives work for the corporation, not the government. And, in many cases, you can buy stock in a quasi-public corporation, expecting to share in its profits.

Many quasi-public corporations were originally federal agencies that have been privatized. Among the best known are the Federal National Mortgage Association (FNMA) and the Student Loan Marketing Association (Sallie Mae), which securitize mortgages and student loans respectively and sell

them in the secondary market. The US Postal Service is also a quasi-public corporation, as is the Tennessee Valley Authority (TVA).

Quotation (Quote)

On a stock market, a quotation combines the highest bid to buy, and the lowest offer to sell, a stock. For example, if the quotation on Daveco stock is "20 to 20⅝," it means that the highest price that's been offered is \$20, and the lowest price that any seller wants to take is \$20.625.

How that spread is resolved depends on whether the stock is traded on an auction market, such as the New York Stock Exchange (NYSE), or on an electronic market, such as the Nasdaq Stock Market (Nasdaq), where the price is negotiated by market makers.

Qubes

The Nasdaq National Market (Nasdaq) sells shares in a unit investment trust (UIT) that tracks the Nasdaq 100 Stock Index. This market capitalization—weighted index includes the largest 100 companies trading on the Nasdaq—most of them technology companies—and is adjusted quarterly to keep it focused on the strongest performers. The name Qubes comes from the UIT's trading symbol: QQQ.

Qubes resemble Standard & Poor's Depositary Receipts (SPDRs), which reflect the performance of the Standard & Poor's 500-stock Index (S&P 500) and the DIAMONDS Trust (DIA), which tracks the Dow Jones Industrial Average (DJIA).

Rally

A rally is a significant short-term recovery in the price of a stock or commodity, or of a market in general, after a period of decline or sluggishness. Stocks that make a particularly strong recovery in a particular sector or in the market as a whole are often said to be leading the rally, a reference to the term's origins in combat, where an officer would lead his rallying troops back into battle. While a rally may signal the beginning of a bull market, it doesn't necessarily do so.

Random walk theory

The random walk theory holds that it is futile to try to predict changes in stock prices. Advocates of the theory base their assertion on the belief that stock prices react to information that becomes known at random, and that, because of the randomness of this information, prices themselves change as randomly as the path of a wandering person's walk.

Supporters of efficient market theory hold a similar belief that market performance can't be predicted, and both schools of thought stand in opposition to technical analysis, which predicts future stock prices based on statistical patterns of prior performance.

Rate of return

The rate of return is your annual income on an investment. With a stock, your return, known as the dividend yield, is your annual dividend divided by the price you paid for the stock. In the case of bonds, return is the current yield, or the annual interest you receive, divided by the price you paid for the bond. For example, if you paid $900 for a bond with a par value of $1,000 that pays 6% interest, your rate of return is $60 divided by $900, or 6.67%.

Rating service

A rating service, such as A.M. Best, Moody's Investors Service, or Standard & Poor's, evaluates bond issuers to determine the level of risk they pose to would-be investors. Though each rating service focuses on somewhat different criteria in making its evaluation, the assessments tend to agree on which investments pose the least risk and which pose the most.

These rating services also evaluate insurance companies, including those offering fixed annuities, in terms of how likely a provider is to meet its financial obligations to policyholders.

Real estate investment trust (REIT)

REITs are publicly traded trusts or associations that pool investors' capital to invest in a variety of real estate ventures, such as apartment and office buildings, shopping centers, medical facilities, industrial buildings, and hotels. After a REIT has raised its investment capital, it trades on a stock market just as a closed-end mutual fund does.

There are three types of REITs: Equity REITs buy properties that produce income. Mortgage REITs invest in real estate loans. Hybrid REITs usually make both types of investments. All three are income-producing investments, and most of a REIT's annual income is distributed to investors. That means the yields on REITs are often higher than on other equity investments.

Real interest rate

Your real interest rate is the interest rate you're getting on an investment minus the rate of inflation. For example, if you're earning 6.25% on a bond, and the inflation rate is 2%, your real rate is 4.25%. That's enough higher than inflation to maintain your buying power and have some in reserve to build your investment base. But if the inflation rate were 5%, your real rate would be only 1.25%.

Real property

Real property is what's more commonly known as real estate, or realty. A piece of real property includes the actual land as well as any buildings or other structures built on the land, the plant life, and anything that's permanently in the ground below it or the air above it. In that sense, real property is different from personal property, which you can move from place to place with you.

Real rate of return

The rate of return on an investment minus the rate of inflation gives you a real rate of return. For example, if you are earning 6% interest on a bond in a period when inflation is running at 2%, your real rate of return is 4%, which is large enough to increase your buying power. But if inflation were at 4%, your real rate of return would be only 2%.

Finding your real rate of return, however, is generally a calculation you have to do on your own. It isn't provided in annual reports, prospectuses, or other publications that report investment performance.

REAL RATE OF RETURN	
Earned interest rate	10%
− Inflation rate	− 3%
REAL RATE OF RETURN	= 7%

Real time

When an event is reported as it happens—such as a quick jump in a stock's price or the constantly changing numbers on a market index—you are getting real-time information.

Traditionally, this type of information was available to the public with a 20-minute time delay or was reported only periodically by news services. With the increasing popularity of the Internet and cable TV, however, more and more individual investors have access to real-time financial news. Knowing what's happening enables you and others to make buy and sell decisions based on the same information that institutional investors and financial services organizations are using.

Realized gain

When you sell an investment for more than you paid, you have a realized gain. For example, if you buy a stock for $20 a share and sell it for $35 a share, you have a realized gain of $15 a share. But if the price of the stock increases, and you don't sell, your gain is unrealized, or a paper profit.

Realizing your gains means you lock in any increase in value, which could potentially disappear if you continued to hold the investment. But it also means you owe tax on that profit unless the investment is tax-exempt or you hold it in a tax-deferred account when you sell. In the latter case, you can postpone paying the tax until you begin withdrawing from the account.

However, if taxes are due and you have owned the investment for a year or more when you sell, you pay tax at the long-term capital gains rate, which is always lower than the rate at which you pay federal income tax.

Recapture

When you recapture assets, you regain them, usually because of the provisions of a contract or legal precedent. Most of the time, recapture benefits you, but depending on the situation, it can also mean a financial loss. When a contract is involved, you may be entitled to recapture a percentage of the revenues from something you produce in addition to the cost of producing it. For example, a hotel developer might be entitled to recapture a portion of the hotel's profits.

A negative form of recapture occurs when the government makes you repay tax benefits that you've profited from in the past. For example, say that your divorce settlement calls for you to pay $150,000 to your ex-spouse over three years. If you pay all of the money in the first two years in order to qualify for a tax deduction, and pay nothing in the

third year, the IRS may force you to recapture part of your deduction in the third year and pay taxes on it.

Recession

Broadly defined, a recession is a downturn in a nation's economic activity. If national productivity, or gross domestic product (GDP), declines for at least two consecutive quarters, it is usually considered a recession. The consequences typically include increased unemployment, decreased consumer and business spending, and declining stock prices.

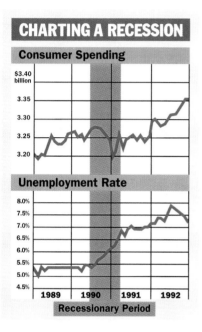

CHARTING A RECESSION

Consumer Spending
Unemployment Rate
1989 1990 1991 1992
Recessionary Period

Record date

To be paid a stock dividend, you must own the stock on the day that the corporation's board of directors names as the record date, also known as the date of record. For example, if a company declares a dividend of 50 cents a share payable on September 1 to shareholders of record as of August 10, you have to own the shares on August 10 to be entitled to the dividend.

Any shares bought between the record date and the day on which the dividend is paid are ex-dividend, which means those new owners will get no dividend for the period.

Red herring

When a security is offered to the public for the first time, the underwriter prepares a preliminary prospectus, called a red herring. While the name may refer to the parts of the document printed in red ink, the implication is that the document is an attempt to present the company in the best possible light. The reference is to the rather distinctive odor of the fish in question, which fleeing fugitives sometimes used to throw bloodhounds off their scent.

Although the preliminary prospectus contains important information about the company, its offerings, financial projections, and investment risk, it is frequently revised before the final version is issued.

Redemption

When a fixed-income investment matures, and you get your investment amount back, the repayment is known as redemption. Bonds are usually redeemed at par, or face value (traditionally $1,000 per bond). However, if a bond issuer calls the bond, or pays it off before maturity, you may be paid a premium, or a certain dollar amount over par, to compensate you for lost interest.

You can redeem, or liquidate, mutual fund shares at any time. The fund buys them back at their net asset value (NAV), which is the dollar value of one share in the fund. In order to discourage quick shifting of assets among mutual funds, many funds charge a redemption fee if you take your money out of the fund within a limited period after you invest.

Redemption fee

Some open-end mutual funds impose a redemption fee when you sell shares in the fund, often during a specific (and sometimes brief) period of time after you purchase those shares. The fee is usually a percentage of the value of the shares you sell, but it may also be a flat fee, or fixed amount.

The purpose of the fee is to prevent large-scale withdrawals from the fund in response to changes in the financial markets, which might require the fund manager to sell holdings at a loss in order to meet the fund's obligation to buy back your shares.

Regional exchange

Stock exchanges in cities other than New York are called regional exchanges. They list both regional stocks (which may or may not be listed on the New York exchanges) as well as stocks that are listed in New York.

Using the Intermarket Trading System (ITS), specialists on one exchange can execute a trade on any other exchange if the price there is

better than the price on the exchange where the specialist is located. There are currently eight such exchanges, with offices in nine cities, including Boston, Chicago, Los Angeles, Philadelphia, and San Francisco.

Registered bond

When a bond is registered, the name of the owner and the particulars of the bond are recorded by the issuer or the issuer's agent. When registered bonds are issued in certificate form, a bond can be sold only if the owner endorses the certificate, or signs it over to someone else. In contrast, bearer bonds are considered the property of whoever holds them, since there is no record of ownership.

Currently, however, bonds are increasingly registered electronically, so there are no certificates to endorse. Instead, you authorize the transaction over the phone or by computer.

Registered investment advisor (RIA)

Investment advisors who register with the Securities and Exchange Commission (SEC) and agree to be regulated by SEC rules are known as registered investment advisors.

Only a small percentage of all investment advisors register. And while the designation doesn't mean that the SEC vouches for their effectiveness, being registered is often interpreted as a sign that the advisor meets a higher standard.

Registered representative

Registered representatives are licensed by the Securities and Exchange Commission (SEC) to give investment advice and act on investors' orders to buy and sell. They are paid a salary or by commission, usually a percentage of the market price of the investments their clients buy and sell. Registered reps work for a broker/dealer that belongs to the exchange where the trades

are handled. They must pass a series of exams administered by the National Association of Securities Dealers (NASD) to qualify for their licenses.

Reinvestment risk

When you use the money from a maturing fixed-income investment, such as a certificate of deposit (CD) or a bond, in order to make a new investment of the same type, there's no guarantee that you will earn the same rate of return on your new investment as on the one coming due. In fact, the return could be significantly lower (or higher), based on what's happening in the economy at large.

This unpredictability is known as reinvestment risk. For example, if a bond paying 10% interest matures when the current rate is 5%, you must settle for a lower return if you buy a new bond or choose some other type of investment.

One way to limit reinvestment risk is by using an investment technique known as laddering, which means splitting your investment among a number of bonds (or CDs) with different maturity dates. That way only part of your total investment will mature and have to be reinvested at any one time.

Reserve requirement

The Federal Reserve requires member banks to keep a certain percentage of their deposits in cash and other liquid assets in reserve at all times.

The required percentage, which is revised periodically, is a key factor in determining how much money a bank can lend. It therefore affects the rate of economic growth. When the reserve requirement is raised, banks have less cash to lend, and the economic growth rate slows.

Restricted security

Restricted securities are stocks or warrants that you acquire privately, through stock options or a corporate merger, rather than by buying them in the open market. For example, you may receive restricted stock if you put money into a start-up company.

If the company has not yet registered with the Securities and Exchange Commission (SEC) for an initial public offering (IPO), its securities cannot be transferred or resold until the issuing company meets the SEC registration requirements for publicly traded securities. Or, if you exercise stock options and buy stock at a reduced price, you may be required to hold those stocks for a period of time before liquidating them.

Return

Your return is the profit you make on your investments, usually expressed as an annual percentage. For example, if you bought a stock at $25 a share and sold it for $30 a share, your return would be $5. If you bought on January 2, 1999, and sold on January 2, 2000, that would be a 20% annual percentage return, or the $5 return divided by your $25 investment. But if you held the stock for five years before selling at $30 a share, your annual return would be 4%, or the 20% gain divided by five years.

Return on equity

Return on equity measures how much a company earns within a specific period in relation to the amount that's invested in its common stock. It is calculated by

$$\frac{\text{Current value} - \text{Cost of investment}}{\text{Cost of initial investment}} = \text{RETURN (\%)}$$

RETURN

dividing the company's net income before common stock dividends are paid by the company's net worth, which is the stockholders' equity.

In general, it's considered a sign of good management when a company's performance over time is at least as good as the average return on equity for other companies in the same industry.

Return on investment

Your return on investment is the profit you make on the sale of a security or other asset divided by the amount of your investment, expressed as an annual percentage rate. For example, if you invested $5,000 and got $7,500 back

RETURN ON INVESTMENT

$7,500	Current value	
− 5,000	Investment amount	
$2,500	Profit	
÷ 5,000	Investment amount	
50%	Percentage return	
÷ 2	Years investment held	
25%	Annual percentage return (return on investment)	

after two years, your annual return on investment would be 25%.

Revenue

Revenue is the money you collect for providing a product or service. Revenue is different from earnings, which is what's left of your revenue after subtracting the costs of producing or delivering the product or service and any taxes you paid on the amount you took in.

When corporations release their financial statements, those that provide services, such as power or telecommunications companies, describe their income as revenues, while those that manufacture products, such as lightbulbs or books, describe their income as sales.

In either case, they're reporting the amount they take in before expenses, taxes and other charges are subtracted. The money a government collects in taxes is also called revenue, and in the US the department that collects those taxes is called the Internal Revenue Service (IRS).

Revenue bond

Revenue bonds are municipal bonds issued to finance public projects, such as airports, roadways, and dams. The bonds are backed by revenue to be generated by the project. For example, if the construction of a tunnel is financed with municipal revenue bonds, the tolls paid by motorists are used to pay back the bondholders. However, bondholders usually have no claims on the bond issuer's other assets or resources.

Reverse stock split

If a company's stock is trading at a very low price, the company may decide to reduce the number of outstanding shares and increase their price by consolidating the shares.

For example, a 1-for-2 reverse stock split halves the number of existing shares and doubles the price. In that case, if you hold 100 shares of a stock selling at $5 a share, for a combined value of $500, in a 1-for-2 reverse stock split, you would own 50 shares valued at $10 a share, which would still give you a combined value of $500.

Stocks may be reverse split 1-for-5, or 5-for-10, or in any ratio the company chooses. Reverse splits are generally used to discourage small investors or to encourage institutional investors, who may not buy stocks priced below a specific point.

Rights offering

In a rights offering, also known as a sub-scription right, a company offers existing shareholders the opportunity to buy additional shares of company stock at a discount, or less than the price at which those shares will be offered to the public.

To act on the offering, you turn over the rights you receive (typically one for each share of stock you own) and the money needed to make the purchase within the required period, often two to four weeks.

You don't have to buy the additional shares, and you can transfer your rights to someone else if you prefer. But buying helps you maintain the same percentage of ownership you had in the company be-fore the new shares were issued rather than having that percentage diluted.

Risk

According to modern investment theory, the greater the risk you take in making an investment, the greater your return should be if the investment succeeds. For example, investing in a start-up company carries substantial risk, since there is no guarantee that it will be profitable. But if it is, you're likely to realize a greater gain than if you had in-vested a similar amount in an already established company.

As a rule of thumb, if you are unwill-ing to take some investment risk, you are

likely to limit your investment reward. For example, if you put your money into an insured bank deposit, which protects your principal, your real rate of return is unlikely to exceed inflation.

Risk-adjusted performance

When you evaluate an investment's risk-adjusted performance, you aren't looking simply at its straight perfor-mance figures but at those figures in relation to how much risk you'd be taking to get the potential return the investment could produce. You might compensate for risk by creating a balanced portfolio in which you com-bined risky and less risky investments. But you might also want to look at the risk posed by various investments individually.

One method is to investigate the investment's price volatility over various periods of time, including different market environments. For example, you might consider how far the price fell in the most recent bear market against its price in a bull market, or how it per-formed in a recent market correction. In general, the greater the volatility, the greater the risk.

However, many analysts believe that looking exclusively at past performance can be deceptive in evaluating the risk you are taking in making a certain investment, since it can't predict what will happen in the future.

Risk-free return

When you buy a US Treasury bill that matures in 13 weeks, you're making a risk-free investment in that there's virtually no chance of losing your principal (since the bill is backed by the US government) and no threat from inflation (since the term is so short).

Your yield, or the amount you earn on that investment, is described as risk-free return. By subtracting the risk-free return from the return on an investment that has the potential to lose value, you can figure out the risk premium, which is one measure of the risk of choosing an investment other than the 13-week bill.

Risk premium

A risk premium is one way to measure the risk you'd take in buying a specific investment. Some analysts define risk premium as the difference between the current risk-free return—the yield on a 13-week US Treasury bill—and the total return on the investment you're considering.

Other measures of risk premium, which are applied specifically to stocks, are a stock's beta, or the volatility of that stock in relation to the stock market as a whole, and a stock's alpha, which is based on an evaluation of the stock's intrinsic value.

Similarly, the higher interest rates that bond issuers typically offer on riskier bonds may be considered a risk premium, since the higher rate, and potentially greater return, is a way to compensate for the greater risk.

Risk ratio

Some investors and financial analysts try to estimate the risk an investment poses by speculating on how much the investment is likely to increase in value as opposed to how much it could decline. For example, a stock priced at $50 that analysts think could increase to $90 or decrease to $30 has a 4:2 risk ratio (the stock could go up $40 but down $20).

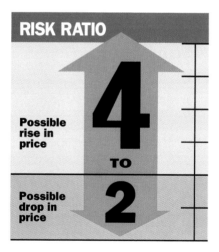

Rollover

If you move your assets from one investment to another, it's called a rollover. For example, if you move money from one individual retirement account (IRA) to another IRA, that transaction is a rollover.

Similarly, when a bond or certificate of deposit (CD) matures, you can roll over the assets into another bond or time deposit. In the same vein, if you move money from a qualified retirement plan into an IRA, you create an IRA rollover.

Roth IRA

The Roth IRA is a variation on a traditional IRA. It allows you to withdraw your earnings completely tax-free any time after you reach age 59½, provided your account has been open at least five years.

You may also be able to withdraw money earlier without penalty if you qualify for certain exceptions, such as using up to $10,000 toward the purchase of a first home. And since a Roth IRA has no required withdrawals, you can continue to accumulate tax-free earnings as long as you like. You can make a nondeductible contribution of up to $2,000 any year you have earned income, even after age 70½, though you can never contribute more than you earn.

In order to contribute to a Roth IRA, your modified adjusted gross income (AGI) must be less than the annual limit set by Congress. You can make a full contribution with a modified AGI of up to $95,000 if you're single, and up to $150,000 if you are married and file a joint return.

You may make partial contributions on a sliding scale if your AGI is between $95,001 and $110,000 if you're single, and between $150,001 and $160,000 if you're married. You may also qualify to convert a traditional IRA to a Roth IRA if your modified AGI in the year you convert is less than the cap, currently $100,000, which applies whether you are single or married.

Round lot

A round lot is the normal trading unit for stocks and bonds on a securities exchange or market. For example, on the New York Stock Exchange (NYSE), shares traded in multiples of 100 are typically considered round lots, as are bonds with par values of $1,000 and $5,000. If you trade fewer shares of stock—called odd lots—you may have to pay a higher brokerage commission.

Russell 2000 Index

This index, published by the Frank Russell Company of Tacoma, Washington, tracks the stocks of 2,000 small American companies, with an average market capitalization of $255 million. It includes many of the initial public offerings (IPOs) of recent years and is considered the benchmark index for small-cap investments.

Salary reduction plan

A salary reduction plan is a type of qualified, employer-sponsored retirement savings plan. Typical examples are 401(k)s, 403(b)s, 457s, and SIMPLE IRAs.

A salary reduction plan allows you to contribute pretax income to a retirement account in your name and to accumulate tax-deductible earnings on those contributions. Your employer may also match some or all of your contribution according to a formula that applies equally to all participating employees. Each type of salary reduction plan has an annual contribution cap that's set by Congress.

TAKE HOME PAY

SALARY REDUCTION PLAN

Sales charge

A sales charge is the fee you pay to buy shares of a load mutual fund, typically figured as a percentage of the amount you invest. As the size of your investment increases, the rate at which you pay the sales charge may decrease. Each dollar amount at which there is a corresponding reduction in the charge is known as a breakpoint. For example, the rate may drop from 4.5% to 4.25% with an investment of $25,000.

The sales charge may be imposed as a front-end load when you buy (also known as a Class A share), as a back-end load when you sell (also known as a Class B share), or as a level load each year you own the fund (also known as a Class C share).

Savings bond

The US government issues three types of savings bonds: Series EE, Series HH and Series I. The interest they pay is free from state and local tax, and they are all considered risk-free since they're backed by the federal government.

Series EE bonds, which you buy for a percentage of their face value and typically hold at least until they reach full value at maturity, are probably the best known. Series I bonds are sold at face value and are indexed for inflation, which means the interest you earn fluctuates with changes in the Consumer Price Index (CPI). Series HH bonds are also sold at face value and pay regular interest, but you can't pay cash for them. You must exchange Series EE bonds to buy them.

The biggest difference between savings bonds and US Treasury bills, notes, and bonds is that there is no secondary market for savings bonds since they can not be traded among investors. You buy them in your own name or as a gift for someone else and redeem them by turning them back to the government, usually through a bank or other financial intermediary.

Screen

In searching for stocks that meet certain investment criteria, you may screen a large sample to identify one or more to invest in. You can also establish a screen, which is a set of criteria against which you measure stocks (or other investments) to find those that meet your criteria.

For example, you might screen for stocks that meet a certain environmentally or socially responsible standard, or for those with current price-to-earnings ratios (P/E) less than the current market average.

Scrip

Scrip is a certificate or receipt that represents something of value but has no intrinsic value. For example, after a corporate stock split or spin-off, a company might issue scrip representing a fractional share of stock for each existing share you own. On or before a specific date, you can convert the value they represent into full shares. What's essential is that the issuer and the recipient must agree on the value that the scrip represents.

Scripophily

Although scripophily sounds like a dread disease, it's actually the practice of collecting antique stocks, bonds, and other securities. The most valuable documents are usually the most beautiful, or those that have some historical significance because of the role the issuing company played in the economy. Sometimes those with distinctive errors are also especially valuable.

Secondary market

When stocks and bonds are bought and sold after the date they are first issued, they trade on what's known as the secondary market. The issuer, or company that offers the stock or bond, gets no proceeds from these secondary trades, as it does when it issues these securities the first time in the primary market. In fact, most securities trading occurs in the secondary market.

Secondary offering

The most common form of secondary offering occurs when an investor (usually a corporation, but sometimes an individual) sells to the public a large block of stock or other securities it has been holding in its portfolio. In a sale of this kind, all of the profits go to the seller rather than the company that issued the securities in the first place.

Secondary offerings can also originate with the issuing companies themselves. In these cases, a company issues shares of its stock over and above those sold in its initial public offering (IPO), usually in order to raise additional capital. However, because an increase in the number of shares devalues those that have already been issued, many companies make a secondary offering only if their stock prices are high.

Sector

A sector is a group of stocks, often in one industry. The performance of any single stock in a sector can be measured against the performance of the sector as a whole, showing where that stock ranks in relation to its peers.

Mutual funds that concentrate on the stocks of a specific sector are known as sector funds. These funds can be more volatile than other funds, reflecting the current strength or weakness of that sector in the overall economy. Technology stocks or health care stocks, for example, might be hot in some periods and in the doldrums in others.

Sector fund

Also called specialty or specialized funds, sector mutual funds concentrate their investments in a single industry, such as biotechnology, natural resources, utilities, or regional banks, for example.

Sector funds tend to be more volatile and erratic than more broadly diversified funds, and often dominate both the top and bottom of annual mutual fund performance charts. A sector that thrives in one economic climate may wither in another one.

Secured bond

The issuer of a bond or other debt security may guarantee, or secure, the bond by pledging, or assigning, collateral to investors. If the issuer defaults, the investors may take possession of the collateral.

A mortgage-backed bond is an example of a secured security, since the underlying mortgages can be foreclosed and the properties sold to recover some or all of the amount of the bond. Holders of secured bonds are at the top of the pecking order if an issuer misses an interest payment or defaults on repayment of principal.

Securities and Exchange Commission (SEC)

The SEC is an independent federal agency that oversees and regulates the securities industry in the US, and enforces securities laws. It requires registration of all securities offered in interstate commerce, and of all individuals and firms who sell those securities.

Established by Congress in 1934, the SEC sets high standards for disclosure about publicly traded securities, including stocks, bonds, and mutual funds, and works to protect investors from misleading or fraudulent practices, including insider trading.

The SEC has also helped to establish a competitive national market system known as Intermarket Trading System (ITS) for trading securities, and set up a system for clearing and settling securities transactions.

Securities Investor Protection Corporation (SIPC)

The SIPC is a nonprofit corporation created by Congress to insure investors against losses caused by the failure of a brokerage firm. Through the SIPC, assets in your brokerage account are insured up to $500,000 (including up to $100,000 in cash)—but only against losses from the brokerage going bankrupt, not against market losses caused by your trading decisions.

All brokers and dealers registered with the Securities and Exchange Commission (SEC) are required to be SIPC members.

Securitization

Securitization is the process of pooling various types of debt—mortgages, car loans, or credit card debt—and packaging them as bonds, which are then sold to investors. These bonds may also be known as asset-backed securities because the interest and return of principal they promise are based on the value of the underlying assets. Those assets could be the property, such as cars or homes purchased with the original loans, or accounts receivable, which are monies owed to the lender.

Security

Generally speaking, a security is a financial instrument that shows you own shares in a company (by owning stocks), have loaned money to a company, government, or municipality (by investing in bonds), or have rights to future ownership (as with options, rights, or warrants).

Traditionally, securities were physical documents, such as stock or bond certificates. But with the advent of electronic recordkeeping, paper certificates have increasingly been replaced by electronic documentation.

Self-regulatory organization (SRO)

All securities and commodities exchanges in the US are self-regulatory organizations (SROs). So is the National Association of Securities Dealers (NASD), whose members operate in the over-the-counter markets (OTC), and the Municipal Securities Rulemaking Board, which oversees municipal bond trading.

These bodies establish the standards under which their members conduct business, monitor the way that business is conducted, and enforce their own rules. For example, the New York Stock Exchange (NYSE) requires that client orders delivered to the floor of the exchange be filled before orders that originate with traders on the floor, who buy and sell for their own accounts.

Sell-off

A sell-off is a period of intense selling of securities and commodities triggered by declining prices. Sell-offs—sometimes called dumping—usually cause prices to plummet even more sharply.

Sell short

Selling short is a trading strategy that takes advantage of an anticipated drop in a stock's price. To sell short, you borrow shares from your broker, sell them, and keep the proceeds until the stock price drops. If it does, you then buy back the shares at a lower price, return the borrowed shares to your broker (plus interest and commission), and pocket the difference.

Suppose, for example, you sell short 100 shares of stock priced at $10 a share. When the price drops, you buy 100 shares at $7.50 a share, give them back to your broker, and keep the $2.50-per-share profit (minus commission). Of course, if the share price rises instead of falls, you may have to buy back the shares at a higher price and suffer the loss.

Settlement date

The settlement date is the date by which a securities transaction must be finalized. Depending on the type of trade, it's either the date when the buyer must pay the broker for securities purchased, or the date by which the seller must deliver the sold securities and receive the proceeds from them.

For stocks and bonds, the settlement date is three business days after the trade date, or what's referred to as T+3. For options and government securities, the settlement date is one day, or T+1, after the trade date. In figuring long- and short-term capital gains on your tax return, you use the trade date—the date you buy or sell a security—rather than the settlement date as the date of record.

Share

A share is a unit of ownership in a corporation or mutual fund, or an interest in a general or limited partnership. Though the word is sometimes used interchangeably with the word stock, you actually own shares of stock.

HOW SELLING SHORT WORKS

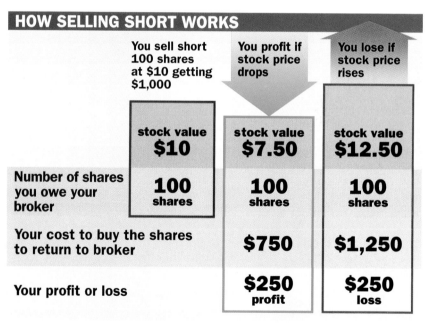

	You sell short 100 shares at $10 getting $1,000	You profit if stock price drops	You lose if stock price rises
	stock value **$10**	stock value **$7.50**	stock value **$12.50**
Number of shares you owe your broker	**100** shares	**100** shares	**100** shares
Your cost to buy the shares to return to broker		**$750**	**$1,250**
Your profit or loss		**$250** profit	**$250** loss

Senior bond

If a bond issuer defaults, or runs into difficulty paying off debt, holders of senior bonds get priority in receiving whatever monies are available. Senior bonds offer slightly lower interest rates than other types of bonds (such as subordinated bonds) because they are considered less risky.

Share class

Some stocks and certain mutual funds subdivide their shares into classes or groups to designate their special characteristics. For example, the differences between Class A shares and Class B shares of stock may focus on voting rights, resale rights, or other provisions that limit the power of certain shareholders. In some overseas countries, Class A shares can be purchased by citizens only, while Class B shares can be purchased by noncitizens only.

In the case of mutual funds, class designations indicate the way that sales charges, or loads, are levied. Class A shares have front-end loads, Class B shares have back-end loads, also called contingent deferred sales charges, and Class C shares have level loads.

Shareholder

If you own stock in a corporation, you are a shareholder of that corporation. You're considered a majority share-holder if you (alone or in combination with other shareholders) own more than half the company's outstanding shares, which allows you to control the outcome of a corporate vote. Otherwise, you are considered a minority shareholder.

In practice, however, it is possible to gain control by owning less than 51% of the shares, especially if there are a large number of shareholders.

Sharpe ratio

One way to compare the relationship of risk and reward in following different investment strategies, such as empha-sizing growth or value investments, is to use the Sharpe ratio. To figure the ratio, you subtract the risk-free return from the average return of an invest-ment portfolio made up of these investments over a period of time, and then divide the result by the standard deviation of the return. A strategy with a higher ratio is less risky than one with a lower ratio. This approach is named for William P. Sharpe, who won the Nobel Prize in economics in 1990.

Short interest

Short interest is the total number of shares of a particular stock that in-vestors have sold short in anticipation of a decline in the share price and have not yet repurchased.

Short interest is often considered an indicator of pessimism in the market and a sign that prices will decline. However, some analysts see short interest as a positive sign, pointing out that short sales have to be covered, and that the need to repurchase can trigger higher prices.

Short position

If you sell stock short and have not yet repurchased shares to replace the ones you borrowed, you are said to have a short position in that stock. Similarly, if you buy a futures contract that commits you to sell a commodity at a specific price at some date in the future, you have a short position in that commodity.

Simple interest

If you earn simple interest on money you deposit in a bank or use to pur-chase a certificate of deposit (CD), the interest is figured on the amount of your principal alone. For example, if you had $1,000 in an account that paid 5% simple interest for five years, you'd earn $50 a year ($1,000 x .05 = $50) and have $1,250 at the end of five years.

In contrast, if you had been earning compound interest, you'd have $1,276.29 at the end of five years, since the interest you earned each year, as well as your principal, would have earned interest.

Simplified employee pension plan (SEP)

A SEP is a quali-fied retirement plan set up as an individual re-tirement account (IRA) in an employee's name. You can establish a SEP for yourself if you own a small business, or you may participate as an employee if you work for a company that sponsors such a plan. The federal government sets the requirements for participation, the maximum annual contribution limits, and the rules governing withdrawals.

Small order execution system (SOES)

The small order execution system auto-matically executes and clears trades in

Nasdaq securities at market makers' best displayed prices in response to buy and sell orders placed through order-entry firms. The negotiation-free transactions include small market orders and limit orders in set quantities between 100 and 1,000 shares.

The SOES, which is designed to give individual investors open access to trading in a volatile market, was mandated by the Securities and Exchange Commission (SEC) after the stock market crash of 1987, when many small investors found themselves unable to sell their stocks as prices plummeted because they could not reach their brokers by telephone.

Small-capitalization (small-cap) stock

Shares of relatively small publicly traded corporations, with a total market value—or capitalization—of less than $500 million, are typically considered small-capitalization, or small-cap, stocks. Stocks of companies with a capitalization of less than $150 million are considered microcap stocks.

Small-cap stocks, which are tracked by the Russell 2000 Index, tend to be volatile, since they are issued by young, potentially fast-growing companies whose successes can't be guaranteed. Over the long term—though not in every period—small-cap stocks as a group have produced stronger returns than any other investment category. Mutual funds that invest in this type of stock are known as small-cap funds.

Socially responsible fund

When these mutual funds, also known as green funds or conscience funds, select securities to meet their investment goals, the securities must also satisfy the fund's commitment to certain principles spelled out in the fund's prospectus.

For example, a socially responsible fund might not buy shares of a manufacturing company that operates factories that fund managers consider sweat shops. Or the fund might not buy shares of a food company that sells out-of-date products in emerging markets. Since the priorities of these funds vary, you may need to do some investigating to find one that matches your values.

Soft market

A soft market, also known as a buyer's market, is one in which supply exceeds demand. In the financial world, the term often refers to a time in which there are more stocks or bonds for sale than there are customers eager to buy them. The lack of interest creates a wide spread, or gap, between the prices being asked for securities and the prices being bid. As a result, trading is often sluggish.

Special situation

An undervalued stock that one or more analysts expects to increase in price in the very near future because of an anticipated—and welcome—change within the company is known as a special situation. That change could be the introduction of a major new product, a corporate restructuring, or anything else that has the potential to increase earnings.

In some cases, the fact that a stock is identified as a special situation creates a flurry of investor interest and actually helps drive the price up even before the change has had time to take effect. A stock that is extremely volatile over the short term because of important recent news about the company, such as a takeover or spin-off, is also described as a special situation.

Specialist

A specialist or specialist unit maintains a fair and orderly market in a specific security or securities on the floor of an exchange. Typically, that means acting both as agent and principal. As agent, the specialist handles transactions for floor brokers who want to buy or sell one of the securities, collecting a percentage of the commission the client pays for the transaction.

As principal, the specialist buys for his or her own account to help maintain a stable market in a security. For example, if the spread, or difference, between the bid and ask (the highest price offered by a buyer and the lowest price asked by a seller) gets too wide, and trading in the security hits a lull, the specialist might buy, sell, or sell short shares to narrow the spread and stimulate trading.

Speculator

When you invest in futures contracts or buy or sell options strictly to take advantage of anticipated price changes and have no interest in buying or selling the underlying investment, you're a speculator.

THE SPECULATORS

Seek to profit on price changes	Buy when they think prices are lowest	Sell when they think prices are highest

In contrast, hedgers buy futures and options to protect their financial interests. For example, a baker who buys a wheat futures contract in order to protect the cost of producing bread is a hedger. But someone who buys the same contract on the chance that contract will increase in value is a speculator.

Spin-off

In a spin-off, a company sets up one of its existing subsidiaries or divisions as a separate company. Shareholders of the parent company receive stock in the new company in addition to the stock they hold in the parent based on an evaluation established for the new entity.

The motives for spinoffs vary. In some cases, a company may want to refocus its core businesses, shedding those that it sees as unrelated. Or it may want to set up an Internet company to capitalize on investor interest. In other cases, a corporation may face regulatory hurdles in expanding its business and spin off a unit to be in compliance.

In some cases, a group of employees will assume control of the new entity through a buyout, an employee stock ownership plan (ESOP), as the result of negotiation.

Spot market

Commodities and foreign currencies are traded for immediate delivery and payment on the spot market—also known as a cash market. The term refers to the fact that the full cash price is paid "on the spot," or within a short period of time.

A cash sale, whether arranged in person, over the telephone, or electronically, is the opposite of a forward contract, where delivery and settlement are set for a date in the future, or a futures contract, which is an agreement to trade a commodity for a set price on a specific date in the future.

Spot price

The spot, or cash, price is the price of commodities and foreign currencies that are being sold for immediate delivery with payment in cash.

Spread

In the most general sense, a spread is the difference between two similar measures. In the stock market, for example, the spread is the difference between the highest price offered and the lowest price asked.

With fixed-income securities, such as bonds, the spread is the difference between the yields on securities having the same investment grade but different maturity dates. For example, if the yield on a long-term Treasury bond is 6%, and the yield on a Treasury bill is 4%, the spread is 2%.

The spread is also the difference in yields on securities that have the same maturity date but are of different investment quality. For example, there is a 3% spread between a high-yield bond paying 9% and a Treasury bond paying 6% that both come due on the same date.

Standard & Poor's (S&P)

Standard & Poor's is an investment services company that rates bonds, stocks, commercial paper, and insurance companies. It also compiles influential stock market indexes and publishes a broad range of reports, guides, and handbooks on financial topics. The S&P 500-stock Index is one of the key

measures of stock market performance and is also the benchmark for a large number of stock index funds.

Standard & Poor's 500-stock Index (S&P 500)

This benchmark index tracks the performance of 500 widely held large-cap stocks in the industrial, transportation, utility, and financial sectors. A capitalization-, or market value-, weighted index, it gives greater weight to stocks with the greatest number of outstanding shares and highest share prices. The stocks included in the index, their relative weightings, and the number that represent each sector vary from time to time, at S&P's discretion.

Standard & Poor's Depositary Receipt (SPDR)

When you buy SPDRs—pronounced spiders—you're buying shares in a unit investment trust (UIT) that owns a portfolio of stocks included in Standard & Poor's 500-stock Index (S&P 500). A share is priced at about $\frac{1}{10}$ the value of the S&P 500.

Each quarter you receive a distribution based on the dividends paid on the stocks in the underlying portfolio, after trust expenses are deducted. If you choose, you can reinvest those distributions to buy additional shares.

Like an index mutual fund that tracks the S&P 500, SPDRs provide a way to diversify your investment portfolio without having to own shares in all the S&P 500 companies yourself. However, while the net asset value (NAV) of an index fund is set only once a day, at the end of trading, the price of SPDRs, which are listed on the American Stock Exchange (AMEX), changes throughout the day, reflecting the constant changes in the index.

Standard deviation

Standard deviation is a statistical measurement of how far a variable quantity, such as the price of a stock, moves above or below its average value. The wider the range of performances, or the higher the standard deviation, the riskier an investment is considered to be.

Some analysts use standard deviation to predict how a particular investment or portfolio will perform.

They calculate the range of the investment's possible future performances based on a history of past performance, and then estimate the probability of meeting each performance level within that range.

Standard & Poor's/BARRA Growth and Value Indexes

Some investors favor growth stocks while others favor value stocks. Since 1992, results of those investment styles, which tend to produce different returns over time, have been tracked separately by the Standard & Poor's(S&P)/BARRA Growth and Value Indexes.

To create the indexes, about half the 1,500 companies tracked in the S&P equity indexes are assigned to the value index and about half to the growth index, based on book-to-price ratio, or the book value of a stock divided by its market capitalization.

The value index includes companies with higher book-to-price ratios, and the growth index includes companies with lower ratios. Both indexes are rebalanced and adjusted on a regular schedule to reflect changes in the stocks' market capitalizations and in the underlying S&P indexes.

Start-up

While any new company could be considered a start-up, the description is usually applied to aggressive young companies that are actively courting private financing from venture capitalists, including wealthy individuals and investment companies. In many cases, the start-ups plan to use the cash infusion to prepare for an initial public offering (IPO).

Statutory voting

When shareholders vote for candidates nominated to serve on a company's board of directors, they usually cast their ballots using statutory voting. Under that system, each shareholder gets one vote for each share of stock he or she owns, and may cast that number of votes for or against each candidate.

For example, if you owned 100 shares, and there were three candidates, you could cast 100 votes for each of them. That means the shareholders owning greater numbers of shares have greater influence on the outcome of the election.

In cumulative voting, on the other hand, a shareholder may cast the total number of his or her votes—one vote for every share of stock multiplied by the number of candidates for the board—for or against a single nominee, divide them between two nominees, or cast an equal number of shares for each of them.

For example, if you owned 100 shares, and there were three candidates, you could cast 300 votes for one of them and ignore the others. With this system, people owning a smaller number of shares can concentrate on one or two candidates. So they may have a better chance of influencing the makeup of the board.

Step up in basis

When you inherit assets, such as securities or property, they are stepped up in basis. That means they are valued at the amount they are worth when your benefactor dies, or the date on which his or her estate is valued, and not on the date they were purchased.

For example, if your father bought 200 shares of stock for $40 a share in 1965, and you inherited them in 1999 when they were selling for $95 a share, they would be valued at $95 a share. If you wanted to sell them, your cost basis would be $95, not the $40 your father paid for them originally. If you sold them for $95 a share, you would not have a capital gain and would owe no tax on the amount you received in the sale.

In contrast, if your father had given you the same stocks as a gift, your basis would be $40 a share. So if you sold at $95 a share, you would have a taxable capital gain of $55 a share (minus commissions).

Stochastic modeling

Stochastic modeling is a statistical process that uses probability and random variables to predict a range of probable investment performances. The mathematical principles behind stochastic modeling are complex, however, so it's not something you can do on your own. But based on information you provide about your age, retirement plans, and risk tolerance, a number of online financial sites perform calculations that can help you evaluate the probability that your investment portfolio will allow you to meet your financial

goals. Appropriately enough, the term stochastic comes from the Greek word meaning "skillful in aiming."

Stock

A stock is an investment that represents part ownership in a corporation and entitles you to part of that corporation's earnings and assets. Common stocks provide voting rights to shareholders but no guarantee of dividend payments. Preferred stocks provide no voting rights but guarantee a dividend payment. Although common stocks are riskier, and their prices are more volatile than preferred stock, they also offer the greater potential for growth.

In the past, as a shareholder you received a paper stock certificate—called a security—verifying the shares you owned. Today, share ownership is usually recorded electronically, and the shares are held in street name by your brokerage firm.

Stock certificate

A stock certificate is a paper document that represents ownership in a corporation. In the past, when you bought stock, you got a certificate that listed your name as owner, and showed the number of shares and other relevant information. When you sold the shares, you endorsed the certificate and sent it to your broker.

Stock certificates are being phased out, however, and replaced by electronic records. That means you don't have to safeguard the certificates, and can sell

them by giving an order over the phone or on the Internet. The chief objection that's been raised to the new system is largely nostalgic and esthetic, since the certificates, with their finely engraved borders and images, are distinctive and often beautiful.

Stock option

A stock option is an agreement that gives you the right to buy or sell a specific stock at a preset price during a certain time period. If you don't exercise the option within that time period, it expires, and you forfeit the money you paid to buy the option. You can buy stock options, which are listed on various stock and options exchanges, through your broker.

Stock options are also a form of employee compensation that gives employees—often corporate executives—the right to buy shares in the company at or below market price. Often, these options are restricted, which means there are certain conditions, such as particular time periods, under which employees can exercise their options and sell the stock. If the stock price rises enough, and an employee has a substantial number of options, the rewards can be extremely handsome.

Stock split

When a company wants to make its shares more attractive and affordable to a greater number of investors, it may split its shares to create more shares at a lower price.

A 2-for-1 stock split, for example, doubles the number of outstanding shares. So if you own 100 shares of a stock priced at $50 a share, for a total value of $5,000, and the company's directors authorize a 2-for-1 stock split, you would own 200 shares priced at $25, with the same total value of $5,000. If the stock again increases in value, and the price moves back up to its presplit price, you would own 200 shares valued at $50 a share, for a total value of $10,000.

Announcements of stock splits, or anticipated stock splits, often generate a great deal of interest in a stock, since it becomes attractive to buyers who want to take advantage of the lower share price or believe that the split stock will soon increase in value.

While 2-for-1 splits are the most common, stocks can be also be split 3-to-1, 10-to-1, or in any other combination. In addition, a company can reverse the process and consolidate shares to reduce the number of shares outstanding in a reverse stock split.

Stop order

You can issue a stop order to your broker to buy or sell a security once it trades at a certain price, usually called the stop price. Stop orders are entered below the current price if you are selling and above the current price if you are buying. For example, if you owned a stock currently trading at $35 a share that you feared might drop in price, you could issue a stop order to sell if the price dropped to $30 a share.

Once the stop price is reached, your order becomes a market order. If the price dropped very quickly, and other orders had been placed before yours, the stock could actually end up selling for less than $30. You can give a stop order as a day order or as a good 'til canceled (GTC) order.

Stop-limit order

A stop-limit is a combination order that instructs your broker to buy or sell a stock once its price hits a certain target, known as the stop price, but not to pay more for the stock, or sell it for less, than a specific amount, known as the limit price. For example, if you give an order to buy at "40 stop 43 limit," you might end up spending anywhere from $40 to $43 a share to buy a stock, but not more than $43.

A stop-limit order can protect you from a rapid run-up in price—such as those that sometimes occur when there's an initial public offering (IPO) in a hot stock—but you also run the risk that your order won't be executed because the stock's price leapfrogs your limit.

The Stock Lineup

There are some handy clues to help you tell the usual suspects apart.

All stocks share some common features. They all represent equity, or ownership shares in a corporation, and they increase or decrease in value based on how much somebody is willing to pay to own them. But each stock also has distinctive characteristics—size, style, and sector—that can help you compare it to other stocks of the same type.

Measuring Size

Size is one of the easiest distinctions you can make among stocks, or, more precisely, among the corporations that issue stocks. The scale, which is measured in dollars, runs from huge to tiny—though the official language is less dramatic. Depending on the issuing company, stock may be large, medium, small and very small, or micro.

These words describe the corporation's **market capitalization**, which is determined by multiplying the number of shares of stock by the current price per share. The more shares there are, and the higher the price, the larger the capitalization, or market cap.

Size isn't fixed. As the price per share goes up or down, the market cap changes. The same is true if the **stock splits**, adding more shares, or if the corporation issues additional shares in a **secondary offering**. In fact, a small-cap company can grow quickly into a mid-cap or even large-cap. For example, several Internet stocks with very large market caps have very short histories.

Does Size Matter?

A stock's market cap isn't the primary reason to invest in it, but knowing what the cap is can alert you to some poten-

tial advantages and some potential drawbacks that characterize stocks of different sizes.

Large-cap stock corporations tend to have more financial reserves than smaller companies. So they are often less affected by an economic slowdown and may provide a more consistent return over time.

On the other hand, smaller companies have the potential to increase more rapidly in value than large companies, in part because large company stock is often more expensive to begin with. If you buy a small company stock when the price is low, and the company

grows dramatically, your investment can pay big rewards.

Large corporations are more likely than smaller ones to pay dividends on their earnings, so if you're investing in part to collect income, bigger can be better. Younger companies, in contrast, often reinvest any earnings to build their businesses.

Put another way, large and mid-cap company stocks, on average, pose less risk than smaller company stocks and much less risk than micro-caps. But smaller companies may provide greater returns, especially if they evolve into large ones.

How Big is Large? How Small is Micro?

Large-cap	$5 billion or more
Mid-cap	$500 million to $5 billion
Small-cap	$150 million to $500 million
Micro-cap	less than $150 million

What's in a Style?

Expensive blue chip stocks have a distinctive style and reputation. So do penny stocks, though it's somewhat less flattering. You expect strong, consistent performance from the former, and, if you're realistic, not much from the latter. Two other styles that get lots of attention are the ones described as **growth stocks** and those described as **value stocks**.

Growth

Growth stocks have a reputation to live up to. Investors, typically, expect them to deliver increases in value, sometimes dramatic ones. For example, a stock that doubles in price shows growth. So does a company whose stock splits and splits again, especially if the value of the shares continues to increase.

But growth stocks are typically riskier investments than blue chips, whose growth is likely to occur at a slower rate.

Value

If a stock isn't growing at the same pace as other stocks you're considering, if its price is very low, or its yield is very high, you may want to investigate whether it has some attractive, though hidden, features. Stocks that seem to be undervalued, or not currently worth what some investors think they should be worth, may be good deals. That's why they're sometimes described as value stocks.

However, buying value stocks means taking an added measure of risk, since there are no guarantees that the company's stock price will rebound.

What Is a Sector Anyway?

Corporations are usually described as part of an industry sector, a type of extended family with whom they share characteristics. For example, companies that produce medical supplies are part of the health care sector and those that manufacture cars are part of the automotive sector.

In fact, experts identify roughly 100 sectors in the US economy, each made up of hundreds of companies. Some sectors produce stronger returns than

others in any given period, though which ones those are does change. Similarly, within each sector, some corporations are stronger than others—and so may be better investment choices.

Stock mutual funds described as sector funds buy stocks in a number of companies in the same or similar businesses for investors who want to diversify their holdings in a particular area of the economy.

Stop price

When you give an order to buy or sell a stock or other security once it has reached a certain price, the price you quote is known as the stop price. When you ask your broker to buy, your stop price is higher than the current market price. When you're selling, the stop price is lower than the current price.

In either case, once the stop price has been reached, your broker will execute the order even if a flurry of trading drives the stock's price up or down quickly. That might mean you end up paying more than the stop price if you're buying or get less than your stop price if you're selling.

Straddle

A straddle is an options-buying strategy that lets you profit from the potential price changes of a particular stock, stock index, or commodities futures contract without actually speculating on whether the price will move up or down.

To use a straddle, you buy an equal number of put options (to sell a particular underlying investment) and call options (to buy the same underlying investment) at the same strike price. On or before the expiration date, at a point at which your potential profit on one half of the straddle outweighs your potential loss on the other half, you can exercise, or offset, the options, making more on one than you lose on the other. That spread, or difference in price, minus what the options cost you, is your profit.

Although straddling costs more than buying puts or calls alone, you may increase your chance of making money (and reduce your chances of losing money) by hedging your investment in this way.

Strangle

A strangle is an options-buying strategy in which you buy an equal number of put options (to sell) and call options (to buy) on the same underlying stock, stock index, or commodities futures contract at different strike prices that are equally out of the money—that is, equally far above and below the current market price of the underlying investment.

A strangle is essentially a bet that the stock will be valued between these two strike prices so you can exercise your options before they expire, realizing a greater profit on one of them than you lose on the other. For example, if a stock is selling at $100 a share, you might strangle it by buying call options at a higher strike price (say $110 a share) and put options at a lower strike price (say $90 a share). If the value of the underlying investment moves dramatically toward either strike price, you stand to benefit. If not, the strategy has not paid off. A strangle costs less than a straddle, but because both options are out of the money, the likelihood of making a profit is also smaller.

Street name

If you have a brokerage account, you can either have your stocks registered in your own name or in the name of the brokerage firm, which is called street name. The advantage of having your stocks registered in street name is that shares can be traded more easily. That's because you don't have to sign and deliver the stock certificates before a sale can be completed.

In addition, having your broker hold your stocks in street name is often safer because it reduces the risk of losing or misplacing the certificates.

Strike price

The strike price, also called the exercise price, is the price at which you can buy the stock or commodity underlying an option. While the strike price is set by the exchange on which the option trades, the price of the underlying investment rises and falls, depending on its performance and market conditions.

As a result, the underlying investment might be selling at a price that would make buying at the strike price a good deal, or it might not. If not, you simply let the option expire.

STRIPS

STRIPS, an acronym for separate trading of registered interest and principal of securities, are special issues of US Treasury zero-coupon bonds. The bonds are prestripped, which means that the Treasury separates a bond into the principal and individual interest payments, and then offers each of those parts separately as a zero-coupon security.

Student Loan Marketing Association (SLMA)

This corporation, commonly known as Sallie Mae, purchases student loans from various lenders, such as banks, and packages the loans as bonds, or as short-term or medium-term notes. After issue, these debt securities trade on the secondary market.

Sallie Mae guarantees repayment of the bonds and notes, and uses the money it raises through the sale of these securities to provide additional loan money for post-secondary-school students. Sallie Mae also arranges financing for state student loan agencies. Its shares trade on the New York Stock Exchange (NYSE).

Subordinated debt

Subordinated debt generally refers to debt securities that have a weaker claim for repayment than unsubordinated debt, should the issuer default on its obligations. In fact, there are also levels of subordinated debt, with senior subordinated debt having a higher claim to repayment than junior subordinated debt.

Subscription right

Before a company offers a new issue of securities to the public, it may offer existing shareholders the opportunity to buy shares of the issue at a discounted price. That's known as a subscription right, or a rights offering. Usually you receive one right for every share you already own, although the number of rights you need to buy a share may vary.

Rights are transferable, and may be bought and sold on the secondary market. They expire quickly—generally within a month—so you typically must act promptly to take advantage of them.

SuperDOT

The New York Stock Exchange (NYSE) SuperDOT, or designated order turnaround, is an electronic routing system used to handle market orders and day limit orders on trades of up to 31,000 shares (in 1999). The order is sent directly to a specialist on the trading floor who completes the transaction and sends back a response confirming the details.

Swap

When you swap or exchange securities, you sell one security and buy a comparable one almost simultaneously. Swapping enables you to change the maturity or the quality of the holdings in your portfolio. You can also use swaps to realize a capital loss for tax purposes by selling securities that have gone down in value since you purchased them.

More complex swaps, including interest rate swaps and currency swaps, are used by corporations doing business in more than one country to protect themselves against sudden, dramatic shifts in currency exchange rates or interest rates.

Systematic risk

Systematic risk, also known as market risk, is the risk that's inherent in, or characteristic of, a particular type or class of security, such as stocks or bonds, as opposed to the risks posed by an individual security of that type.

For example, the prices of existing bonds characteristically drop when interest rates go up. So a systematic or market risk of owning bonds is that you would probably realize less than the par value of a bond if you sold it in the secondary market after a jump in interest rates. That loss of value, however, would not reflect whether or not the individual bond was a good credit risk.

12b-1 fee

A number of load and no-load mutual funds levy 12b-1 fees on the value of your mutual fund account to offset the fund's promotional and marketing expenses.

These asset-based fees, which get their name from the Securities and Exchange Commission (SEC) ruling that describes them, typically amount to somewhere between 0.5% and 1% annually of the net assets in the fund. A fund that charges 12b-1 fees must detail those expenses, along with other fees it imposes, in its prospectus.

Tax-deferred

When an investment you make or the earnings on your investment are tax-deferred, it means that you can post-pone paying income tax until you begin withdrawing from the account in which the investment is held. That allows your earnings to compound more quickly.

You can make tax-deferred contributions to qualified retirement plans, such as a 401(k). You collect tax-deferred earnings in those plans as well as in traditional individual retirement accounts (IRAs), fixed and variable annuities, and some insurance policies.

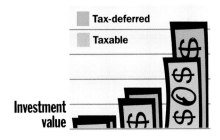

Tax-efficient funds

When mutual funds distribute their earnings and any short- or long-term capital gains, its shareholders must report those amounts as taxable income (unless they own the fund in a tax-sheltered retirement plan). If the fund can reduce taxable income, it may be described as a tax-efficient fund. However, the goal is to be tax-efficient while still producing a strong positive return.

One approach stock fund managers may use to create tax efficiency is to emphasize stocks expected to grow in value over those that produce current income, or yield. Another approach is to reduce turnover, which means buying and holding stocks for long-term gains.

In general, the smaller a fund's turnover, or buying and selling, the more tax-efficient it can potentially be. That's one reason that index funds are tax-efficient. Since these funds mirror a particular index, they buy and sell investments only when the composition of the index changes.

Tax-exempt

Some investments are tax-exempt, which means you don't have to pay income tax on the earnings they produce. For example, the interest you receive on a municipal bond is generally exempt from federal income tax, and

also exempt from state and local income tax if you live in the state where the bond was issued. (However, if you sell the bond before maturity, any capital gain is taxable.)

Similarly, dividends on bond mutual funds that invest in municipal bonds are exempt from federal income tax. And for residents of the issuing state for single-state funds, the dividends are also exempt from state and local taxes. (However, capital gains on these funds are never tax exempt.)

If you have a Roth IRA, any earnings are tax-exempt when you withdraw them, provided your account has been open for five years or more and you're at least 59½ years old.

When an organization such as a religious, educational, or charitable institution, or a not-for-profit group, is tax-exempt, it does not owe tax of any kind to federal, state, and local governments. In addition, you can take an income tax deduction for gifts you make to such organizations.

Technical analysis

Technical analysts study trading histories to identify price trends in particular stocks, mutual funds, commodities, or options in market sectors or in the overall financial markets. They use their findings to predict probable, often short-term, trading patterns in the areas that they study. The speed (and advocates would say the accuracy) with which the analysts do their work depends on the development of increasingly sophisticated computer programs.

Tender offer

When a corporation offers to buy outstanding shares of another company, called the target company, at a price higher than the market price, it is called a tender offer. The tender is usually part of a bid to take over the target company.

If a corporation accumulates 5% or more of another company, it has to report its holdings to the Securities and Exchange Commission (SEC), the target company, and the exchange or market on which the target company's shares are traded.

Thin market

A thin market can be an entire securities market (such as one in an emerging nation), a specific class of securities (such as microcap stocks), or an individual security. Thin means infrequently traded.

Thinly traded

A particular stock, sector, or market is said to be thinly traded if it is traded only infrequently, and there are a limited number of interested buyers and sellers. Prices of thinly traded securities tend to be more volatile than those traded more actively because just a few trades can affect the market price substantially.

It can also be difficult to sell shares of thinly traded securities, especially in a downturn, if there is no ready buyer. Shares of small- and micro-cap companies are most likely to be thinly traded.

Third market

Exchange-listed securities, such as those that are traded on the New York Stock Exchange (NYSE) or the American Stock Exchange (AMEX), are also bought and sold off the exchange, or over the counter (OTC), in what is known as the third market. Typically, third-market transactions are large block trades involving securities firms (that may or may not be members of the exchange) and institutional investors, such as investment companies and pension funds.

With the advent of electronic communications networks (ECNs), however, more investors are buying and selling in this way. Among the appeals of the third market are speed, reduced trading costs, and anonymity.

Tick

A tick is the minimum movement by which the price of a security, option, or index changes. With stocks, a tick represents $\frac{1}{16}$ of a point. With bonds, it may represent an increment as small as $\frac{1}{32}$ of a point. An uptick represents an increase in price, and a downtick a drop in price.

Ticker symbol

A ticker symbol, also known as a stock symbol, is a string of letters that identifies a particular stock on one of two electronic tapes that report market transactions. The consolidated tape includes companies that trade on the New York Stock Exchange (NYSE), the American Stock Exchange (AMEX), regional exchanges and other markets, such as Instinet. A second tape includes companies that trade on the Nasdaq Stock Market.

Most corporations have a say in what their symbol will be, and many choose one that's clearly linked their name, such as IBM or AMZN for Amazon.com. Various letters may be added to a ticker symbol to indicate where the trade took place or that there was something a typical about the transaction.

For example, IBM.Pr would indicate that the trade involved preferred stock. A stock's ticker symbol is the same as the one that identifies it on the exchange or market where it trades, but it isn't always the one that's used in newspaper stock columns.

Ticker (tape)

While the stock markets are in session, there is a running record of trading activity in each individual stock. Today's computerized system, still referred to as the ticker or ticker tape, actually replaces the scrolling paper tape of the past.

Time deposit

When you put money into a bank or savings and loan account with a fixed term, such as a certificate of deposit (CD), you are making a time deposit. Time deposits may pay interest at a higher rate than demand deposit accounts, such as checking or money market accounts, from which you can withdraw at any time. But if you withdraw from a time deposit account before the term ends, you may have to pay a penalty—sometimes as much as all the interest that has been credited to your account. Some other time deposits require you to give advance notice if you plan to withdraw money.

Time value of money

The time value of money is money's potential to grow in value over time. Because of this potential, money that's available in the present is considered more valuable than the same amount in the future. For example, if you were given $100 today and invested it at an annual rate of only 1%, it could be worth $101 at the end of one year, which is more than you'd have if you received $100 at that point.

In addition, because of money's potential to increase in value over time, you can use the time value of money to calculate how much you need to invest now to meet a certain future goal. Many personal investment handbooks and online financial services help you calculate these amounts based on different interest rates.

Inflation has the reverse effect on the time value of money. Because of the constant decline in the purchasing power of money, an uninvested dollar is worth more in the present than the same uninvested dollar will be in the future.

Total return

Total return is your annual gain or loss on an equity or debt investment. It includes reinvested dividends or interest, plus any change in the market value of the investment. When total return is expressed as a percentage, it's figured by dividing the increase in value, plus dividends or interest, by the original purchase price. On bonds you hold to maturity, however, your total return is the same as your yield to maturity (YTM).

TOTAL RETURN

$$\frac{\text{Change in value} + \text{dividends}}{\text{Cost of initial investment}} = \text{TOTAL RETURN (\%)}$$

Tracking stock

Some corporations issue tracking stock, a type of common stock whose value is linked to the performance of a particular division or business within a larger corporation rather than to the corporation as a whole. Tracking stock separates the finances of the division from those of the parent company, so that if the division falters or takes time to become profitable, the value of the traditional common stock won't be affected.

If you own tracking stock, you actually are invested in the parent company, since it continues to own the division that's being tracked, though typically you have no shareholder's voting rights in the corporation.

General Motors issued the first tracking stock, which was linked to Electronic Data Systems (EDS), in 1984. In the fall of 1999, there were about 30 on the market, with many of them tracking Internet operations.

Trade date

The trade date is the day on which you buy or sell a security, option, or futures contract. The settlement date occurs one or more days after the trade date, depending on the type of security that you're trading. The terms T+1 and T+3 are used to indicate the number of days you have to settle—one day in the case of government securities and options, and three days in the case of stocks.

Trader

Traders, also known as competitive or floor traders, are individuals who buy and sell securities for their own accounts. They don't pay commissions, so they can profit on small differences in price, but they must abide by the rules established by the exchange on which they trade. The term trader also describes people who execute trades at asset management firms.

Trading floor

The trading floor is the active trading area of a stock exchange, such as the New York Stock Exchange (NYSE). Securities are traded auction-style on an exchange trading floor. That means the prices are set by competitive bidding between brokers, following a series of clearly established exchange rules.

Many brokerage firms that are market makers also refer to the space they have allocated for trading as their trading floor. The same term is used to describe the trading areas in banks.

Trading range

A trading range means slightly different things on different types of exchanges. On a stock exchange, it's the spread between the highest and lowest prices at which a particular stock or market as a whole has been trading over a period of time. On a commodities exchange, the trading range for a particular futures contract is set by the exchange. Prices can't go above or below those limits during the trading day.

Trading symbol

All companies listed on the New York Stock Exchange (NYSE), the American Stock Exchange (AMEX), or the Nasdaq Stock Market (Nasdaq) are represented by one to five letters of the alphabet. Some, but not all, trading symbols are easily associated with their companies, such as IBM for International Business Machines or YHOO for Yahoo!.

Sometimes, the exchange trading symbol varies slightly from the way the company is designated on the ticker.

TICKER SYMBOLS

The Single-letter Elite

F	Ford Motor Co. (NYSE)
U	US Airways (NYSE)
S	Sears Roebuck (NYSE)

Symbols for Smiles

FLY	Airlease Ltd. (NYSE)
UGLY	Ugly Duckling (NasdaqNM)
SING	Singing Machine Co. (OTC)

Simple Symbols

MSFT	Microsoft Corp. (NasdaqNM)
IBM	International Business Machines (NYSE)
EBAY	eBay Inc. (NasdaqNM)

Trading volume

Trading volume is a measure of the number of stocks, bonds, futures contracts, options, or other investments that are sold in a specific period of time, such as a day. The volume of trades is often linked to volatility in the market, since as more investors buy and sell, prices are apt to rise and fall more rapidly. The financial media regularly report the trading volume in different markets.

Tranche

Certain securities, such as collateralized mortgage obligations (CMOs), are made up of a number of classes, called tranches, that differ from each other because they pay different interest rates, mature on different dates, carry different levels of risk, or differ in some other way.

When the security is offered for sale, each of these tranches is sold separately. Similarly, a large certificate of deposit (CD) may be subdivided into

Reading a Stock Ticker

The ancestor of the stock market's high-speed electronic ticker is good old-fasioned tape.

News about the current trading price of a stock is about as public as information gets. The reason is that transactions are recorded virtually as they occur.

Market reporters use digital scanning devices to report the stock symbol and price of every New York Stock Exchange (NYSE) trade to an electronic ticker almost instantly. Trades on other exchanges are consolidated in the same band, while trades on the Nasdaq market are presented in a separate, parallel band. Then both bands are flashed electronically around the country—typically with a 15-minute delay.

The catch is that the stream of letters and numbers the tickers produce takes some deciphering. That's because even though the technology that powers the tickers has changed dramatically, the system of symbols and abbreviations that has remained largely the same over the years.

Just Ticking Along

The first stock ticker (which got its name from the loud ticking of its printing mechanism) was invented by Edward Calahan and installed in New York in 1867. But it was lightbulb inventor Thomas Edison who perfected the design several years later and made it his first commercial success.

Edison's ticker listed the price and size of each transaction on the long stream of narrow paper known as ticker tape. By the 1880s, stock tickers had gone interstate, with Western Union sending trading reports from New York to tickers in other major cities. Brokers from New York to Philadelphia and beyond would crowd around the tape as it flowed out, jockeying to get the first look.

The Big Screen and Beyond

In the early 1920s, Percival N. Furber invented the Trans-Lux Movie Ticker, a camera that projected the ticker tape's information onto a large screen on the exchange wall.

In 1964, the 900 ticker sped up trade reporting from the original 500 characters a minute to 900—the maximum readable speed—to keep up with increasing volume. Today, small transactions and trades at the same or similar prices usually aren't reported. Even so, only a small fraction of a day's trading volume makes it to the ticker, and when trading is really hectic additional shortcuts are introduced.

Stock Symbols

A stock symbol is the unique code of one to five letters that identifies an individual stock on the ticker.

A Blast From the Past

The Financial Literacy Center will begin selling working replicas of Edison's ticker in May 2000. While they're selling for far more than the $6 a week the NYSE paid to rent the first ticker, you get today's technology as well as yesterday's for the higher price, since these tickers can display e-mail as well as stock quotes.

Reading a Stock Ticker

The information on the ticker is presented in two parts. Traditionally the symbol is on the top line, and the price and volume beneath it to the right. That's a carryover from the original ticker, when one wheel printed letters on one paper tape and the other wheel printed numbers on a second. But you may also see the information in one line, with the price and volume numbers to the right of the symbol.

The stock price shows the last price at which the stock traded. The price is reported in points and fractions of a point with one point equal to $1. So 15½, for example, means $15.50. Sixteenths are displayed with decimals (as in 11.16 for eleven sixteenths).

Volume is the number of shares traded, and when it is included on the ticker, it is printed before the price. In that case a separator (s) is inserted between the volume and the price.

15 When trades involve one round lot (100 shares), volume is omitted, leaving only the price. Here, it's $15 a share.

6s15 In trades involving 200-9,900 shares, the number of round lots is indicated to shorten the quote. This symbol reports that 600 shares were traded at $15 a share.

12.000s15 Trades involving 10,000 or more shares are displayed in full. Here it's 12,000 shares at $15 a share.

6ss 15 Trades in odd lots are indicated by ss following the number of lots. If this trade were on the NYSE, it would mean 60 shares, or six odd lots of 10 shares, had been traded at $15 a share.

OXY   A   CIRC   SVP⟩

15   P/R 63⅜   12.000s 15

Unsecret Codes

There are several additional symbols that can be attached to the stock symbol to indicate special conditions attached to the trade or to designate different types of securities. Among those you might see are

CV	Convertible preferred stock
ERR	Error, so ignore
PR	Preferred stock
OPD	Significant price change from closing price
RT	Rights
SLD	Trade reported out of sequence
WD	When distributed
WI	When issued
WS	Warrants
XD	Ex-dividend

Different classes of common stock are indicated by a letter designating the class following the stock symbol, and transactions on specific exchanges are indicated with an ampersand plus a distinguishing letter, such as "&P" for the Pacific Stock Exchange.

Smart Symbols

Companies have a fair amount of say in what their stock symbols will be, and many choose to remind investors of their brand identity — GE for General Electric, for example, or IBM for International Business Machines. But some companies take this on-the-ticker advertising a step further, letting their symbols show their products:

FUN (NYSE): Cedar Fair, L.P., amusement park owner and operator.

FIZ (AMEX): National Beverage Corp.

BUNZ (Nasdaq): Schlotzsky's, Inc., a fast-food sandwich chain.

SAM (NYSE): Boston Beer Company, Inc., brewers of Samuel Adams.

smaller certificates for sale to individual investors. Each smaller certificate, or tranche, matures on the same date and pays the same rate of interest, but is worth a fraction of the total amount.

Transparency

Transparency is a measure of how much information you have about the markets where you invest and the corporations whose stocks or bonds you buy. For example, in order to achieve maximum transparency in US markets, the Securities and Exchange Commission (SEC) requires corporations to disclose all information that might have an impact on their financial status so that investors can make fully informed decisions.

Real-time trading information, increasingly available to individuals as well as institutional investors, and linked pricing systems are other steps toward complete transparency.

Treasury bill (T-bill)

Treasury bills are short-term government debt securities with a maturity date of 13, 26, or 52 weeks. The 13- and 26-week bills are sold weekly by competitive auction to institutional investors, and to individual investors through Treasury Direct for the average price paid by the competitive bidders.

You buy T-bills at a discount to the face value of $1,000 per bill, but the bill is redeemed at maturity for the full face value. The difference between what you pay and the $1,000 you get back is your interest. That interest is federally taxable but exempt from state and local tax.

Because they are highly liquid short-term investments, Treasury bills are often described as ideal parking places for money you may need access to or are waiting to invest.

Treasury bond

Treasury bonds are long-term government debt securities with a maturity date of 10 to 30 years. They are issued in denominations of $1,000, though investors can buy any number of bonds

they wish, to a maximum of $1 million per issue.

While Treasury bonds are federally taxable, they are exempt from state and local taxes. Treasury bonds are considered among the most secure investment in the world, since they are backed by the federal government.

Treasury Direct

This direct investment system, offered through the Federal Reserve banks and their branches, lets you make noncompetitive bids for US Treasury bills, notes, and bonds.

Once you open a Treasury Direct account, you can buy, sell, or roll over your investments by mail, telephone, or online, avoiding the expense of buying and selling through a bank or brokerage firm. Interest paid on your investments, and the value of any securities you redeem at maturity, are deposited directly into your bank account.

Treasury Investor Growth Receipt (TIGER)

A TIGER is a US Treasury security that has been stripped, or divided into principal and each of its interest payments, by a brokerage firm. Each part is sold separately as a zero-coupon security.

Since each of the interest payments and the repayment of principal come due at a different date, TIGERs and other stripped securities give investors a choice of investments that provide lump-sum payments at different, or staggered, intervals, when the investors might need the money.

Treasury note

Like US Treasury bills and bonds, Treasury notes are debt securities issued by the US government and backed by its full faith and credit. They are available at issue through Treasury Direct in denominations of $1,000 to $1 million and are traded in the secondary market after issue.

While bills are short-term issues and bonds are long-term, notes are intermediate-term securities, with a maturity date that ranges from two to 10 years.

The interest you earn on Treasury notes is exempt from state and local, but not federal, taxes. And while the rate at which the interest is paid is generally less than on long-term corporate or Treasury bonds, the shorter term means less inflation risk.

Triple witching

Once every quarter—on the third Friday of March, June, September, and December—options, index options, and futures contracts expire on the same day in the US. In the past, when they expired at the same hour of the day, trading could be extremely volatile. But in recent years, the timing has been adjusted so that they expire at different times throughout the day, somewhat reducing the potential frenzy of trading.

Trust

When you create a trust, you transfer money and/or other assets to the trust. You give up ownership of those assets in order to accomplish a specific financial goal or goals, such as protecting assets from estate taxes, simplifying the transfer of property, or making provision for a minor or other dependents.

YOU ARE THE DONOR
You set up the trust.
You transfer property to the trust.
You name the trustee.
You name the beneficiaries.

YOUR TRUST
The trust earns income and pays taxes.

In Trust

YOUR BENEFICIARIES
They receive the assets of the trust according to its terms.

YOUR TRUSTEES
Trustees manage the trust's investments, control the property in the trust, and oversee payments.

When you establish the trust, you are the grantor, and the people or institutions you name to receive the trust assets at some point in the future are known as beneficiaries. You also designate a trustee or trustees, whose job is to manage the assets in the trust and distribute them according to the instructions you provide in the trust document.

Turnover ratio

A mutual fund's turnover ratio measures the percentage of holdings that the fund sells, or turns over, in a year. For example, if a stock fund manager has a portfolio of 100 stocks at the beginning of the year, sells 75 of them and buys 75 different stocks, the turnover rate of the fund is 75%. Some investors look for funds with lower turnover ratios, since limited trading may help to minimize capital gains taxes and trading costs. However, a high turnover ratio can also produce strong returns, which can offset the added costs and produce a net gain.

Uncovered option

An uncovered option, also known as a naked option, is an option you sell, giving the buyer the right to buy the underlying investment from you at a specific strike price. The catch is that you don't own the underlying investment, or enough of it to meet your obligation to sell. If the buyer exercises the option, you will have to buy the underlying investment to be able to deliver it according to the terms of the contract.

While you might realize a profit from the premium you receive for selling the option, you could also suffer a loss, if in order to sell, you had to buy the investment at a market price that was higher than the strike price. And that's the situation under which the person holding the option would exercise it.

Underlying investment

An underlying investment is a security (such as a stock) or other type of financial product (such as a stock index or futures contract) whose value determines the value of a related investment. For example, if you own a stock option, the stock you have the right to buy or sell with that option is the option's underlying investment.

Similarly, the investments a mutual fund makes are considered the fund's underlying investments, since the net asset value (NAV) of the fund is based on the combined values of all of the investments the fund owns.

Undervaluation

Any stock that trades at a lower price than the issuing company's reputation, earnings outlook, or financial situation would seem to merit is considered undervalued, or what is known as a value stock. Undervaluation may occur when a company loses market appeal.

Some investors concentrate on identifying and investing in undervalued stocks, drawn by their bargain prices. However, there's no way to be sure when, if ever, the price will increase enough to justify the purchase.

Underwriter

An underwriter, typically an investment banker, buys an entire new securities issue from the company or government offering it, and resells the issue as individual stocks or bonds to the public.

Part of the underwriter's job is to weigh the risks involved in taking on the financial responsibility of finding buyers against the profit to be made on the difference between the price paid for the issue and the amount it will generate. Typically, a number of bankers join forces as a purchase group, or syndicate, to spread the risk around and to reach the widest possible market.

Insurance policies also need an underwriter. In this case, the term refers to a company that is willing to take the risk of insuring your life, property, income, or health in return for a premium, or payment.

Uniform Gifts to Minors Act (UGMA)

Under the UGMA, an adult can set up a custodial account for a minor and put assets such as cash, securities, and mutual funds into it. You pay no fees or charges to set up the account, and there is no limitation on the amount you can put in. (To avoid owing gift tax, however,

you may want to limit what you add each year to an amount that qualifies for the annual gift tax exclusion—$10,000 per contributor in 1999.)

One advantage of the UGMA is that you can transfer assets you expect to increase in value, so that the long-term value of the account can grow substantially. One disadvantage may be that the gift is irrevocable. That means the assets become the property of the minor from the moment they go into the account, even though the minor cannot legally take control until the age of 18 or 21, depending on state law. At that point, called majority, the child can use those assets as he or she wishes.

In addition, if you are both the donor and the custodian, and die while the child is still a minor, the assets are considered part of your estate. That could make the estate's value large enough to be vulnerable to estate taxes.

Uniform Transfers to Minors Act (UTMA)

The UTMA allows an adult to set up a custodial account for a minor, who then owns any assets placed in the account. The UTMA is similar to the Uniform Gifts to Minors Act in many respects. You can use an UTMA to gift assets in addition to cash and securities, including real estate, fine art, antiques, patents, and royalties.

In addition, in all 50 states, the child must be 21 to gain control of the assets in the account. In some states, the UTMA has replaced the UGMA, while in others, both are available.

Unit investment trust (UIT)

A UIT is generally a fixed portfolio of bonds with specific maturity dates, of income-producing stocks, or, in some cases, of all of the securities included in a particular index. Examples of the latter include the DIAMONDS Trust (DIA), which mirrors the composton of the Dow Jones Industrial Average (DJIA), and Standard & Poor's Depositary Receipts (SPDR), which mirrors the Standard & Poor's 500-stock Index (S&P 500).

UITs resemble mutual funds in the sense that they offer the opportunity to diversify your portfolio without having to purchase a number of separate securities. You buy units, rather than shares, of the trust, usually through a broker. However, most UITs trade more like stocks than mutual funds in the sense that you trade them in the sec-ondary market if you want to sell rather than redeeming your holding by selling your units back to the issuing fund.

Further, the price of a UIT fluctuates constantly throughout the trading day, just as the price of an individual stock

does, rather than being repriced only once a day, after the close of trading. As a result most UITs (though not DIAMONDS or Spiders (as SPDRs are known) trade at prices higher or lower than their net asset value (NAV).

Unit of trading

When you buy stocks, bonds, options and commodities futures, it's typical to buy in a particular volume or for a particular dollar value, called a round lot or a unit of trading. For example, stocks are usually traded in lots of 100 shares and bonds in multiples of $1,000. However you can buy an odd lot, which is more or fewer shares or bonds, at any time. The drawback is that the commission on an odd lot may be more than the commission on a round lot.

Unit trust

The category of investment known as a mutual fund in the US is called a unit trust in other parts of the world.

United States savings bond

Series EE savings bonds are issued by the US government in face value denominations ranging from $50 to

$10,000 and are sold directly to investors by banks, credit unions, and savings and loan associations at a discount. They are also available through payroll deduction plans offered by some employers.

Series EE bonds pay interest for 30 years at a rate that's readjusted every six months. Series HH bonds, which you can buy at face value only through an exchange for Series EE bonds, pay a fixed rate of interest for up to 20 years. With both

types of bonds you earn less if you keep the bonds for fewer than five years.

In addition, Series I bonds, which are sold at face value, are indexed for inflation. The interest rate you earn varies, based on changes in the consumer price index (CPI).

The interest on US savings bonds is exempt from state and local taxes and is federally tax-deferred until the bonds mature or are cashed in. At that point, the interest may be tax-exempt if you use the bonds to pay college expenses, provided that your adjusted gross income (AGI) falls in the range set by federal guidelines.

Universe

In the world of investments, the word universe refers to a specific group or category of investments that share certain characteristics, though the characteristics vary from universe to may be the stocks that are included in a particular index, the stocks evaluated by a particular analytical service, or all of the stocks in a particular industry.

Unlisted security

A security, such as a stock, is unlisted when it cannot meet the listing requirements of any of the organized exchanges or markets. The stock can be traded over the counter (OTC), however, and may be included in the pink sheets published by the National Quotation Bureau or on the OTC Bulletin Board.

Since in order to be listed, a company has to have a certain market capitalization, a minimum number of outstanding shares, or comparable indication of staying power, many unlisted stocks are those of small companies that may someday meet those requirements and be listed.

In most cases, unlisted stocks are thinly traded because they do not get much attention from the media or financial analysts, and are judged to be too risky for many investors.

Unrealized gain

If you own an investment that has increased in value, your gain is unrealized until you sell and take your profit.

In most cases, the value continues to change as long as you own the investment, either increasing your unrealized gain or creating an unrealized loss. You owe no income or capital gains tax on unrealized gains, sometimes known as paper profits, though you typically compute the value of your investment portfolio based on current—and unrealized—values.

Unrealized loss

If the market price of a security you own drops below the amount you paid for it, you have an unrealized loss. The loss remains unrealized as long as you don't sell the security while the price is down. In a volatile market, of course, an unrealized loss can become an unrealized gain, and vice versa, at any time.

One reason you might choose to sell at a loss, other than needing cash at that moment, is to prevent further losses in a security that seems headed for a still-lower price.

Unsecured bond

When a bond isn't backed by collateral or security of some kind, such as a mortgage, that can be used to repay the bondholders if the bond issuer defaults, the bond is described as unsecured. However, most unsecured bonds pose little risk of default, since the companies that issue them are usually financially sound. Unsecured bonds are also known as debentures.

Uptick

An uptick is the smallest possible incremental increase in a security's price, which, for stocks, is currently $1/16$ of a point. So when there's an uptick in a stock selling at $40^{15}/_{16}$, the new price is 41. When US markets convert to decimal pricing, which is expected in the summer of 2000, an uptick will be measured in decimals rather than fractions.

Valuation

Valuation is the process of estimating the value, or worth, of an asset or investment. Sometimes it means determining a fixed amount, such as establishing the value of your estate after your death.

Other times, valuation means estimating future worth. For example, fundamental stock analysts estimate the outlook for a company's stock by looking at data such as the stock's price-to-earnings (P/E), price-to-sales, and price-to-book (or net asset value) ratios. In general, a company with a high P/E is considered overvalued, and a company with a low P/E is considered undervalued.

However, as the prices of many rapidly growing Internet stocks are moving skyward, often in the presence of little—or even no—earnings, many analysts are reconsidering the old valuation models and looking more closely at a company's long-term potential to develop its products and expand its markets.

Value fund

When a mutual fund manager buys primarily undervalued stocks for the fund's portfolio with the expectation that these stocks will increase in value, that fund is described as a value fund. A value fund may be limited to stocks of a certain size, such as those included in a small-cap value fund, or it may include undervalued stocks with different levels of capitalization.

There is a running debate among financial analysts about whether, over the long term, an investor makes out better buying shares in a value fund or in a fund that may buy high-priced stocks with strong growth potential.

Value Line, Inc.

Value Line is an investment research company that provides detailed analysis on a range of stocks, mutual funds, and convertible

investments. Their publications include *The Value Line Investment Survey* and *The Value Line Mutual Fund Survey*, which contain regularly updated rankings of specific investments that the company covers.

The company uses a dual ranking system in its evaluations. For example, Value Line ranks stocks for their safety and timeliness, and mutual funds both for their overall performance and for their risk-adjusted performance.

Value Line Composite Index

Value Line, an independent investment research service, tracks the performance of approximately 1,700 common stocks in its composite index. The index, which is equally weighted, is considered a reliable indicator of overall market trends.

Value stock

Value stocks, also known as under-valued stocks, trade at a lower price than the company's reputation, earnings outlook, or financial situation would seem to merit. Investors who seek them out expect the company's fortunes to turn around, and the price of the stock to increase accordingly.

Variable annuity

Unlike the guaranteed rate of return you receive with a fixed annuity, the return on a variable annuity fluctuates with the performance of the underlying investments in your subaccounts. You can allocate your assets among the various subaccounts, which resemble mutual funds, offered in your annuity contract. For example, you could allocate 70% to a growth portfolio, 15% to a bond portfolio, and 15% to a fixed-income account.

Variable annuities also provide insurance protection, promising that if you die before you begin to receive income, your beneficiaries will get at least as much as you put into the annuity, even if your underlying investments have lost money. This assurance encourages some people to invest their annuity assets more aggressively in the hopes of realizing greater portfolio growth.

HOW VARIABLE ANNUITIES WORK

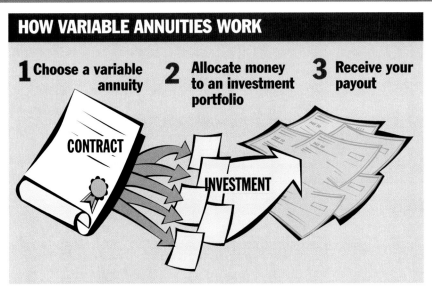

1 Choose a variable annuity

2 Allocate money to an investment portfolio

3 Receive your payout

CONTRACT

INVESTMENT

Another appeal of variable annuities is that you can move money among sub-accounts without owing income tax on any gains. The downside is that the cost of added insurance protection, and the promise of a stream of income for life, can make owning a variable annuity more expensive than owning comparable mutual funds. In addition, withdrawals before you reach age 59½ can be subject to a 10% early withdrawal penalty.

Venture capital (VC)

Venture capital is financing provided by wealthy independent investors, banks, and financing companies to help new businesses get started and grow. In return for the money they put up, also called risk capital, the investors may play a role in the company's management as well as receive some combination of equity, profits, or royalties.

Vesting

If you are part of an employer pension plan or participate in an employer-sponsored retirement plan, such as a 401(k), you become fully vested—or entitled to the contributions your employer has made to the plan, including matching and discretionary contributions—after a certain period of service with the company.

If you leave your job before becoming fully vested, you forfeit all or part of your employer-paid benefits. If you become entitled to full benefits gradually over several years, this process is called graded vesting. But if your benefits become payable only after a specified

number of years of service, and you forfeit all employer-paid benefits if your employment ends before this waiting period is up, the process is called cliff vesting.

Volatility

Volatility indicates how much and how quickly the value of an investment, market, or market sector changes. For example, stocks of small, newer companies are usually more volatile than those of established, blue chip companies because their values tend to rise and fall very sharply over short periods of time.

The volatility of a stock relative to the overall market is known as its beta, and the volatility triggered by internal factors, regardless of the market, is known as a stock's alpha.

Volume

Volume is the number of shares traded in a company's stock or in an entire market over a specified period, typically a day. For example, the average volume of trading on the New York Stock Exchange (NYSE) was 822 million shares a day in 1999. On the Nasdaq Stock Market (Nasdaq), it was 1.02 billion shares. Volumes are reported daily in the business sections of newspapers.

Voting right

Investors who own shares of a common stock or shares in a mutual fund typically have voting rights, which allow them to participate in the election of boards of directors. These shareholders can also vote for or against certain propositions put forward by management. In contrast, investors who own preferred shares or corporate bonds have no voting rights.

Warrant

For a small fee, you can purchase a warrant that allows you to buy a company's stock at a fixed price. The warrant is valid for a specific period of time, often for several years. Sometimes there is no expiration date.

For example, a warrant priced at $1 per share might guarantee you the right to buy a certain stock at $10 within the next 10 years. If the price goes up to $15, you can exercise, or use, your warrant, save $4 per share, and resell the security at a profit. If the price of the stock falls over the life of the warrant, however, the warrant becomes worthless.

Warrants are listed with a *wt* following the name of the stock in the stock tables of the newspaper and are traded independently of the underlying stock.

Weighted stock index

In weighted stock indexes, price changes in some stocks have a much greater impact than price changes in others in computing the direction of the overall index. By contrast, in an unweighted index, prices changes in all the stocks have an equal impact.

A price-weighted index, such as the Dow Jones Industrial Average (DJIA), counts changes in the prices of high-priced securities more than changes in the prices of low-priced securities. Similarly, a market capitalization-weighted index, such as the Nasdaq Composite Index, emphasizes price changes in securities with the highest market caps. (A capitalization-weighted index may also be called a market value-weighted index.)

The theory behind weighting is that price changes in the largest or most expensive securities have a greater impact on the overall economy than price changes in smaller-cap or less expensive stocks. However, some critics argue that strong market performance by the biggest or most expensive stocks can drive an index up, masking stagnant or even declining prices in large segments of the market, and providing a skewed view of the economy.

Will

A will is a legal document you use to transfer assets you have accumulated during your lifetime to the people and institutions you want to have them after your death. The will also names an executor—the person or people who will carry out your wishes. You can leave those assets directly, or you can use your will to establish one or more trusts to receive the assets and distribute them at some point in the future.

The danger of dying without a will is that a court in the state where you live will decide what happens to your assets. Their decision may not be what you would have chosen.

Wilshire 5000 Index

The Wilshire 5000 is a market capitalization-weighted index of more than 7,000 stocks, prepared by Wilshire Associates, Inc., of Santa Monica, California. It is the broadest US stock market index, tracking all the stocks traded on the New York Stock Exchange (NYSE), the American Stock Exchange (AMEX), and the Nasdaq Stock Market (Nasdaq). There's a difference between the index's name (the 5000) and the number of stocks it tracks because additional stocks are being offered for trading all the time.

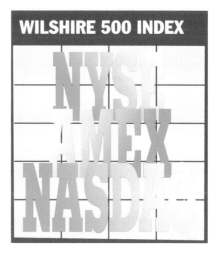

Wire house

International and national brokerage houses with multiple branches used to have an advantage over smaller firms because they were linked by private networks that enabled them to transmit important about the financial markets almost instantaneously.

Although the Internet now makes it possible for all firms—and even individual investors—to benefit from high-speed communication, the largest brokerage houses are still sometimes referred to as wire houses because of the technological edge they used to enjoy.

Wire room

The wire room is the back office of a brokerage firm. People who work there send the buy or sell orders that come in from brokers to the firm's trading department or floor traders. The wire room also gets notifications when the transactions are completed and sends those notifications back to the brokers who took the orders.

Working capital

Working capital is the money that allows a corporation to function by providing money to pay the bills and keep operations humming. Some working capital is provided by earnings, but corporations can also get infusions of working capital by borrowing money, issuing bonds, and selling stock.

World Bank

Formally known as the International Bank for Reconstruction and Development (IBRD), the World Bank was established in 1944 to aid Europe and Asia after the devastation of World War II. To fulfill its current roles of providing financing for developing countries and making interest-free and low-interest long-term loans to poor nations, the World Bank raises money by issuing bonds to individuals, institutions, and governments in more than 100 countries.

World fund

US-based mutual funds that invest in securities from a number of countries, including the US, are known as world funds or global funds. Unlike international funds that buy only in overseas markets, world funds may keep as much as 75% of their investment portfolio in US stocks or bonds.

Because world fund managers can choose from many markets, they are often able to invest in those companies providing the strongest performance in any given period.

Wrap account

A wrap account is a professionally managed investment plan in which all expenses, including brokerage commissions, management fees, and administrative costs, are "wrapped" into a single annual charge, usually amounting to 2% to 3% of the value of the assets in the account.

Wrap accounts combine the services of a professional money manager, who chooses a personalized portfolio of stocks, bonds, mutual funds, and other investments, and a brokerage firm, which takes care of the trading and recordkeeping on the account.

Writer

In the options market, a writer is someone who sells put and call options, an activity known as writing a call or writing a put. Unlike the buyer of an option, who can let the option expire, a seller must go through with a trade if the party holding the option wants to exercise it.

Yankee bond

Yankee bonds are bonds issued in dollars in the US by overseas companies and governments. The purpose is to raise more money than the issuers may be able to borrow in their home markets, either because there is more money available for investment in the US, or because the interest rate the issuers must pay to attract investors is lower.

US investors buy these bonds as a way to diversify into overseas markets without the potential drawbacks of currency fluctuation, foreign tax, or different standards of disclosure that may be characteristic of other markets.

Yellow sheets

Every trading day, the National Quotation Bureau publishes bid and ask prices of unlisted corporate bonds being traded over the counter (OTC). The data, which comes from dealers who make a market in the bonds, is printed on yellow paper, which is where the name comes from.

Yield

Yield is the rate of return on an investment, paid in dividends or interest and expressed as a percent.

In the case of stocks, the yield on your investment is the dividend you receive per share divided by the stock's price per share. With bonds, it is the interest divided by the price.

In the case of bonds, the yield on your investment and the interest rate your investment pays are sometimes— but by no means always—the same.

If the price of a bond moves higher or lower than par, the yield will be different from the interest rate. For example, if you pay $950 for a bond with a par value of $1,000 that pays 6% interest, your yield is 6.3%. But if you paid $1,100 for the same bond, your yield would be only 5.5%.

Yield can usually be calculated by dividing the amount you receive annually in dividends or interest by the amount you spent to buy the investment.

YIELD

$$\frac{\text{Dividends or interest you receive}}{\text{What you invested}} = \text{YIELD}$$

for example

$$\frac{\$60 \text{ interest}}{\$950 \text{ invested}} = 6.3\% \text{ YIELD}$$

Yield curve

A yield curve is a graph that shows the relationship between the yields on short-term and long-term bonds of the same investment quality. Most of the time, the curves are created by comparing the return on short-term Treasury bills to the return on 30-year Treasury bonds. Since long-term rates are characteristically higher than short-term rates, a yield curve that confirms that expectation is described as positive. In contrast, a negative yield curve occurs when short-term rates are higher.

Yield to maturity (YTM)

Yield to maturity is the most precise measure of a bond's return over time. It takes into account the interest rate in relation to the price, the purchase or discount price in relation to the par value, and the years remaining until the bond matures. Although YTM figures are complex to calculate, brokers will supply this information if you ask, or you can use a calculator programmed to provide YTM figures.

Zacks Investment Research

This Chicago-based company tracks changes in earnings estimates, as well as buy, sell, and hold recommendations for approximately 5,000 stocks. The information is provided by more than 3,500 financial analysts at over 210 brokerage firms.

Based on its research, Zacks compiles consensus earnings estimates, industry group reports, and company reports that are widely followed by both individual and institutional investors. The service is available to all investors by subscription.

Zero sum

A zero-sum market is one in which one investor's profits mirrors another investor's losses. For every dollar one person makes, someone else loses a dollar. Commodities and options markets are examples of zero-sum markets.

Zero-coupon bond (Zero)

These bonds are issued at a deep discount but pay no interest until they mature. You buy zeros, usually in denominations of $1,000 per bond, at prices far below par value. While you hold the bonds, say over a 10-year period, you receive no interest—hence the term zero coupon—since coupon means interest in bond terminology.

When the bond matures, you are paid the face value, including the interest that's accumulated over the intervening 10 years. For example, you may purchase a $20,000 zero-coupon bond with a six-year term for $13,500.

One advantage of zeros is that you can invest relatively small amounts up front and choose maturity dates to coincide with times you know you'll need the money—for example, when college tuition bills come due.

One drawback to zeros, however, is that taxes are due annually on the interest that accrues, even though you don't receive the actual payment until the bond matures. The exception occurs if you buy tax-exempt municipal zeros, on which no tax is due either during the term or at maturity. Another drawback is that zero-coupon bonds are very volatile in the secondary market, so if you have to sell them before maturity, you might have to sell at a loss.

BOOKS FROM LIGHTBULB PRESS

Lightbulb Press books are available in bookstores everywhere. Visit us on the World Wide Web at www.lightbulbpress.com. Contact us at (917) 256-4900 for information on bulk discounts.

THE WALL STREET JOURNAL GUIDE TO UNDERSTANDING MONEY & INVESTING
by Kenneth M. Morris
and Virginia B. Morris

DICTIONARY OF FINANCIAL TERMS
by Virginia B. Morris
and Kenneth M. Morris

THE WALL STREET JOURNAL GUIDE TO UNDERSTANDING PERSONAL FINANCE
by Kenneth M. Morris
and Alan M. Siegel

A WOMAN'S GUIDE TO INVESTING
by Virginia B. Morris
and Kenneth M. Morris
Introduction by Bridget A. Macaskill

USER'S GUIDE TO
THE INFORMATION AGE

by Kenneth M. Morris
Introduction by David C. Nagel

CREATING RETIREMENT INCOME

by Virginia B. Morris

THE WALL STREET JOURNAL GUIDE
TO PLANNING YOUR FINANCIAL FUTURE

by Kenneth M. Morris, Alan M. Siegel
and Virginia B. Morris

THE WALL STREET JOURNAL GUIDE
TO UNDERSTANDING YOUR TAXES

by Scott R. Schmedel, Kenneth M. Morris
and Alan M. Siegel

THE WALL STREET JOURNAL GUIDE
TO UNDERSTANDING MONEY AND
INVESTING IN ASIA

by Kenneth M. Morris, Alan M. Siegel
and Beverly Larson